TRANSIT COOPERATIVE RESEARCH PROGRAM

Report 9

Transit Operations for Individuals with Disabilities

EG&G DYNATREND
Burlington, MA
and
CRAIN & ASSOCIATES, INC.
Menlo Park, CA

Subject Area

Public Transit

Research Sponsored by the Federal Transit Administration in Cooperation with the Transit Development Corporation

TRANSPORTATION RESEARCH BOARD
NATIONAL RESEARCH COUNCIL

NATIONAL ACADEMY PRESS
Washington, D.C.   1995

TRANSIT COOPERATIVE RESEARCH PROGRAM

The nation's growth and the need to meet mobility, environmental, and energy objectives place demands on public transit systems. Current systems, some of which are old and in need of upgrading, must expand service area, increase service frequency, and improve efficiency to serve these demands. Research is necessary to solve operating problems, to adapt appropriate new technologies from other industries, and to introduce innovations into the transit industry. The Transit Cooperative Research Program (TCRP) serves as one of the principal means by which the transit industry can develop innovative near-term solutions to meet demands placed on it.

The need for TCRP was originally identified in *TRB Special Report 213—Research for Public Transit: New Directions,* published in 1987 and based on a study sponsored by the Urban Mass Transportation Administration—now the Federal Transit Administration (FTA). A report by the American Public Transit Association (APTA), *Transportation 2000,* also recognized the need for local, problem-solving research. TCRP, modeled after the longstanding and successful National Cooperative Highway Research Program, undertakes research and other technical activities in response to the needs of transit service providers. The scope of TCRP includes a variety of transit research fields including planning, service configuration, equipment, facilities, operations, human resources, maintenance, policy, and administrative practices.

TCRP was established under FTA sponsorship in July 1992. Proposed by the U.S. Department of Transportation, TCRP was authorized as part of the Intermodal Surface Transportation Efficiency Act of 1991 (ISTEA). On May 13, 1992, a memorandum agreement outlining TCRP operating procedures was executed by the three cooperating organizations: FTA, the National Academy of Sciences, acting through the Transportation Research Board (TRB), and the Transit Development Corporation, Inc. (TDC), a nonprofit educational and research organization established by APTA. TDC is responsible for forming the independent governing board, designated as the TCRP Oversight and Project Selection (TOPS) Committee.

Research problem statements for TCRP are solicited periodically but may be submitted to TRB by anyone at any time. It is the responsibility of the TOPS Committee to formulate the research program by identifying the highest priority projects. As part of the evaluation, the TOPS Committee defines funding levels and expected products.

Once selected, each project is assigned to an expert panel, appointed by the Transportation Research Board. The panels prepare project statements (requests for proposals), select contractors, and provide technical guidance and counsel throughout the life of the project. The process for developing research problem statements and selecting research agencies has been used by TRB in managing cooperative research programs since 1962. As in other TRB activities, TCRP project panels serve voluntarily without compensation.

Because research cannot have the desired impact if products fail to reach the intended audience, special emphasis is placed on disseminating TCRP results to the intended endusers of the research: transit agencies, service providers, and suppliers. TRB provides a series of research reports, syntheses of transit practice, and other supporting material developed by TCRP research. APTA will arrange for workshops, training aids, field visits, and other activities to ensure that results are implemented by urban and rural transit industry practitioners.

The TCRP provides a forum where transit agencies can cooperatively address common operational problems. The TCRP results support and complement other ongoing transit research and training programs.

TCRP REPORT 9

Project B-1 FY '92
ISSN 1073-4872
ISBN 0-309-05712-4
Library of Congress Catalog Card No. 96-60006

Price $27.00

Published reports of the

TRANSIT COOPERATIVE RESEARCH PROGRAM

are available from:

Transportation Research Board
National Research Council
2101 Constitution Avenue, N.W.
Washington, D.C. 20418

Printed in the United States of America

FOREWORD

By Staff
Transportation Research
Board

This report will be of interest to transit managers and planners in urban rural areas engaged in providing accessible services to individuals with disabilities. In response to national laws and policies promoting nondiscrimination on the basis of disability and promoting greater independence for individuals with disabilities, transit agencies in North America have developed many innovative approaches to better serve customers with disabilities. Providing such transportation services, cost-effectively, to individuals with disabilities may require the integration of several services into one comprehensive transportation system. This report provides alternative operating models and possible enhancements to traditional public transit services that can be employed to encourage individuals with disabilities to use fixed-route services when appropriate.

Under TCRP Project B-1, research was undertaken by a team headed by EG&G Dynatrend to develop a methodology to design and evaluate integrated transit systems that (1) provide accessible integrated service complying with the Americans with Disabilities Act of 1990 (ADA); (2) facilitate the appropriate use of the ADA paratransit service; and (3) support service or system enhancements to encourage travel on accessible fixed routes by individuals with disabilities. Phase I of the study, described in this report, identified and defined possible options and enhancements; determined the applicability of each option to various situations and areas; and noted key implementation issues. An extensive literature search and a survey of all public transit providers in the United States and Canada was conducted. The survey identified 624 agencies that have implemented various service options and enhancements to better serve customers with disabilities. Many of these agencies have improved services to persons with disabilities by strengthening basic elements of their operation, such as vehicle and station design, equipment maintenance, driver training, accessible information, and communications. Beyond these basic and often required service improvements, 20 innovative service options and enhancements were identified. In some cases, these are innovations; in other cases, they are long-standing concepts that are being rediscovered. These 20 options and enhancements are discussed in detail in Chapter 3. Follow-up telephone contact was made with those transit providers who indicated that they had successfully implemented one or more of the identified service options. Information on service, cost, and implementation issues was obtained through these calls.

This report will assist transit managers and planners in designing and evaluating integrated services that can be employed to encourage individuals with disabilities to use fixed-route services. An unpublished companion document, prepared under this project and entitled *Evaluating Transit Operations for Individuals with Disabilities*, provides evaluation methodologies for analyzing five successful service options identified and described in this report. It also examines, in detail, the implementation of these innovations by five selected transit systems. The options evaluated in the companion document are service routes, feeder service, route deviation, low-floor buses, and fare incentives.

This companion document (which analyzes the costs, savings, and operating issues of each service and then compares the cost-effectiveness of the different options used) is available on loan through the TCRP, 2101 Constitution Avenue, N.W. Washington, D.C. 20418.

CONTENTS

ACKNOWLEDGMENTS

The research described in this report was performed under TCRP Project B-1 by EG&G Dynatrend and by Crain & Associates, Inc. EG&G Dynatrend was the primary contractor for the study. Work performed by Crain & Associates was under a subcontract with EG&G Dynatrend.

Russell Thatcher of EG&G Dynatrend was the principal investigator and was responsible for general supervision of the research. David Koffman coordinated the research activities of researchers at Crain & Associates.

Guidance was provided throughout the project by Stephanie Nellons Robinson, the TCRP Technical Advisor for the project, and a steering committee of transit professionals.

Descriptions of the various service options and enhancements included in this report were developed by a number of researchers. Linda Aeschliman of Crain & Associates researched and prepared descriptions of accessible taxi services and accessible bus stop programs. Karla Karash of EG&G Dynatrend prepared descriptions of service routes/community bus programs, marketing programs, fixed-route planning, subscription bus services, flag-stop and request-a-stop services, and automated information and communication systems. David Koffman wrote sections describing low-floor buses, travel training, and facilitated travel. Lawrence Harman of EG&G Dynatrend researched and prepared sections on route deviation services, point deviation services, and general public dial-a-ride. Russell Thatcher wrote the descriptions of on-call, accessible, fixed-route bus programs; bus identifier systems; destination card programs; and trip planning services. Richard Weiner of Crain & Associates prepared descriptions of fare incentive programs, fare simplification mechanisms, and feeder services.

Carol Schweiger and Marsha Gangi of EG&G Dynatrend assisted in the design of the database that was created to store survey and follow-up call information. Follow-up calls to survey respondents were made by Linda Aeschliman, Russell Thatcher, and Richard Weiner.

TRANSIT OPERATIONS FOR INDIVIDUALS WITH DISABILITIES

SUMMARY   In response to national laws and policies prohibiting discrimination on the basis of disability and promoting greater independence for persons with disabilities, transit agencies in North America have developed many innovative approaches for better serving customers with disabilities. In the United States, innovations have been developed to more cost-effectively implement the Americans with Disabilities Act of 1990 (ADA). In Canada, new operating models and services have been developed in response to national and provincial policies and mandates.

A survey of transit agencies in North America, conducted in 1994 at the start of this study, identified 624 agencies that have implemented various service options and enhancements to better serve customers with disabilities. Many of these agencies have improved services to persons with disabilities by strengthening basic elements of their operation such as vehicle and station design, equipment maintenance, driver training, accessible information, and communications. Beyond these basic and often required service improvements, 20 innovative service options and enhancements were identified. In some cases, these are innovations; in other cases, they are long-standing concepts that are being rediscovered.

Eight new approaches for designing and operating paratransit, fixed-route, and hybrid modes have been documented. These include

- Service routes/community bus programs;
- On-call, accessible, fixed route bus services;
- Route deviation services;
- Point deviation services;
- Paratransit to fixed-route feeder programs;
- General public dial-a-ride services;
- Subscription bus services; and
- Flag stop and request-a-stop services.

Several new technologies are also being employed to improve the accessibility of public transit service. These include low-floor vehicle designs, including low-floor minibuses, full-size buses, and minivans for use in accessible taxi programs. Numerous technologies to improve information and communication access are also being employed, including

- Talking bus stops and signs,
- Talking buses and trains,
- Auditory maps and pathways,
- Automated speech recognition,
- Electronic information signage,

- Assistive listening devices, and
- Telecommunications systems.

Finally, a number of support services are being employed to make fixed-route transit a more attractive and usable travel alternative. Efforts in this area include

- Travel training and facilitated transportation,
- Fare incentive programs,
- Fare simplification mechanisms,
- Trip planning services,
- Targeted marketing and planning efforts,
- Accessible bus stop programs,
- Bus identifier systems, and
- Destination card programs.

Many of these options and enhancements appear to be applicable to transit agencies regardless of size and setting and are rapidly gaining popularity, in both the United States and Canada. One hundred and thirty-five systems reported that they have implemented travel training programs. Targeted marketing efforts were reportedly being used by 160 systems. Low-floor vehicles, which were being tested in only a few sites in the early 1990s, were reportedly being used by 77 systems with another 72 systems considering their use. On-call, accessible, fixed-route bus programs also appear to be widespread, with 74 systems reporting active programs.

Other options and enhancements are being used in more specific settings or are still being explored for more widespread use. Of the 63 systems reporting the use of route deviation programs, most were in rural areas. Some variations of the route deviation concept that limit the impact on fixed schedules are, however, being successfully used in urban settings. Similarly, paratransit feeder to fixed-route service is being used primarily in rural areas although interest is high among urban transit providers as they expand their paratransit service areas.

Initial research findings indicate that a number of transit agencies have employed a combination of these options and enhancements to successfully encourage the appropriate use of fixed-route and paratransit service. The following are a few of the exemplary programs described in this report:

- Madison County Transit (Madison County, Illinois) reported an increase in general public ridership (from 4,000 to 6,500 trips per day) as well as a decline in the need for paratransit service (from 12,000 trips per month to 7,500 trips per month) after establishing a network of service routes throughout the county. The service route program was supported by a travel training program and an aggressive marketing campaign.
- Successful on-call, accessible, fixed-route bus programs have been implemented by the Massachusetts Bay Transportation Authority (Boston, Massachusetts), the Transit Authority of River City (Louisville, Kentucky), the Rogue Valley Transportation District (Medford, Oregon), the Southeastern Pennsylvania Transportation Authority (Philadelphia, Pennsylvania), and the Washington Metropolitan Transportation Authority (Washington, D.C.).
- BC Transit (Vancouver, British Columbia) has established an accessible taxi program to supplement its existing paratransit service. This "Taxi Saver" service provides a 50 percent user-side subsidy while the standard paratransit service is 92 percent subsidized. A total of 50,000 taxi rides are provided each year as part of this program.

- After replacing a traditional, radial, fixed-route system with a sectored, point deviation program, Transit Management of Hamilton, Inc., (Hamilton, Ohio) reported an increase in overall ridership and a 36 percent decrease in bus mileage.
- Island Transit (Coupeville, Washington), which operates long routes connecting communities on Whidbey Island, serves about half of all paratransit customers by providing paratransit feeder service to the fixed routes. Over 3,000 paratransit feeder trips are arranged each month.
- After starting a service route, Richmond Hill Transit (Richmond Hill, Ontario) found that over 50 percent of its paratransit trips could be accommodated by this new route. Cost per trip on the service route was reported as $5 compared to $13 for the paratransit program. The switch made the paratransit service available for other riders who needed this service.
- The Sacramento Regional Transit Authority (Sacramento, California) reported providing transportation for 350 clients of work and work-training programs using a fixed-route subscription bus service. Forty program participants have also been travel trained to use other fixed-route buses.

As innovative service designs are developed and employed, there is a need to document key implementation issues, costs, and benefits. This information will help to guide other transit agencies as they seek to expand and improve services for riders with disabilities.

CHAPTER **1**

INTRODUCTION

PROBLEM STATEMENT

Passage of the Americans with Disabilities Act of 1990 (ADA) fundamentally changed the relationship between paratransit and fixed-route service. Paratransit service is no longer considered a substitute for accessible fixed-route service — both are required. Paratransit is a complementary service to be provided whenever fixed-route service is unable to or not appropriate to meet a customer's needs.

The ADA has also changed the way in which individuals are determined eligible for public paratransit service. Eligibility is no longer to be based solely on a person's particular disability or on the type of mobility aid that a person uses (for example, those who use wheelchairs are eligible for paratransit). Instead, ADA paratransit eligibility is determined on the basis of a person's ability to use the fixed-route system (given that system's current characteristics) and on related environmental factors. ADA-paratransit-eligible individuals are not necessarily granted access to the paratransit service for all travel needs — the fixed-route system is to be used whenever possible and appropriate.

This new relationship between fixed-route and paratransit service has important implications. First, provision of the most efficient, effective transportation now requires that fixed-route and paratransit service be designed, developed, and operated as one system rather than as separate systems. The expressed demand for paratransit service should be considered in the design or redesign of a total public transit program. Options and enhancements that better integrate fixed-route and paratransit service need to be considered.

Second, the transit industry's ability to implement the ADA may depend on its ability to take full advantage of fixed-route services and develop integrated paratransit and fixed-route systems. The Federal Transit Administration's (FTA's) recent review of ADA paratransit plans found that the requirement that posed the greatest problem to the industry is, not surprisingly, the elimination of capacity constraints. Shortcomings in addressing this service criterion were noted in 44 percent of the plans reviewed (*1*). Many transit providers project significant increases in travel demand by customers with disabilities. Expanding paratransit systems to meet this need will require significant increases in funding. Better use of available fixed-route capacity could, however, greatly reduce the financial impact of this aspect of the law.

Third, transit systems, which are likely to incur significant financial burdens meeting the paratransit requirements of the ADA, must consider the most efficient, appropriate integration of fixed-route and paratransit service. Before an undue financial burden can be claimed, providers must demonstrate that para-

transit service is being provided only when it is needed and required. Costs associated with providing paratransit service for trips that could have been accommodated on the fixed-route system cannot be counted in any calculation of undue financial burden. It is vital in these instances that all appropriate service options be explored for meeting the needs of ADA-paratransit-eligible individuals in the most integrated, cost-effective way.

As a result, interest in service options that better integrate fixed-route and paratransit systems and in programs that can enhance fixed-route systems has risen since the passage of the ADA. A significant number of ADA paratransit plans include travel training programs, on-call lift-bus programs, expanded marketing efforts, and other improvements. The development of service options and enhancements has also been promoted and facilitated by programs such as Project ACTION; demonstration programs and policies established by Transport Canada; and by workshops and seminars sponsored by the FTA, industry associations, and state transit agencies.

Technical information and research on the many types of service options and enhancements are limited. Certain types of enhancements (such as travel training, marketing, and employee training) are described in recent Project ACTION reports. For service options (such as route deviation services, feeder services, and service routes), few detailed studies exist that describe costs, benefits, and implementation issues. Available information is limited in many cases to promotional materials and articles in industry journals describing the efforts of specific providers. Without the benefit of research and detailed information, many providers are implementing programs without adequate knowledge of the likely costs, benefits, or effects on existing services and riders.

PURPOSE AND OVERVIEW OF THE STUDY

The goal of this research was to develop information and data to facilitate the efforts of local transit providers to implement appropriate service options and enhancements for serving individuals with disabilities. Specific objectives consistent with this goal include developing a way for transit managers and planners to design and evaluate integrated transit systems that do the following:

• Provide accessible, integrated service that complies with the ADA
• Facilitate the appropriate use of paratransit service
• Support service or system enhancements that encourage individuals with disabilities to travel on accessible fixed routes.

Research was conducted in two phases. In Phase I, service options and enhancements being used by transit systems in North America were identified and described. To develop a comprehensive list and to compensate for the limited body of knowledge that exists, a three-step approach was used. The first step involved an extensive literature review. Second, using readily available mailing lists, a brief information request was mailed to 624 public transit systems in the United States and Canada. This request asked providers to indicate if they had implemented or planned to implement certain service options and enhancements. It also asked for descriptions of other innovative options and enhancements that may not have been identified in the survey. Third, on the basis of the information received from the mailing, follow-up telephone calls were made to 95 transit providers that indicated relative success with one or more options and enhancements. Service and cost information, as well as information about local system characteristics, was collected through these calls.

Phase II of the research involved selecting five transit systems, which had implemented certain service options and enhancements, for a detailed evaluation. Evaluation methodolo-

gies were developed to guide the review of each system and option. The effectiveness of each option was examined, and key implementation issues were determined. Options and enhancements studied included service routes, feeder service, route deviation, low-floor buses, and fare incentive programs. A companion document, *Evaluating Transit Operations for Individuals with Disabilities* (2) was prepared and is available through the Transportation Cooperative Research Program.

ORGANIZATION OF THE REPORT

This report contains descriptions of each of the service options and enhancements identified and detailed information about innovative programs from the 95 systems contacted. Chapter 2 provides a more detailed summary of the research undertaken. Chapter 3 contains descriptions of each of the service options and enhancements identified.

A copy of the survey sent to transit providers is included in Appendix A. Information about selected transit providers, obtained from the survey and follow-up calls is presented in a series of tables in Appendix B.

6

CHAPTER **2**

SUMMARY OF RESEARCH APPROACH

IDENTIFICATION OF CURRENT INNOVATIVE PRACTICES

As discussed previously, research focused on identifying and describing the service options and enhancements being used in North America to promote fixed-route use and the appropriate use of paratransit by individuals with disabilities. To identify current practices, several research activities were undertaken, including an extensive literature search, a review of first-year ADA complementary paratransit plans prepared by public transit providers in the United States, and a survey of transit providers in both the United States and Canada.

Literature search activities included the following:

- A manual search of the holdings at the U.S. Department of Transportation (USDOT) library in Washington, D.C., for information about service options and enhancements
- A search through the Transportation Research Records from 1980 to date and of selected earlier records
- A search of the Massachusetts Institute of Technology's (MIT's) libraries using MIT's on-line search capability
- A search of the Volpe National Transportation Systems Center's library using its on-line search capability
- A search of the bulletin board Tap-In system maintained by the Community Transportation Association of America (CTAA)
- A search of articles, in the American Public Transit Association's (APTA's) *Passenger Transport*, focusing on the last 3 years but also searching indexes covering much of the 1980s
- A search of Project ACTION project summaries and newsletters
- A review of ADA paratransit plans in all ten FTA regional offices
- A review of recent Canadian research projects based on research summaries received from Transport Canada
- A search of National Technical Information Service and Dialog
- A review of national and international conference proceedings.

The researchers wrote an article describing the effort and requesting that readers bring innovative local programs to the attention of the research team by calling a toll-free telephone number, usable in both the United States and Canada. The article was sent to the CTAA, the APTA, and Project ACTION for printing in the *Community Transport Reporter*, *Passenger Transport*, and *Project ACTION Update* respectively.

Finally, an information request was sent to all public transit providers in the United States and Canada. This included 548

transit providers in the United States and 76 providers in Canada. The list of providers was developed with the assistance of Transport Canada, the FTA, and Project ACTION. The survey included a list of options and enhancements identified in the literature search. Respondents were asked whether they had tried, were using, or planned to implement each of the listed options and enhancements. They were also asked to rate the effectiveness of each option with which they had some experience. Finally, they were asked if they were aware of other options and enhancements not listed. A copy of the information request form is provided in Appendix A.

There were 309 responses to the industrywide survey — a return rate of 50 percent. Information from each response was entered into a database, and summary statistics and findings were prepared. Charts listing all providers using each option and enhancement were developed. These charts were used to identify possible case study sites and to direct follow-up call activities.

Follow-up calls were made to providers who indicated that they are using one or more of the listed options and enhancements. Because of the number of respondents, calls were made only to those providers who rated their local efforts as moderately effective to very effective (ratings of 3 or better). Calls were also focused on options and enhancements that were considered most appropriate for further study. Options and enhancements targeted for follow-up data collection included the following:

- Feeder services
- Travel training and facilitated travel
- Low-floor buses
- Service routes/community buses
- Route deviation services
- Point deviation services
- Accessible taxi programs
- On-call, accessible, fixed-route bus service
- Fare incentives programs.

The follow-up calls served several purposes. First, they verified that the provider was using the option or enhancement as described. In several cases, providers misunderstood the descriptions provided in the survey. For example, several agencies reported that they provide feeder service but understood this to mean general public feeder service using two fixed-route modes (such as bus feeder to rail service). Once it was confirmed that the provider was indeed operating an option/enhancement as described, additional information about the provider and the service was obtained. This included the following information:

- The population of the service area
- The size of the service area
- The total fixed-route fleet size
- The percent of fixed-route vehicles that are accessible
- The number of paratransit trips provided yearly
- The date when the option/enhancement was implemented.

If the contact person did not have this information readily available, data from available Section 15 reports were used. The tables in Appendix B provide this service information for selected systems identified through the survey.

Finally, follow-up calls were used to determine the suitability of the systems contacted for possible case study work. Information about local consumer involvement, such as the existence of advisory groups and how frequently such groups meet, was obtained. A general sense of the receptiveness of the provider to being studied was also noted.

Ninety-five transit providers were contacted for more detailed information about local services and programs. Where appropriate, this information was used in preparing the detailed description contained in Chapter 3 of this report. Data tables summarizing the information collected are provided in Appendix B.

DESCRIPTION OF OPTIONS AND ENHANCEMENTS

The second major task of the study involved preparing detailed descriptions of the service options and enhancements identified. From the literature review and survey, 20 basic service options and enhancements were identified. Four other aspects of the operation of an accessible transportation system (vehicle and facility design, equipment maintenance, employee training, and the provision of accessible information and communications) were identified as essential elements rather than options.

Chapter 3 provides, in a consistent format, descriptions of options and enhancements. Each begins with a concise definition. The definition is followed by a detailed description of the option or enhancement. Next, information is provided concerning the following:

- Ways in which the option/enhancement can promote fixed-rate use and the appropriate use of paratransit
- Applicability to particular situations and areas
- Key implementation issues
- Service and cost information.

Most sections end with a graph indicating the effectiveness of the service option as reported by transit systems responding to the survey. In a few cases, descriptions of options identified during the follow-up calls to the survey do not contain this information.

A list of additional sources of information discovered during the literature search and used to develop this report is provided after the list of references. These sources are grouped by option and enhancement.

CHAPTER **3**

DETAILED DESCRIPTIONS OF SERVICE OPTIONS AND ENHANCEMENTS

ESSENTIAL ELEMENTS OF AN ACCESSIBLE TRANSPORTATION SERVICE

This study and report focus on how traditional fixed-route and demand-responsive services can be changed and enhanced to promote the most appropriate use of fixed-route and paratransit services and to provide transportation service in the most integrated setting. Various operating models and technologies are presented and reviewed. Support services that can encourage the use of fixed-route service are discussed.

Certain aspects of the design and operation of accessible transportation services are essential and should not be considered options or enhancements to be studied and implemented if cost-effective. These essential elements of an accessible transit system include accessible vehicle and facility design, equipment maintenance, employee training, and information communications. Every transit system purporting to serve individuals with disabilities should address these issues, which are discussed in the following sections.

Accessible Vehicle and Facility Design

For transit providers in the United States, ADA regulations specify minimum accessibility design standards for vehicles and facilities. Vehicles and facilities should meet or exceed these minimum standards.

In Canada, the Ontario Ministry of Transportation has developed recommendations for improved access to transportation systems as part of its Easier Access Program. The recommendations, being implemented by several transit agencies throughout the province, were developed by a task force composed of representatives of transit systems and disability user groups.

Equipment Maintenance

To attract persons with disabilities to transit, and to fixed-route systems in particular, service must be safe and reliable. All access features, including lifts and ramps, securement systems, kneeling features, and information and communications systems, must be maintained in working order. Each feature should be checked regularly as part of any daily inspection and malfunctions should be reported and repaired promptly.

For all transit providers in the United States, the ADA regulations include provisions specific to lift and equipment maintenance. Section 37.161 of the USDOT's regulations contains general provisions that apply to all providers of transportation

services. Section 37.163 details additional requirements for public entities.

Employee Training

Adding lifts, ramps, and other features to vehicles and facilities is only the first step in providing transportation services that are truly accessible. A well-trained work force is also essential to ensure that equipment is used correctly and that all customers, including those with disabilities, receive appropriate assistance and are served courteously.

All transportation providers in the United States are required, by the USDOT's ADA regulations, to train employees "to proficiency." Training should address use of all access equipment, providing appropriate assistance to individuals with disabilities, knowledge of system policies and practices, and basic customer service and sensitivity skills.

Accessible Information and Communications

To be able to understand and use the transit system, customers (including those with vision, speech, and hearing impairments) need to have access to service information. This includes written materials, schedules, and any other communications that may be provided, such as those in terminals, at transit stops, and in vehicles.

Section 37.167 (f) of the USDOT's ADA regulations includes specific requirements for ensuring access to information and communications. Information must be provided in formats usable by the person with a disability and must be provided in formats appropriate to their use. Systems and technologies must be employed to ensure that individuals with hearing and speech impairments have equal access to any communications provided both prior to the trip and during the trip.

SERVICE OPTIONS AND ENHANCEMENTS

Beyond these essential system features, numerous other options and enhancements can be considered. These include 1) alternative operational models, 2) alternative technologies, and 3) support services.

Alternative operational models are various approaches to the basic design and operation of fixed-route and demand-responsive systems. Options in this category include the following:

- Service routes and community bus

- On-call, accessible, fixed-route bus
- Route deviation
- Point deviation
- Feeder service
- General public dial-a-ride (DAR)
- Subscription bus
- Flag-stop and request-a-stop programs.

Alternative technologies include new vehicle and equipment designs that specifically address the needs of customers with disabilities. Although this category could include numerous recent technologies, the researchers have focused this study on the following:

- Low-floor buses
- Accessible taxis
- Automated information and communication technologies.

Finally, support services are activities and programs that supplement the basic services being provided. Support services promote, encourage, and facilitate the use of appropriate modes by persons with disabilities. The following support services were examined during this study:

- Travel training and facilitated transportation
- Fare incentive programs
- Fare simplification mechanisms
- Marketing
- Trip planning
- Service planning
- Accessible bus stop programs
- Vehicle identifier programs
- Destination card programs.

PRESENTATION OF OPTIONS AND ENHANCEMENTS

The remainder of this chapter contains detailed descriptions of each of the options and enhancements noted above. Operational models are addressed first, alternative technologies are provided second, and the various support services identified are discussed last. Each description contains a concise definition of the option, a discussion of the applicability of the option to specific situations and areas, and important implementation considerations. Certain descriptions also contain service information and cost data, if these were available in the literature. The references and sources of information used to prepare the descriptions are listed at the end of this chapter.

If the option or enhancement being described was included in the study survey, information about the option's or enhancement's reported use and effectiveness is also provided. Charts of selected transit providers reporting the use of each option are contained in Appendix B and referenced in each of the following sections.

SERVICE ROUTES AND COMMUNITY BUS

Fixed routes are designed to reduce the distances that elderly persons and persons with disabilities must travel to get to and from bus stops. Typically, smaller vehicles are used, and vehicles travel on neighborhood streets or to mall or hospital doorways to reduce walking distances. Although routes are designed to better meet the needs of persons with disabilities and elderly persons, they are open to the public. Services can be planned as feeders to other fixed-route services and can include a "route deviation" option.

Service routes (also known in Canada as community bus services) were first identified as a service option in Boras, Sweden, in 1983 (3). Service routes are designed to bring fixed-route buses as close as possible to the residences and destinations of the target population (i.e., users of paratransit services). The service in Boras was considered successful and has been introduced in more than 50 cities in Sweden. Other European countries (such as Denmark, Finland, Norway, and Holland) had implemented service routes by late 1991.

In Canada, the Toronto Transit Commission implemented the service route concept in 1989 (4). Since then, more than six other Canadian cities have implemented service routes, and more are planned. Canadian cities that have implemented services include Ottawa, St. Catherine, Hamilton, Oakville, Welland, Edmonton, Winnipeg, and Calgary (5, 6). Early implementers in the United States include Madison County Transit of Madison, Illinois (1985), and Madison Metro of Wisconsin (1992) (7, 8). Many other transit agencies in the United States are planning or implementing service routes so as to improve the cost-effectiveness of services provided to ADA-eligible persons.

Characteristics of service routes include the following:

- A route layout that minimizes walking distance for the target population. Route planning considers demographics, housing for the target population, topography, and important destinations such as care centers, clinics, hospitals, shopping, and connections to regular fixed-route service. Service route planning also considers the pattern of travel requests coming from paratransit services. Figure 1 illustrates the different route pattern for service routes versus regular fixed-route service.
- Service routes feature convenient bus stops. Buses stop at entrances to malls, hospitals, and so forth. Usually patrons can flag buses anywhere on the route and exit the buses anywhere on the route. Some services also feature route deviation service, where the patron can request that the vehicle make a small diversion from the regular route for pick up or drop off.
- Service routes use vehicles smaller than those typically used by fixed-route public transit programs. The vehicles used have included accessible vehicles similar to those used in

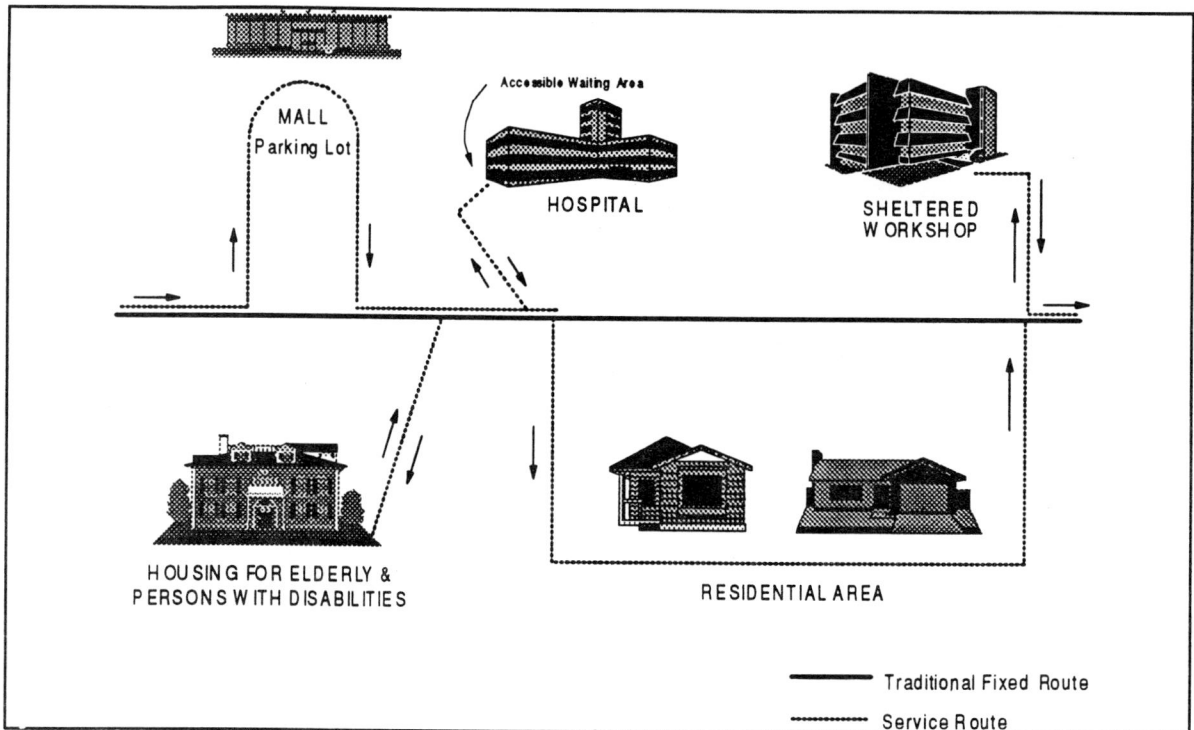

Figure 1. Service route as compared to regular fixed route.

paratransit and special low-floor buses (24 to 29 ft long) with two or three wheelchair positions.

• Service routes use streets that cannot be serviced by regular transit buses. These include narrow streets in residential and central areas and pedestrian-only areas.

• Service routes operate with sufficient time in the schedule to allow for driver assistance and for entrance and exit by persons needing additional time.

• Most service routes operate on hourly schedules; however, the schedules need to be coordinated with the service needs of the target population—for example, the services can be designed to accommodate the schedule of sheltered workshops or other local programs.

Service routes have been developed as additions to fixed-route services, as in Toronto, Ontario, and Madison, Wisconsin, and have been used to replace fixed-route services with low patronage as in Madison, Illinois.

Promoting Integration and Appropriate Use of Fixed-Route and Paratransit Services

Service routes allow users of paratransit systems to use fixed-route services because the service routes reduce walking distance and the vehicles used often are low-floor buses, which eliminate the need for users to climb the steps of full-sized buses. The advantage of service routes for users of paratransit systems is that use of service routes does not require reserva-

tions—this increases the possibility for spontaneous travel. There may also be a fare advantage—paratransit system fares may be twice those of fixed-route services. Service routes allow persons with disabilities to travel on the same system with the general public, thereby promoting independence and mainstreaming.

For service routes to promote appropriate use of paratransit services, they should be closely coordinated with those services. If this is not the case, service routes can still provide excellent service to a community (providing service at higher productivities than the paratransit service) but may not succeed in attracting trips from the paratransit service.

Applicability to Particular Situations and Areas

Service routes have been used in cities of various sizes in Europe and in North America. In Sweden, for example, service routes have been implemented in cities the size of Stockholm (population 724,000) and Boras (population 60,000). The overall density of the service area is less important than the density of origins and destinations along any potential fixed-route corridor.

Service routes can be used to replace low-use, regular, fixed-route services and to replace certain trips on the paratransit services. Service routes could be used, for example, to replace off-peak, fixed-route service where ridership is low. In Madison County, Illinois, a system of service routes has replaced the local fixed-route service previously provided by the Bi-State

Development Agency, leaving Bi-State to provide fixed-route service for commuters in the peak periods. Madison County Transit has been able to increase ridership on the fixed-route system (including Bi-State and Madison County Transit) from around 4,000 trips daily in 1985 to 6,500 daily in 1993 while Bi-State's overall ridership was declining.

For service routes to be successful in relieving demand for paratransit services, there must be sufficient demand density to require a fixed-route service, that is, the fixed-route service should be able to carry more ADA-eligible patrons per hour than the paratransit service. If the pattern of paratransit tripmaking is characterized by many-to-many trips, and there is little regularity to the travel demands of the target population, service routes may not be appropriate. In assessing the applicability of service routes, transit agencies should consider whether the ADA paratransit service is likely to experience new demand for many-to-one trips such as to sheltered workshops for persons with cognitive disabilities who may not have previously qualified for paratransit services.

Key Implementation Issues

Several factors affect how service routes substitute for paratransit and/or existing fixed-route services. Issues to consider include the following:

- Design of the service routes should consider the patterns of trip demand of the target population, and the routes should be laid out and scheduled to best accommodate these patterns. Regular trips, such as subscription trips or trips to senior centers or sheltered workshops, can indicate likely fixed routes. Use of service routes to provide regularly scheduled trips should result in the paratransit system's providing more many-to-many trips.

- Paratransit service operators need to encourage patrons to use the service routes. This can best be done where the paratransit dispatchers know the travel needs of their customers and where they have some incentive to endorse the use of the service routes. Flexibility is important—ADA-eligible patrons may be able to use service routes on some occasions but not always (such as when there is snow or ice).

- Travel training, facilitated travel programs, and other hands-on methods will help paratransit users to become familiar with the service routes (9).

- Use of similar vehicles and familiar drivers (such as those who drive for the paratransit service) will help patrons feel comfortable in transitioning to service routes from paratransit services.

- A close working relationship with the community of persons with disabilities and with agencies serving that community will facilitate the planning and marketing of the service.

- Where social service agencies have a financial stake in the success of service routes, they may be more likely to support their use by clients. For example, agencies providing transportation or paying "agency" fees to the transit agency will have an incentive to encourage use of service routes.

- Patrons of ADA paratransit service may be more likely to use service routes if there is an advantage such as a lower fare than paratransit service or if convenience is greater (for example, no need to call for reservations).

Service and Cost Information

The existing limited experience with service routes shows a wide range of operating results. Following are some of the statistics collected on overall tripmaking, conversion of paratransit trips to fixed-route trips, and financial results.

Experience with the service routes in Boras, Sweden, indicates how much the mobility of target populations can be enhanced. Before and after studies in an area with service routes found that daily tripmaking by the elderly had increased by 12 percent per day overall. Data from Madison, Wisconsin, also seem to indicate that service routes encourage new tripmaking. Surveys conducted on service routes after implementation indicated that paratransit registrants had increased their tripmaking by 12 percent. Initial plans projected a decline in use of the paratransit system of 12 percent, but this has not occurred.

Systems varied in their success in transferring patrons from paratransit services to fixed-route services. Of those entitled to paratransit services in Boras, Sweden, the percentage using public transit rose from 28 to 53 after service routes were introduced. Of those entitled to paratransit, 15 percent found the distance to the bus stop too great, even with service routes. Of those entitled to paratransit service and who also use public transportation, 35 percent reported difficulties when using public transit after service routes were introduced, as compared to 91 percent before service routes.

In Madison County, Illinois, the monthly trips provided by the paratransit service declined from 12,000 to 7,000 after the fully developed service-route system was introduced. Madison County Transit undertook several steps to encourage this switch, including the introduction of travel training, marketing of the service routes to community groups and agencies, and using trained paratransit drivers for the service routes. Because Madison County Transit has a policy of not rejecting requests for service, a reasonable assumption is that the 5,000 monthly trips switched onto the service routes. Assuming no overall increase in tripmaking, the service routes would then carry around 42 percent of the trips carried by the paratransit system.

The Boras system and the Madison County, Illinois, system saved money by introducing service routes, whereas the Toronto system and the Madison, Wisconsin, system did not. In Boras, the savings on the paratransit service were estimated to be twice the net operating cost of the service routes. In addition, Boras was able to eliminate some fixed-route services equivalent to 66 percent of the net cost of the service routes.

In Madison County, Illinois, the service route network was used to replace off-peak and local fixed-route services provided by Bi-State Development Corporation of St. Louis. Because the service routes cost about one-quarter as much per hour as the Bi-State routes, they could offer much more area coverage. The total daily ridership on both the Bi-State routes and the service routes increased from around 4,000 daily in 1985 to around 6,500 daily. In addition, the service routes reduced the demand for paratransit service by 42 percent. The productivity

12

of the service routes for ADA-eligible persons is higher than that experienced by the paratransit service.

In Toronto, Ontario, and in Madison, Wisconsin, the service routes were added to the existing fixed-route network; therefore, there were no savings resulting from eliminating existing fixed-route services. In Madison, Wisconsin, the productivity of the service routes for paratransit-eligible persons was similar to that of the paratransit service. In addition, as mentioned previously, service route use did not replace or reduce paratransit service use. Therefore, the Madison, Wisconsin, service routes were an additional system cost.

Surveys taken of the Toronto service route ridership found that 12 percent of the users were registered for paratransit service and another 7 percent of the users thought they might be eligible for paratransit. Toronto estimated that the cost to provide the service routes for those paratransit users amounted to $33 per trip as compared to $30 per trip for paratransit service. If all of the users and potential paratransit users were counted, the service route cost would have been $21 per trip. This analysis does not reflect any increase in overall tripmaking that may have resulted from the service routes. Also this analysis does not consider the benefits obtained by the more than 80 percent of the riders who are not paratransit eligible.

These varied results indicate that service route design is very important if service routes are to provide enhanced mobility for persons with disabilities, relieve the demand for paratransit service, and save money. Clearly, there is more potential for savings when the service routes replace existing, low-demand, fixed-route services.

Reported Use and Effectiveness

Of the 309 respondents to the study survey, 55 indicated that they operate service routes. Follow-up calls revealed, however, that most of these providers incorrectly considered prescheduled paratransit services or fixed-route charter services to be service routes. Twelve examples of service route programs were, however, confirmed from the survey. Table B-1 in Appendix B provides information about these systems.

The survey asked respondents to rate the effectiveness of each option employed on a scale of 1 to 5 (with 1 being "not effective" and 5 being "very effective"). Among the 12 confirmed examples of service route programs, the reported effectiveness of this option was quite high. As shown in Table B-1 in Appendix B, all nine of the agencies that rated this option indicated an effectiveness of between 3 and 5.

ON-CALL, ACCESSIBLE, FIXED-ROUTE BUS SERVICE

On-call, accessible, fixed-route bus service (also known as call-a-lift bus service) allows individuals who need to use accessible fixed-route vehicles to call in advance and request that an accessible bus be placed on a particular route at the time they wish to travel.

The transition from an inaccessible, fixed-route system to one using accessible buses can take several years. In larger systems with staggered fleet replacement schedules, the first few orders of accessible vehicles may leave the system with a fleet that is only partially accessible. During this period, the most effective, efficient distribution of accessible buses throughout the fixed-route system becomes important. In such cases, transit providers have the following basic options:

(1) Assign accessible buses to particular routes and designate a few routes as 100-percent accessible

(2) Assign accessible buses to more routes and operate these routes as partially accessible (for example, every other bus is accessible)

(3) Establish an on-call, accessible, fixed-route bus program and allow individuals to call in advance and request that accessible vehicles be assigned to routes they will be using at the time they plan to travel

(4) Combine an on-call program with designated accessible or partially accessible routes.

The successful use of the first two options requires that the transit agency predict the likely demand for fixed-route service by individuals with ambulatory disabilities. Paratransit trip records can be examined to determine common origins and destinations. Major trip generators and attractors can also be plotted and compared to the fixed-route network. Involving customers with disabilities is also recommended. The transit agency's advisory committee, local service agencies, and local advocacy organizations should be consulted regarding the routes that they or their members are most likely to use.

Even if a transit agency is successful in assigning new accessible buses to the most appropriate and heavily used routes, designating only certain routes as fully or partially accessible still restricts travel options for people with disabilities. A much-reduced network will be available to them. Trips in areas served by non-accessible buses will not be possible. Similarly, trips that typically involve transfers will not be possible if one of the routes is not designated as accessible.

On-call, accessible, fixed-route bus programs offer a short-term solution to this problem. By distributing accessible vehicles throughout the system and allowing individuals to request accessible vehicles on any route at any time, the entire fixed-route network can be made available to customers with disabilities.

Transit providers in the United States can also use on-call, accessible, fixed-route service programs to help satisfy the requirements of the ADA (10). The USDOT regulations implementing the ADA recognize on-call service as an acceptable form of complementary paratransit service for the purpose of meeting the needs of Category 2, ADA-paratransit-eligible individuals (persons who can get to and from fixed-route stops and can otherwise navigate the fixed-route system but who can only board a bus if it is accessible) (11). By implementing an on-call bus program, transit agencies effectively make their entire fixed-route system accessible to these individuals. Complementary paratransit service can then be focused on other ADA-paratransit-eligible persons.[1]

Typically, an on-call, fixed-route, bus program works in the following way: Customers needing to use accessible, fixed-route vehicles call ahead to indicate the route they will be using and the time they will be traveling. If the program is being used to meet ADA-complementary paratransit service requirements, requirements for advance notice cannot exceed "next day" standards (requests must be taken up to the close of the typical administrative hours on the day before travel). If the program is used only to supplement the complementary paratransit service, greater advance notice can be required. Many systems in this situation require requests to be made by early or mid-afternoon on the day preceding service to allow staff in fixed-route operations to arrange the necessary scheduling.

As in the scheduling of paratransit service, certain information, such as the type of mobility aid used, should be collected from the customer to ensure that service is appropriate and efficient. This information will be needed partly to ensure that the vehicle lift or other access features will be able to accommodate the passenger. Given that requests may be made by individuals with ambulatory disabilities who do not use wheelchairs, this information will be needed to ensure that a securement location is available on the route and at the time it is requested. In addition, any particular assistance that may be needed by the individual or the need to travel with a personal care attendant or service animal could be noted.

Depending on where requests are received, it may be necessary to establish formal communications with the appropriate fixed-route operations staff. The Massachusetts Bay Transportation Authority (MBTA) in Boston, for example, takes requests at their Office for Transportation Access (OTA), the administrative office responsible for all fixed-route and paratransit programs for individuals with disabilities (12). OTA then calls the appropriate fixed-route garage (there are eight garages throughout the system) and follows this verbal contact with a facsimile copy of the request form. The MBTA has also formally designated fixed-route staff at each garage; these individuals are responsible for accepting requests and making the necessary arrangements.

Requests for accessible buses could also be taken at other locations within the system. In less complex systems with only one fixed-route bus garage, a phone line could be designated within the fixed-route dispatch office. Requests could also be taken by the office that provides the public with route and schedule information. Another alternative would be to assign the function of accepting accessible bus requests to the in-house or contractor staff who schedule paratransit service. This latter alternative would promote greater integration between paratransit and fixed-route services.

Once the request has been received and transmitted, as needed, to the appropriate fixed-route staff, an accessible bus

is scheduled. The request may also be noted on the driver manifest along with any pertinent information about the customer. In some systems, a second bus, on the next run on that route will also be scheduled. Should the customer be late in arriving at the designated stop or if the accessibility features on the first bus malfunction, service can still be delivered with a minimum delay.

Arrangements can also be made to accept standing order requests from individuals making repetitive trips for work, school, and so forth. If travel will be made at the same time and on the same route each day for an extended period, an ongoing vehicle assignment can be arranged. The customer may be asked to reconfirm the request periodically, such as every month. The customer would also need to call should the daily routine change or service not be needed on a particular day.

On-call, accessible bus services can be offered as a supplement to paratransit services or can be integrated with paratransit operations. Where the program is used to supplement paratransit, the use of the on-call bus program is voluntary. Individuals with disabilities can choose which mode they prefer to use and request service on either system. Programs integrated with the paratransit service may, on the other hand, require use of the fixed-route system by those determined able to use it. If eligibility determination records show that a customer who is calling for paratransit service can use accessible, fixed-route vehicles and if the customer can get to and from the bus stops for the particular trip in question, on-call bus service can be offered as an alternative to paratransit.

One of the benefits of an on-call, accessible bus program is the ability to identify actual demand. On the basis of actual requests received, routes can be considered for designation as fully or partially accessible. For example, should one or more standing order requests be received for a particular route, it may be cost-effective to assign enough accessible vehicles to that route to allow it to be advertised as fully accessible. As additional accessible vehicles are purchased, the demand for on-call service can be used to help decide the most appropriate distribution of these vehicles within the system.

Promoting Integration and Appropriate Use of Fixed-Route and Paratransit Services

By effectively making the entire fixed-route network accessible, on-call, accessible bus programs can increase opportunities that customers with disabilities have to use fixed-route service. When fully integrated with paratransit operations, such programs can also permit transit providers to make maximum use of fixed-route service and can provide a cost-effective alternative to paratransit.

Although they offer the benefit of expanded opportunities for using a fixed route, on-call programs provide a lower level of service than either fixed-route or paratransit systems. Because customers must request service in advance, on-call programs do not offer the flexibility of scheduling and spontaneity provided by fixed-route service or the convenience of curb-to-curb or door-to-door service available to paratransit riders. On-call, accessible bus programs are, therefore,

---

[1]If an on-call, accessible, fixed-route bus program is used to meet the needs of Category 2, ADA-paratransit-eligible persons, the program must be designed to meet each of the six complementary paratransit service criteria noted in the regulations. For example, it must be offered for no more than twice the base fixed-route fare, must be available during all hours of fixed route operation, must meet "next day" response time standards, and so forth.

recommended only as a short-term system enhancement. As additional, accessible, fixed-route buses become available— beyond the number needed to operate the on-call program— fixed routes should be designated and advertised as fully or partially accessible.

If arrangements for standing orders are permitted, on-call, accessible bus programs may be most attractive to customers traveling to work or to school or for other repetitive trips. Unless required as an alternative to paratransit service, demand for on-call bus service for individual, one-time trips is likely to be limited. Because on-call service is less inconvenient for customers making repetitive trips, transit providers may want to consider reviewing current paratransit subscription trips and offering on-call, fixed-route service to customers making repetitive paratransit trips.

Applicability to Particular Situations and Areas

On-call, accessible, fixed-route bus programs can enhance any fixed-route system that is less than 100-percent accessible. This enhancement is equally beneficial in rural systems, small urban, and large urban systems. It is perhaps most applicable in situations where fixed-route access is less than 50 percent or where the planned capital replacement schedule for fixed-route vehicles will not enable full accessibility to be achieved in the near term. This option may also be attractive if there is no clear alternative for the effective assignment of a few accessible buses. If likely demand is not concentrated along a particular route or set of routes, it may be more effective to offer on-demand access throughout the system rather than designate a few routes as accessible.

Several transit providers contacted during this study also indicated that early attempts at operating lift-equipped buses had been problematic. Older lifts were unreliable and often out of service. Even though these problems had been alleviated with the purchase of newer equipment, the general perception among riders, particularly those who had attempted to use services in years past, was that lifts were unreliable. These systems offered on-call services as a way to assure riders that equipment would be functioning, thereby increasing rider confidence.

Key Implementation Issues

Level of Fixed-Route Accessibility Needed to Start a Program

Although providing on-call, accessible, fixed-route service on a first-come, first-served basis is possible, implementation probably should be considered only after there are sufficient accessible buses in the fixed-route fleet to meet the projected demand. The inconvenience of capacity constraints would further reduce program attractiveness relative to paratransit service and could severely limit program use.

Table B-2 in Appendix B includes information from several systems on the level of fixed-route access when the program was implemented ("% FR Access when Implem."). Although four providers indicated that service was started when the fixed-route fleet was less than 20 percent accessible, one (the Transit Authority of North Kentucky) noted that not all requests could be met in the early stages of the program. Most programs were implemented at 20 percent or greater access. In systems with multiple fixed-route garages, consideration must also be given to having an adequate level of accessibility at each garage.

Location of Staff Receiving Requests

During program design, the most appropriate location at which to take requests for accessible buses should be determined. Requests can be accepted in several locations, including a general administrative office, a public information office, the paratransit operations center, or the fixed-route operations center.

Integration with Paratransit Operation

Combining the operation of paratransit and on-call bus services offers important advantages. First, it allows paratransit schedulers to use the fixed-route system as a cost-effective alternative where appropriate. Arrangements could be made within the same office to serve individuals who call to request paratransit service but who could use the fixed-route system with the guarantee of an accessible bus. Second, the paratransit operations staff is likely to have information, already on file for many on-call bus customers, that can be helpful in ensuring that the best possible service is provided.

Successful integration with the paratransit operation will require, however, that paratransit staff be fully versed in planning trips on the fixed-route system and that they have access to the most recent service information. This will be particularly important in larger, more complex systems.

Establishing a Full Bus Policy

Placing an accessible bus on a route on request does not guarantee that a seat or a wheelchair securement location is available when the bus reaches the stop at which the caller wishes to board. Other persons with disabilities may wish to board the bus at prior stops along the route. Although this is not likely to happen as frequently on routes not designated or advertised as accessible, it is possible on any route; therefore, a clear policy for resolving such situations must be adopted and communicated to potential customers. A call for an accessible bus could either be treated as a reservation for a seat/securement location or simply as a request to place an accessible bus on the route without a guarantee of a seat. If the former policy is adopted, customers needing to use the available securement locations at prior stops may be told that the space is reserved. If the latter approach is taken, the person who originally called for the bus may be denied service. The use of an on-call program as a required alternative to paratransit as opposed to a supplemental/voluntary service should also be considered when determining an appropriate policy.

Regardless of the approach taken, routinely scheduling the bus requested and a following bus can help to resolve such capacity issues. Combining the operation of on-call and paratransit service can also facilitate the quick dispatching of a paratransit vehicle in such circumstances.

Driver Training

Particular attention must be given in on-call bus programs to ensuring that drivers assigned to accessible buses are adequately trained. Often, in systems where only a part of the fixed-route fleet is accessible and routes are designated as accessible, only those drivers who might be assigned an accessible bus are trained. With the implementation of an on-call bus program, an accessible bus may be assigned to any route on any given day. If all drivers have not been fully trained, the person scheduling accessible buses must be careful to ensure that the driver assigned has been trained. Depending on union work rules, this coordination of trained drivers with requested buses may be complicated by the ability of drivers to bid for particular routes. In such a situation, the needs of the program should be discussed with the union and an appropriate process for resolving any conflicts developed.

Reported Use and Effectiveness

Of the 309 respondents to the study survey, 74 indicated that they offer on-call, accessible, fixed-route bus service. The survey asked respondents to rate the effectiveness of each option employed on a scale of 1 to 5 (with 1 being "not effective" and 5 being "very effective"). Of the 28 respondents who completed the effectiveness rating portion of the survey, 23 reported that this option was moderately to very effective in promoting use of fixed-route service. Only five providers reported that it was less than moderately effective. Figure 2 shows the effectiveness rating given to this option by survey respondents.

Table B-2 in Appendix B provides information about the on-call, accessible, fixed-route bus programs at selected transit agencies. As shown, the service is provided by transit agencies in rural and large urban settings. Although several agencies report infrequent use of the service, some provide a significant number of trips per month through the program. In particular, the MBTA, the Transit Authority of North Kentucky, the Rogue Valley Transportation District, and the Southeastern Pennsylvania Transportation Authority reported that on-call service was a significant part of overall fixed-route ridership by persons with disabilities.

ROUTE DEVIATION SERVICE

In a route deviation service, a vehicle operates along a fixed route, making scheduled stops along the way. Vehicles will deviate from the route, however, to pick up and drop off passengers upon request. The

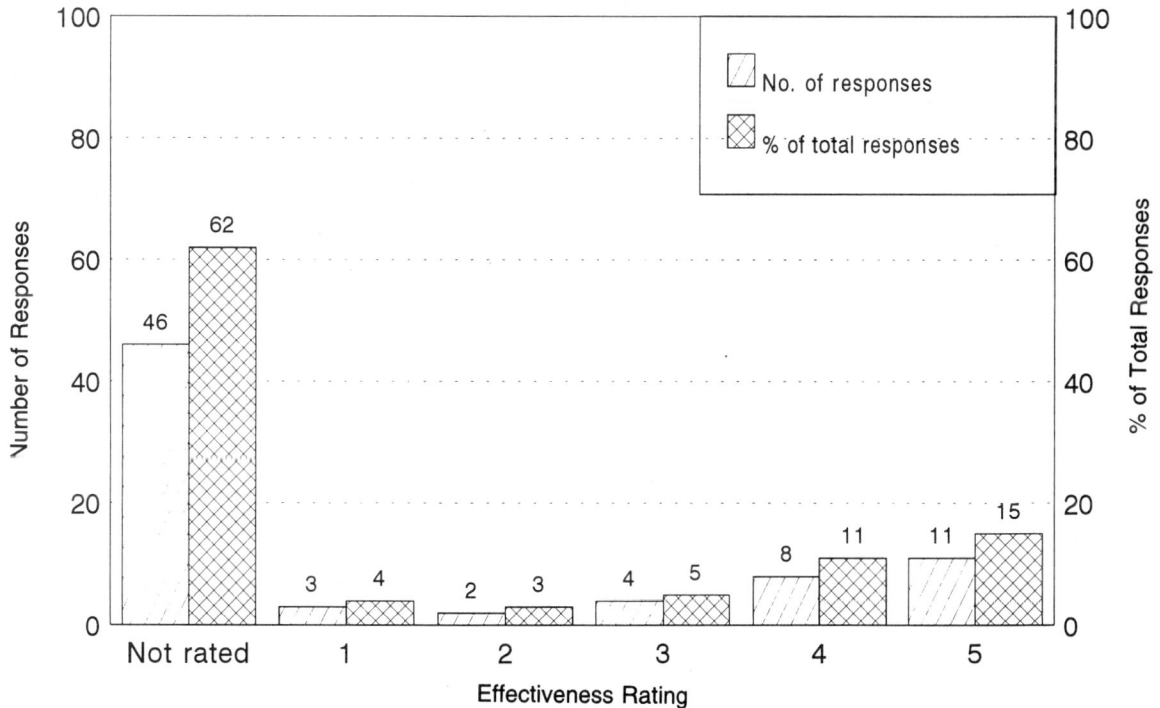

Figure 2. *Reported effectiveness of on-call, accessible, fixed-route bus programs. 1 = not effective; 5 = very effective.*

16

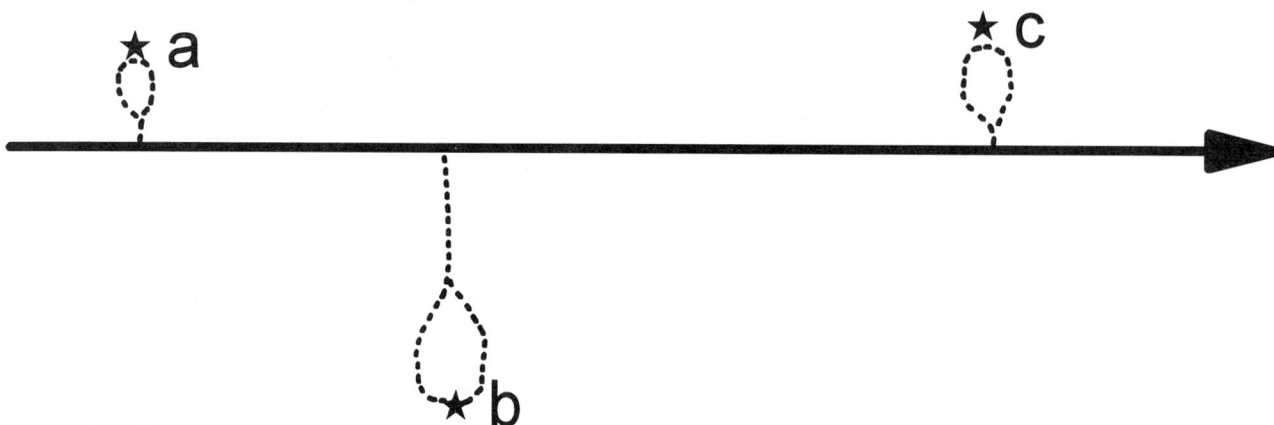

Figure 3.   Illustration of route deviation.

vehicle then returns to the fixed route at the point at which it departed to accommodate the request. Several variations are possible, including client-specific route deviation, and site-specific route deviation.

Route deviation has been described in several publications (*10, 13, 14, 15, 16*) as a hybrid configuration adapting features of fixed-route, fixed-schedule transit service and demand-responsive, curb-to-curb service. In the absence of any requests to "deviate," the service operates as a traditional fixed-route system with vehicles following a specific route and making scheduled stops. Unlike traditional fixed-route service, however, customers are allowed to request that vehicles deviate to either pick them up or drop them off at a specific location off of the advertised route. After accommodating off-route requests, vehicles return to and continue along the advertised route. Because the service accommodates deviation requests as part of an advertised schedule, vehicles leave and return to the same point along the route. This ensures that all customers who may be waiting for the vehicle will still be accommodated. Figure 3 illustrates route deviation service. The solid line depicts the advertised route. The dotted lines show deviations from the route to pick up or drop off riders at points "a," "b," and "c."

Requests for deviations from the advertised route can be made in various ways. For pickups, customers are typically required to call the fixed-route dispatcher or control center in advance. The amount of advance notice required will vary depending on the time needed to arrange for the pickup and communicate the request to the driver of the vehicle. Systems that have radio-equipped vehicles can require minimal notice. If two-way communication with vehicles is not available, systems may require that requests be received before the vehicle has left the garage or other checkpoint to begin the run. Some systems require 24-hour or prior-day notice so that the request can be reviewed and the effect on the advertised schedule can be assessed. If too many off-route requests are received, the request may be denied or the customer may be served by paratransit.

Requests for deviations to reach a particular destination can either be required in advance or given to the driver when the customer boards the vehicle. If vehicles are radio-equipped, drivers can be required to relay deviation requests to the dispatcher for approval. If not, drivers may be given basic operating guidelines to assist in accepting requests.

A major issue in the design of route deviation service is deciding which riders will be allowed to make deviation requests. Systems can be either general public or rider-specific. A general public route deviation service will accept requests from all riders. A rider-specific program might target the service to riders who have difficulty getting to or from the advertised route. The ability to request deviations could be limited to persons with disabilities or even to persons with specific functional disabilities (for example, persons determined ADA paratransit eligible under Category 3—meaning they cannot get to or from stops or stations). It is even possible to use route deviation, fixed-route service to meet the travel needs of individuals who have requested paratransit service. Trip requests received at the paratransit scheduling office could be referred to the fixed-route system if the request could be accommodated by a minor deviation of the fixed-route bus.

For transit providers in the United States, the decision to operate either a general public or a rider-specific route deviation service is often related to overall plans to provide ADA-complementary paratransit service. The USDOT regulations implementing the ADA define general public route deviation services as "demand-responsive" systems (*17*). Public entities operating such services are under no regulatory obligation to provide complementary paratransit service along routes that accept route deviation requests from the general public. If, however, the opportunity to request route deviation is limited to a specific rider group, a paratransit plan must still be developed and submitted.[2] Essentially, the route deviation service becomes part of the transit provider's approach to accommodating individuals determined ADA paratransit eligible. For example, if vehicles deviate only for persons with disabilities, and the service is intended to meet the ADA paratransit requirements, the six service criteria also must be met (for example, vehicles must deviate up to $^3/_4$ mi, deviation requests must be

---

[2]On the basis of internal guidance developed by the FTA during the review of ADA paratransit plans.

accepted on a next-day basis, fares for deviations can be no more than twice the base fare, and so forth). Also, the proposed service must be able to meet the needs of persons who cannot "navigate" the system (that is, Category 1 persons). For example, if the system involves more than one route, transfers must be coordinated or assistance must be provided to ensure that riders can travel throughout the entire service area.

The area throughout which service is provided and the times when deviations are accepted also should be determined when designing the system. Deviation requests can be limited to certain distances from the advertised route. Transit providers using this model typically deviate anywhere from two blocks to $\frac{3}{4}$ mi. Deviations of a few blocks are typical for systems that accept requests from the general public. Systems that deviate $\frac{3}{4}$ mi tend to do so to meet regulatory requirements for complementary service.

Several transit providers using this option also employ route deviation in only certain parts of their service area. Typically, deviations are allowed on routes or portions of routes serving rural and suburban areas. Use of route deviation in these areas has less of an impact on overall service than it would in the core of the service area. It also permits the fixed-route system to service those who may otherwise require paratransit service, which would be expensive to provide in these low-density areas.

Route deviation can also be limited to certain times. The Lakeland Area Mass Transit District in Lakeland, Florida, permits the general public to request deviations only on Saturdays. The Housatonic Area Regional Transit District in Danbury, Connecticut, identifies specific runs on its fixed-route schedules on which deviation requests are permitted.

To limit the effect that deviations could have on overall service, it is also possible to accept deviation requests but provide the service only as appropriate. Several transit providers coordinate the operation of route deviation services with their demand-responsive/paratransit services. Customers whose deviation requests would cause an unacceptable delay on the fixed-route system are served by paratransit if they are eligible. Other systems advertise that they will entertain deviation requests but note in their public information that requests will be met only if possible.

Another popular approach to offering a degree of route flexibility while limiting overall schedule impact is to provide site-specific, route deviation service. Under this alternative, certain major trip generators or destinations, such as public housing or group homes, senior centers, service agencies, and so forth are identified on the advertised schedule. Deviation requests are only accepted for these specific sites. Customers and local agencies can request that new sites be considered and these may be included on the schedule the next time the routes are adjusted or schedules updated. As noted in Table B-3 in Appendix B, use of site-specific route deviation was reported by several providers, including systems in Abilene, Texas; Attleboro, Massachusetts; Danbury, Connecticut; Eugene, Oregon; Fort Worth, Texas; and Rapid City, South Dakota.

Route deviation can be developed in various ways. Table 1 summarizes the various approaches that can be used to design route deviation services.

Promoting Integration and Appropriate Use of Fixed-Route and Paratransit Services

Route deviation integrates the operation of fixed-route and demand-responsive service—it provides regularly scheduled fixed-route service for the general public while permitting requests for more personalized curb-side service.

A significant percentage of persons eligible for paratransit service have difficulty getting to and from traditional fixed-route bus stops. They can otherwise use fixed-route vehicles but have difficulty walking long distances or are affected by architectural or environmental barriers. Route deviation services allow these individuals to use the general public bus system rather than a separate paratransit service.

Applicability to Particular Situations and Areas

Route deviation services appear to be most applicable in rural and suburban areas where the effects of deviations are not as disruptive to general service. Longer routes with longer headways and relatively low ridership may also be appropriate for deviation. Deviation services may also be appropriate where there is a linear pattern of development and where, consequently, most potential origins and destinations are close to advertised fixed routes.

Route deviation may also be appropriate where both fixed-route service and complementary paratransit service are not economically feasible. Many rural and small urban fixed-route systems have introduced route deviation service as a way to maintain fixed-route programs and meet requirements of the ADA. This option can be used more broadly if it is limited in design (for example, site-specific programs) or if it is coordinated with paratransit service and requests are honored only if possible within the fixed-route schedule.

Key Implementation Issues

Scaling the Deviation

The maximum distance for deviations has significant operating consequences as well as a major effect on potential demand. Systems typically deviate from a block or two to $\frac{3}{4}$ mi. Systems for the general public seem to deviate less than programs designed to meet the ADA, which follow the regulatory corridor requirements.

Anticipation of Capacity Constraints

When designing the system, potential demand and the ability to meet all requests must be addressed. Policies concerning the handling of requests and the use of the paratransit system as a backup should be considered.

Receiving and Processing Service Requests

Route deviation systems follow the DAR model of receiving requests for service—scheduling the request within the constraints of a fixed route or fixed schedule and communicating the

TABLE 1 Summary of route deviation design factors and alternatives

Design Factor	Alternatives
Customers served	• general public • persons with disabilities • persons with specific functional limitations • other target groups (older persons, etc.)
Treatment of deviation requests	• accept all requests • accept all requests but serve either with fixed route vehicle or paratransit vehicle (coordinate operations) • accept requests only "if possible"
Area served	• accept requests on all routes • use only on certain routes • use on certain portions of routes (*e.g.*, rural and suburban areas) • identify a limited number of key sites near the route(s) that buses will deviate to on request
Days and hours	• all days and hours • only certain times (*e.g.*, off-peak) • only certain days (*e.g.*, weekends)

request to the operator of the vehicle. This requires considerable organizational commitment, communications capability, and sophistication in customer relations. Some transit properties who were designating route deviation for persons with disabilities as their ADA complementary paratransit service have come to realize the complexity of these deviation services.

Marketing and Public Information

Introducing an innovative service such as route deviation requires aggressive marketing and consumer education. The general riding public as well as those who may request and use the deviation feature need to understand the changes that will be made.

Service and Cost Information

As shown in Table B-3 of Appendix B, systems providing route deviation service report mixed success with this option. Several systems reported very limited use. It is not clear if this reflects a lack of demand for the service or limited marketing by the transit providers. This option appears to be most successful where deviations are limited to specific sites and where transit providers work with local human service agencies to arrange regular, ongoing deviations for clients.

There is also some evidence that deviation services can improve overall service productivity when combined with DAR services. In Idaho Falls, Idaho, the system operator was able to reduce higher cost DAR trips by 40 percent by scheduling

the trip on (or a transfer between) one of three route deviation loops operating through the city.[3]

Reported Use and Effectiveness

Of the 309 respondents to the study survey, 59 indicated that they operate route deviation service. Of the 19 respondents who completed the effectiveness rating portion of the survey, 14 reported that this option was moderately to very effective in promoting use of fixed-route service. Figure 4 shows the effectiveness rating given to this option by survey respondents.

Follow-up calls were made to the systems that reported that route deviation services were relatively effective in meeting the needs of customers with disabilities. Table B-3 in Appendix B provides information about selected transit providers using this option.

———————◆———————

POINT DEVIATION SERVICE

In a point deviation service system, a vehicle operates on a fixed schedule with specific stops but without a fixed route. Vehicles will accommodate requests for pick up and drop off at locations other than specified stops or "points" as long as they can be accommodated within the fixed schedule.

---

[3]Don Thorp, Manager, CART, Inc., Idaho Falls, Idaho.

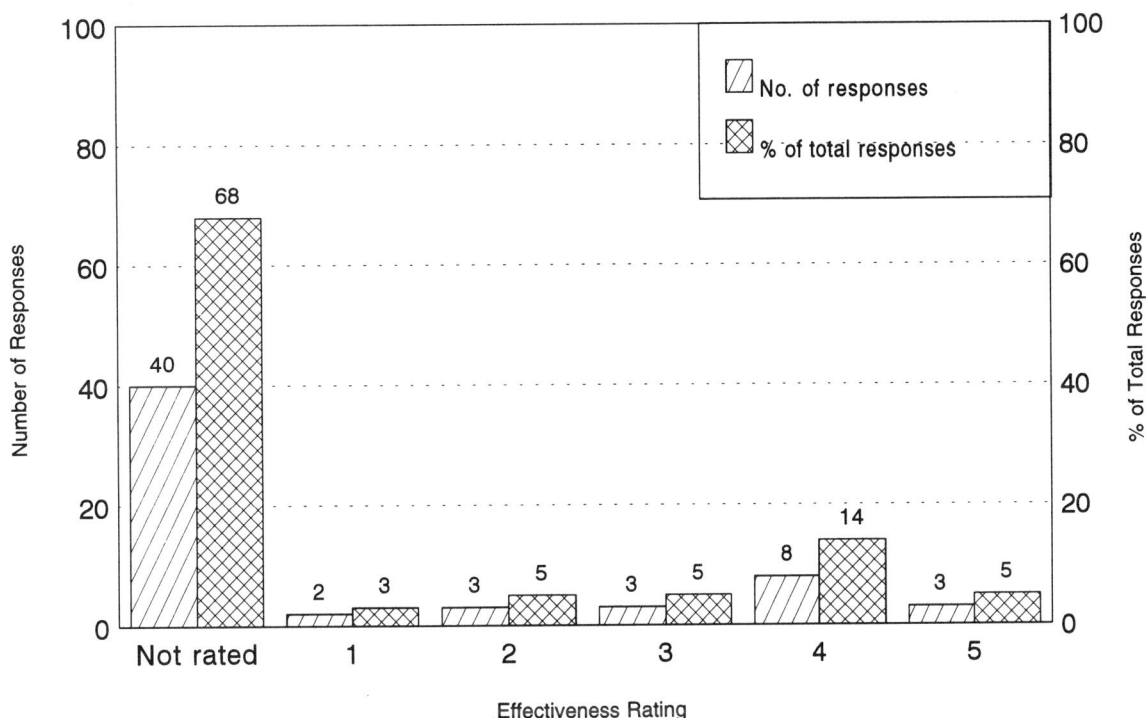

Figure 4. Reported effectiveness of route deviation services. 1 = not effective; 5 = very effective.

With point deviation service, where there are no fixed routes, service is provided within a defined geographic area. The system operates essentially as a DAR program modified to accommodate a series of "checkpoints" on a fixed schedule. Typically, checkpoints are arranged in a particular sequence to reflect local patterns of travel and to allow vehicles to follow a logical scheduling pattern. The operator is free to choose the particular route needed to arrive at these checkpoints at the designated times (*10, 13, 14, 15, 16*).

Customers must know where the nearest checkpoint is to their desired trip origin and trip destination and the scheduled time for the bus to arrive at each point. They can either choose to meet the vehicle at a designated checkpoint or can call in advance to arrange to be picked up at another location within the service area. Typically, as in basic DAR services, requests are made to a central scheduler who can determine if the request can be serviced within the time and space requirements of the fixed checkpoints in the system. Because the system is essentially a modified DAR, it can accept requests for service at a location other than a designated checkpoint on a first-come, first-served basis.

Figure 5 illustrates the basic concept of point deviation service. The checkmarks (✓) represent checkpoints served on a particular schedule. In this illustration, the vehicle arrives at checkpoints on the hour, 10 min past the hour, 20 min past the hour, and so forth. The dotted line represents the general route taken by vehicles in the system (in this illustration, vehicles would be traveling in a general counter-clockwise direction). Although vehicles would travel this general route to get to the next checkpoint on schedule, they would be free to take any

route between checkpoints. In the illustration below, advance requests for service have been made by riders at points "a," "b," and "c." The vehicle would deviate from the general "route" to pick up or drop off passenger "a" at 13 min past the hour, passenger "b" at 35 min past the hour, and passenger "c" at 55 min past the hour.

Point deviation systems can also have more complex designs. A recent variation, being used in the city of Hamilton, Ohio, combines several sectored point deviation "routes" with a timed-transfer center (*18*). This concept is illustrated in Figure 6. Basically, the service area is divided into sectors corresponding to the general areas within which fixed routes might previously have been operated. Rather than advertising a fixed route within each sector, the system advertises checkpoints at which vehicles stop on a set schedule. Although vehicles generally follow a route that takes them from the edge of the service area to the central transfer point, they are also free to make pickups and drop-offs at other locations within their sector. Riders who cannot easily get to a checkpoint can call in advance to request a curb-side pickup. Within each sector, passengers could receive direct curb-to-curb service. As shown in this illustration, passenger "b" is picked up between checkpoints 1 and 2 in Sector B. This passenger is then dropped off by the same vehicle before it arrives at the central transfer point.

Riders wishing to travel between sectors must first transfer at the central terminal. To reduce waiting times and to better coordinate transfers, the system in Hamilton operates as a timed-transfer, "pulse" service with all vehicles arriving at the central terminal simultaneously. In Figure 6, passenger "a" is picked up in sector A between checkpoints 1 and 2. This

20

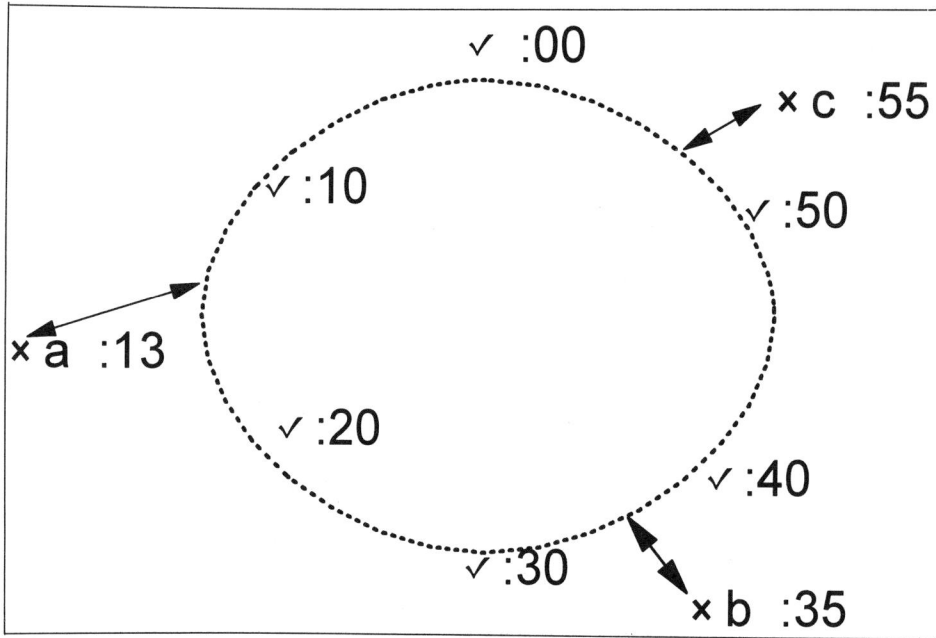

Figure 5.   Illustration of point deviation service.

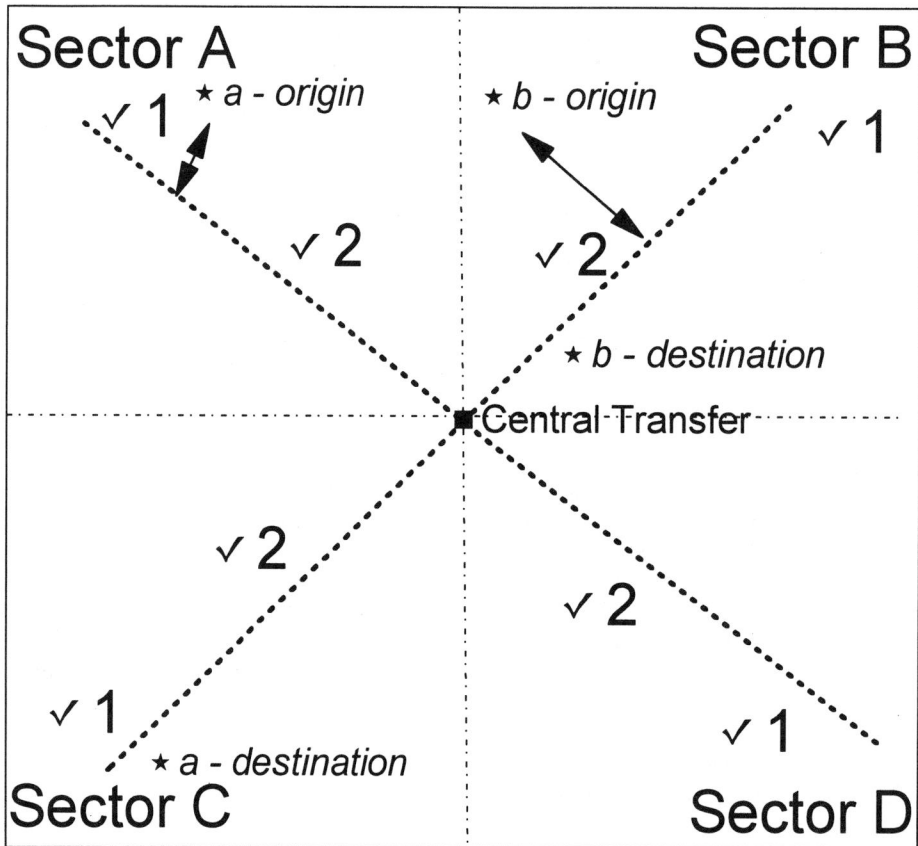

Figure 6.   Illustration of a timed-transfer point deviation system.

passenger travels to the central terminal and transfers to the vehicle serving Sector C and is then dropped off at the desired destination close to checkpoint 1 in that sector.

Although Figure 6 describes a system with four sectors, the system in Hamilton actually operates with six different sectors and point deviation "routes." Passengers can schedule trips by phone from a week in advance to 24 hours in advance for curb-to-curb service. Transit Management of Hamilton, Inc., which provides public transit for the city, reports that ridership on the new system is higher than on the previous fixed-route service. Interestingly, despite the deviations, bus mileage has decreased by 36 percent (18).

Promoting Integration and Appropriate Use of Fixed-Route and Paratransit Services

Like route deviation, point deviation combines operational features of both demand-responsive and fixed-route service. In fact, point deviation systems often develop from pure paratransit or demand-responsive systems. As frequently served origins and destinations are identified, they are built into the schedule on an ongoing basis to consolidate pickups and improve productivity.

By combining the features of both types of service, point deviation can meet general public transportation demands and the needs of persons with disabilities in one, integrated system. The established checkpoints, served at designated and advertised times, provide a structure that can meet general public transportation needs. At the same time, this option provides the operational flexibility needed to serve passengers who cannot get to or from designated stops. Compared to pure paratransit service, higher productivities can be achieved if a significant number of riders can travel to checkpoints to meet the bus.

Applicability to Particular Situations and Areas

Simple point deviation systems are probably best suited to rural communities and suburban neighborhoods. More complex designs, such as the timed-transfer model described above may also be applicable in older, mid-sized cities with a radial street pattern.

The geographic setting also needs to be conducive to a limited checkpoint system. In particular, this option may be more appropriate in areas where a few well-defined origins and destinations (activity centers) can be organized into zones that meet the necessary spatial requirements for this service. From a policy perspective, if the point-deviation service is evolving from a pure DAR, door-to-door service, it would have to be considered by most users to be a drop in level of service.

Point deviation systems, like certain forms of route deviation, can be considered to be demand-responsive systems by the USDOT. For public transit agencies in the United States, this means that there may be no requirement to operate a complementary ADA paratransit program; therefore, point deviation systems may be appropriate in areas where a general public transit system is desired but financial limitations make the operation of both fixed-route and complementary paratransit services infeasible.

Key Implementation Issues

Many of the same implementation issues that apply to route deviation systems are also applicable to this service option. These common issues as well as other considerations include capacity constraints, receiving and processing service requests, marketing and public information, checkpoint locations, service area size, and advertised schedule. These are discussed in the following paragraphs.

Anticipation of Capacity Constraints

When designing the system, potential demand and the ability to meet all requests must be addressed. Policies concerning the handling of requests and the use of the paratransit system as a backup should be considered. The system operator in Hamilton, Ohio, tracks vehicles manually on a map—noting capacity and schedule adherence—and sends a backup van to help out when the bus nears capacity or scheduling problems develop.

Receiving and Processing Service Requests

Point deviation systems follow the DAR model of receiving requests for service, scheduling the request within the constraints of a fixed route or fixed schedule, and communicating the request to the operator of the vehicle. This requires considerable organizational commitment, communications capability, and sophistication in customer relations.

Marketing and Public Information

Introducing an innovative service such as point deviation requires aggressive marketing and consumer education. The general riding public as well as those who may request and use the deviation feature need to understand the changes that will be made. The city of Hamilton, Ohio, conducted an 8-week publicity campaign before initiating a point deviation service.

Location of Checkpoints

For successful operation, the system of checkpoints must be designed to accommodate as many riders as possible without setting the schedule so tightly that deviations throughout the designated area are not possible. The checkpoints also should represent a logical travel pattern that can be easily understood and related to desired trips.

Size of the Service Area and the Advertised Schedule

The size of the service area and the time allowed for travel between checkpoints are closely related. Vehicles should be able to deviate from checkpoints to the outer reaches of the service area, pick up at least one passenger, and be at the next checkpoint on schedule. In general, a larger service area requires more time between checkpoints. It also is important to establish time intervals that allow for reasonable travel times. As with traditional, fixed-route systems, shorter headways and faster travel times will increase demand and ridership.

Service and Cost Information

The literature evaluating point deviation services is dated. A point deviation system operated in Merrill, Wisconsin, in the late 1970s and early 1980s reported higher ridership than their previous fixed-route service, with a sizeable percentage of passengers (up to 70 percent) requesting deviations. In 1980, passengers per vehicle hour were reported to be 10.4, very high for demand-responsive systems (*14*).

Recent experience such as that in Hamilton, Ohio, suggests that ridership can be increased and costs decreased in the right setting and with an innovative design.

Reported Use and Effectiveness

Of the 309 respondents to the study survey, only 34 indicated that they operate point deviation service. Only seven of these respondents completed the effectiveness rating portion of the survey. All rated this option as moderately to very effective. Figure 7 shows the effectiveness rating given to this option by survey respondents.

Follow-up calls were made to the systems that reported that point deviation services were relatively effective in meeting the needs of customers with disabilities. Table B-4 in Appendix B provides information about selected transit providers who use this option.

FEEDER SERVICE

Feeder service is the transportation of people with disabilities on paratransit vehicles to and from a fixed-route bus stop or train station. The service may also occur in the reverse order, with individuals travelling on a bus or train to a point where they may transfer to a paratransit vehicle.

Feeder service is primarily provided through paratransit vehicles that pick passengers up at their homes (although the trip could originate from any location) and transport them for the first leg of their journey to the bus stop or rail station. This is usually the shorter segment of the total trip. This segment is also often the free-fare part of the journey.

Upon arrival at the stop or station, the person disembarks from the paratransit vehicle and, after a short wait or immediately upon leaving the paratransit vehicle, boards the fixed-

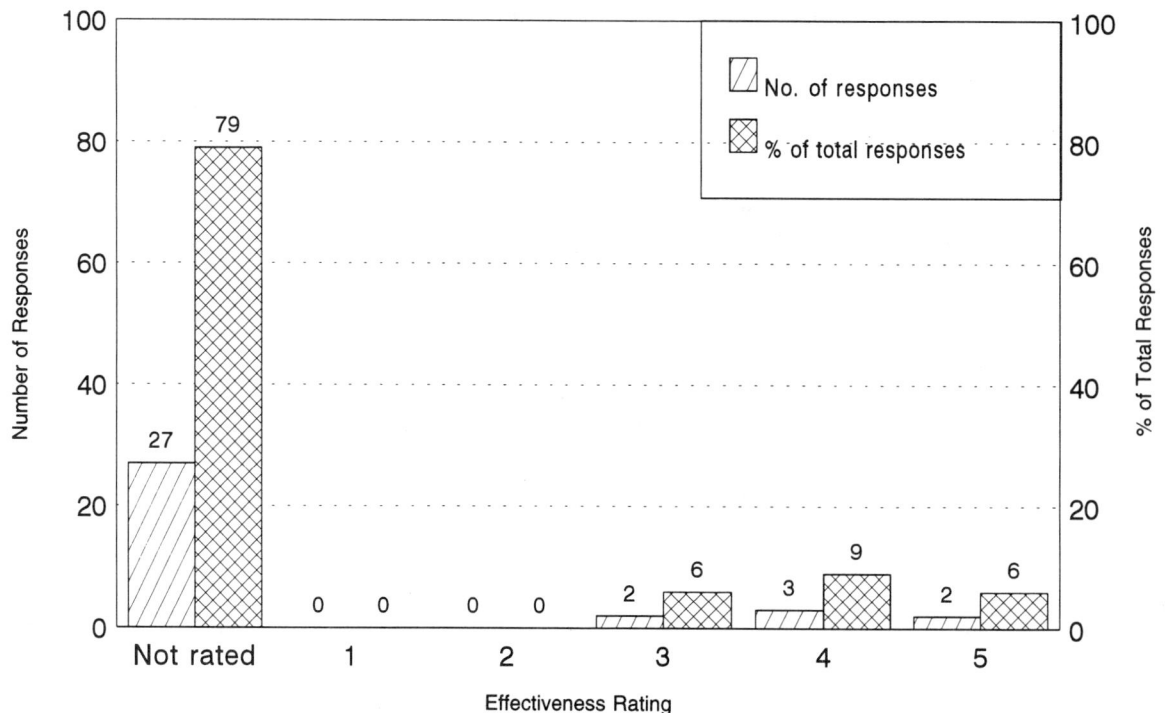

Figure 7. Reported effectiveness of point deviation services. 1 = not effective; 5 = very effective.

route vehicle. The person then travels on the bus or train to a stop closest to his or her final destination. For the return trip, this process occurs in reverse, with the first segment of the journey travelled by fixed route, and the transfer occurring from the bus or train to the paratransit vehicle, which transports the rider to his or her final destination.

Variations on this model include the following:

• The paratransit trip could be provided on either an accessible van or an accessible taxi.

• The paratransit driver may or may not wait with the person until the bus arrives.

• The person may pay a fare on the paratransit vehicle and receive a free transfer onto the bus.

• The journey may be a three-legged trip in each direction, with paratransit feeder service provided on each end of the bus or train segment.

A few examples of feeder service have been identified in this study, particularly in larger urban areas. In 1991, the New York City paratransit program, Access-A-Ride, implemented a limited-scale feeder pilot program for Brooklyn subscription riders. Only 11 people were identified who had trip characteristics that could be efficiently integrated into the fixed-route and paratransit schedules and were willing to volunteer for the program (*19*). For the few who did participate, the program worked surprisingly smoothly, with minimal transfer problems between the two modes.

More common examples of feeder service may be found in general public DARs that feed into fixed-route service. Many of these services include a substantial proportion of seniors, although not necessarily those who are ADA-eligible. The Link system in Wenatchee, Washington, is an example of this kind of feeder service (*20*). Of the 200 daily transfers between the DAR and fixed-route services, almost half are riders with disabilities, and approximately 11 percent are wheelchair users. As a result, over 2.5 percent of fixed-route riders are wheelchair users, higher than most comparable systems.[4]

The feeder service that appears to have the potential for serving the largest number of riders in the United States is a new program being implemented by the Los Angeles County Metropolitan Transportation Authority (LACMTA). With a service area of over 3,000 square mi, feeder service is expected to become an important part of paratransit operations. LACMTA expects to begin providing feeder trips to individuals travelling downtown from the San Gabriel Valley.[5]

Promoting Integration and Appropriate Use of Fixed-Route and Paratransit Services

The two primary goals of this service model are mainstreaming people with disabilities and providing a cost-effective transportation alternative to paratransit. Feeder service promotes the ADA goal of mainstreaming people with disabilities

by enabling individuals to travel by fixed-route, even though they cannot get to the bus stop or rail station by themselves. The model is designed to reduce operating costs by replacing part of the trip with fixed-route service.

Because both fixed-route and paratransit service are integral components of the feeder service model, this model, by definition, embodies the study objective more than most other service enhancements under consideration. Most of the enhancements in this study have a direct bearing on the effectiveness of this model; the more relevant ones include travel training, low-floor buses, accessible taxis, accessible bus stops, service routes, and marketing.

Applicability and Implementation Issues

Feeder service appears well suited to meeting the goals cited above, but its applicability is limited to those persons with disabilities who can use fixed-route service if they have transportation to the stop or station. There are also administrative and cost-effectiveness issues that affect the viability of this model. The following factors must be taken into account in determining the feasibility of a feeder service in a specific location.

Voluntary Versus Mandatory Feeder Service

Setting aside a philosophical commitment to mainstreaming, persons who have a choice between door-to-door service and transferring from a paratransit vehicle to a bus or train will usually prefer the no-transfer option. For feeder service to work, it generally needs to be offered as a mandatory program or be encouraged through an incentive such as a free-fare on both modes.

In the United States, mandatory feeder service complies with the ADA regulations, subject to capacity constraint limitations regarding excessive trip lengths. According to ADA Sections 37.129 (b) and (c), which apply to persons in eligibility categories 2 and 3, complementary paratransit service "may be provided by paratransit feeder service to an accessible fixed route, where such service enables the individual to use the fixed-route bus system for his or her trip."

Trip Length and Time

Feeder service is unlikely to be cost-effective for short trips. The longer the trip, the greater the cost-savings that may result from substituting part of the trip on less-costly, fixed-route service. This is primarily because feeder service involves additional administrative costs for trip planning and coordination and additional operating costs for drivers who may be required to wait with the passenger at the transfer point. These costs offset the benefits of transferring to the cheaper, fixed-route service when applied to shorter trips. For this reason, suburban to urban or rural to urban trips are likely to be better candidates for feeder service than intra-urban trips.

[4]Dennis Davis-Bloom, Link, Wenatchee, Washington.
[5]Chip Hazen, Los Angeles County Metropolitan Transportation Authority, Los Angeles, California.

The transfer between modes often makes the feeder model less competitive in terms of time than a direct paratransit trip. The shorter the trip, the greater the negative effect of the transfer on the total ride time. This raises the issue of a time penalty; the transit agency should consider a standard for an acceptable ratio of feeder ride time to paratransit ride time or for total allowable ride time for various distances.

The type of fixed-route service to be used for feeder trips also will affect trip length and time. In some circumstances, feeder service to express bus or rail may actually be shorter and quicker than direct paratransit. This will be more likely in places where there is heavy peak-hour traffic congestion or where the paratransit trip may involve additional stops on the route to pick up or drop off other passengers. Feeder service to express bus or rail in these situations will probably be more readily accepted by customers and may even be preferred.

Individual Trip Planning

A high degree of confidence in both the fixed-route and paratransit systems' on-time performance is essential. Feeder service involves close coordination between the different modes, so a substantial amount of lead time is needed to plan an individual trip that can fit into the schedule of both systems. Because of the amount of pre-trip planning required, it appears that scheduling non-recurring trips may be simply too cumbersome and time-consuming. For the same reason, systems are more likely to schedule regular trips that occur from the same origin, usually the person's home.

Scheduling transfers for subscription trips, however, which involve trips that can be planned and repeated over an extended period of time, is very productive from the paratransit provider's perspective. The coordination of subscription trips can be refined over time, and, because the same bus drivers probably will transport the individual on a regular basis, fewer drivers need training in the specific requirements of the program. Feeder service is, therefore, more likely to be limited to subscription trips.

Accessible Environment

The applicability of the feeder service model is limited by the number and extent of potential barriers along the route. Barriers generally affect wheelchair users but may affect ambulatory riders. The first potential barrier that should be considered is the accessibility of the bus stop. Although several systems have initiated accessible bus stop programs, many stops remain inaccessible to wheelchair users. Further, particularly for the frail elderly, bus stops need to be well protected from inclement weather and have seating for people to rest on. If shelters do not have a bench, feeder service at that location may only work for wheelchair users, because persons with walkers or other ambulatory devices may not be able to stand for long periods.

Another potential barrier is the fixed-route bus or rail station and car. Although the passage of the ADA has led to the purchase of predominantly wheelchair-lift-equipped buses throughout the United States, some system fleets include inaccessible buses that will remain in use into the 21st century. In Canada, many systems continue to provide service with inaccessible fixed-route buses. Similarly, many older rail stations will remain inaccessible well into the next century.

One factor often overlooked in planning feeder service is the accessibility of the environment once the person completes the bus trip. Generally, densely developed downtown areas or intersections that have recently been renovated are most likely to have curb cuts; however, if curb cuts are not installed, the accessibility of the trip is diminished. These access factors all need to be taken into account for each individual's trip plan.

Transfer Points

The transfer point is a particularly important stage in the feeder trip sequence. The transit agency must decide whether the paratransit driver should wait with the person until the fixed-route vehicle arrives or whether this should only occur during the first few trips until coordination problems have been resolved. Having a driver wait at the transfer point takes time and may perpetuate the individual's dependency.

Bus transit systems employing timed transfers, where buses converge at central locations and then depart after a short time, may find that these locations make ideal feeder transfer points. Such locations, however, are generally limited to a few transportation nodes (such as shopping malls and transit centers); this may be insufficient for transferring individuals whose origins and destinations are geographically dispersed.

Transfers to rail lines may be less problematic if stations provide the rider with a safe, sheltered place to sit and wait.

Wait Times

In addition to standards for overall ride times, the transit agency should set standards for acceptable wait times at the transfer point and ensure that no person will be stranded if a bus is not on schedule or if a wheelchair lift on a specific bus is inoperable. This last point highlights the risks involved in feeder service to fixed-route buses that have long headways. If a person misses one bus, he or she may have an intolerably long wait before the next one arrives. Radio coordination between the modes may alleviate this problem.

Again, feeder to rail service may have an advantage. Rail service is more likely to have short headways. The national average is 6.6 min during peak hours.[6] Timing of transfers to rail systems would, therefore, not be as critical.

Fare Revenue Coordination

In cities where the paratransit and fixed-route systems are operated by separate agencies, an agreement will need to be reached whereby one party is willing to forgo the fare for

---

[6]*The Urban Transportation Monitor*, October 14, 1994.

the feeder passenger. Forgoing the fare may be more feasible administratively for the paratransit provider, because this entity is usually the smaller agency and the one with the greater incentive to provide feeder service. However, it would be more practical for the passenger to pay the fare to a paratransit driver than a fixed-route bus driver.

Alternatively, the transit agency could require the passenger to pay both fares, because the trip is longer than most trips provided on paratransit service. Besides being subject to the double-the-transit fare limit under ADA, this approach may be considered punitive if riders not required to transfer only pay a single fare.

Additional implementation issues that will contribute to the success of a feeder program are travel training, general public DAR, computerized scheduling systems, and policy guidelines. These are discussed in the following paragraphs.

Travel Training

The full effectiveness of the feeder model depends on the ability of individuals with disabilities to use the bus system. It is generally anticipated that persons in ADA eligibility Categories 2 and 3 are most likely to benefit from feeder service. These categories apply to persons who cannot access the fixed-route system because the system is not yet accessible or is temporarily inaccessible and to persons who have a specific impairment-related condition that prevents them from traveling to a boarding location. For persons in those eligibility categories, the potential applicability of this model can be expanded with comprehensive mobility training.

General Public DAR

Feeder service may also be integrated as part of a general public DAR system coordinated with a fixed-route system. This would remove the stigma of segregated paratransit van usage and increase the potential ridership of the DAR system.

Computerized Scheduling Systems

Although not all systems that provide feeder service use computerized scheduling, the need for precision scheduling certainly makes such features as automatic vehicle locators extremely useful in coordinating schedules between paratransit and fixed-route.

Policy Guidelines

The transit agency, after considering implementation issues such as those described above, must set policy and operating guidelines that define the target population and establish which trips are the most viable candidates for feeder service. Involving local officials and community representatives in developing these guidelines should facilitate community acceptance of the feeder concept.

From the riders' perspective, however, feeder service may seem extremely inconvenient and time-consuming. Elected officials and transit operators generally find themselves on the horns of a dilemma: on the one hand, it is extremely unproductive and costly for paratransit vehicles to be transporting passengers over long distances, parallel to an existing fixed-route service. On the other hand, they need to be accountable to a public that demands the most convenient service possible. For feeder service to work successfully, much prior education is required to assure both the community of those with disabilities and elected officials that this model is in their collective best interests.

Reported Use and Effectiveness

Of the 309 respondents to the study survey, 70 indicated that they provide feeder service. Follow-up calls revealed, however, that most of these providers were reporting feeder services that involved two fixed-route systems. Only 13 examples of paratransit-feeder-to-fixed-route were confirmed from the survey. Table B-5 in Appendix B provides information about these systems.

The survey asked respondents to rate the effectiveness of each option employed on a scale of 1 to 5 (with 1 being "not effective" and 5 being "very effective"). Among the 13 confirmed examples of paratransit/fixed-route feeder service, the reported effectiveness of this option was quite high. As shown on Table B-5, seven of the nine agencies that rated this option indicated an effectiveness of either 4 or 5. As would be expected, providers who required that riders transfer found programs to be more effective than those who made transferring voluntary.

GENERAL PUBLIC DAR

General public DAR is a demand-responsive, door-to-door or curb-to-curb service provided to the general public, as well as to persons with disabilities.

DAR is the best known of the demand-responsive paratransit services. It has different names throughout North America to describe the same thing: dial-a-bus, telebus, or call-a-ride. It involves a request in advance of the trip by a consumer for a pickup at his or her desired location and a drop-off at his or her requested location or a designated point. Because of the cost of these services, general public DAR services are operated or sponsored by public agencies. Basically, DAR services take one of three forms:

• Many-to-one. (Transportation is provided from multiple origins to a single location, such as an employment center or intermodal connection with rail or bus service.)

26

- Many-to-few. (Transportation is provided from multiple origins to a few designated destinations, for example, a suburban activity center or medical complex.)
- Many-to-many. (Transportation is provided between any two points within the service area.)

General public DAR services have a long history in North America with some enduring success stories and spectacular failures. The services have been designed to operate both as stand-alone modal services and integrated with other mass transportation services within the region.

One of the well-known, early, federally funded DAR demonstrations was implemented in Haddonfield, New Jersey, in 1972. The service operated with 11 buses in suburban Philadelphia. The service area was approximately 5 square mi. It operated in a many-to-many mode open to the general public. Requests for service were made to a central control center where radio communication was maintained with the entire fleet (13). A legacy of the project was the MIT-developed, fully automated scheduling and routing capability designed as a part of the demonstration. After 4 years, the project was terminated at the conclusion of the demonstration when the local government was unwilling to pick up the high operating costs.

The innovative techniques used at Haddonfield were incorporated into other experimental DAR programs throughout North America. Among these was a service in La Habra, a community in Orange County, California. This program was expanded to cover the entire County by the Orange County Transit District. The key features of the Orange County general public DAR design were: (1) immediate response service (15 to 40 min); (2) centralized computer control of scheduling and dispatching through a fully-automated algorithm derived from the Haddonfield experiment; and (3) 180 vehicles providing intra-zonal DAR service to roughly 12 to 15 communities (21). In response to financial realities, the Orange County services have evolved into an intra-neighborhood transportation program serving more than twice the number of geographic sectors (33) with considerably fewer vehicles than originally planned (109). What remains is the centralized computer routing and scheduling system and the immediate response configuration within the neighborhood service area (14).

During the mid 1970s, the Michigan Bureau of Urban and Public Transportation implemented a Dial-A-Ride Transportation (DART) demonstration program that provided short-notice, demand-responsive services to the general public in smaller cities and towns. Many of the communities that participated in this 1-year demonstration continued the programs with local support (14). In 1977, with the assistance of federal demonstration monies, a rural, general public DAR program was initiated with 10 vans in the 400-square-mi Cape Cod region of Massachusetts. By 1993, the service had expanded to 31 minibuses and 2 vans by consolidating human service transportation with general public DAR service (22). With the availability of federal assistance for small urban and rural transit systems in 1979 (Section 18 of the Federal Transit Act of 1964, as amended), these programs continue to this day. Although many recipients of Section 18 funds advertise that they operate

services open to the general public, they are designed to serve specific populations (e.g. the elderly and persons with disabilities) and are available to the general public on a space-available basis.

Significant innovative efforts have been made to integrate general public DAR with regional fixed-route transportation (bus and rail) and shared-ride taxi. These efforts have been made in Westport, Connecticut; Santa Clara County, California; and Ann Arbor, Michigan (14) among other places. For various reasons, these innovations were reduced in scope or scale.

Promoting Integration and Appropriate Use of Fixed-Route and Paratransit Services

In Norfolk, Virginia, and Edmonton, Alberta, fixed-route operators found that general public DAR services integrated with their fixed-route service could be substituted for low-productivity routes in the low-density periphery of their regional service area. In Alberta, this service was introduced with no loss in ridership and a significant reduction in operating expenses (23). As a direct result of the complementary paratransit requirements of the ADA, the integration of DAR services with accessible fixed-route services has taken on new meaning for fixed-route operators. With the ADA, there is more than just the potential for substituting one costly, low-productivity service for a less-costly, higher-productivity mode. Because DAR is a demand-responsive service itself, there is no requirement for an ADA paratransit service to complement it.

Following an analysis of their fixed-route and demand-responsive ridership using a geographic information system, the Tidewater Regional Transit System in Norfolk plans to implement an integrated, zonal, demand-responsive, paratransit service with their "timed-transfer" or "pulse" fixed-route system. This would, in effect, make their general public Maxi-Ride DAR service and their Hand-Ride services paratransit feeder services to the accessible fixed-route bus system (24).

The Hillsborough Area Regional Transportation Authority in Tampa, Florida, reported plans to substitute DAR service for low-ridership fixed routes in the outlying portions of their service area. DAR vehicles would transport passengers to fixed-route end stops as well as provide local transportation in these lower-density regions.

Applicability to Particular Situations and Areas

General public DAR services have found a niche in situations such as lower-density areas previously served by fixed-route services where they can act as intra-community transportation and feeder services to the regional fixed-route system (for example, Norfolk and Edmonton) and low-density rural and small urban regions—particularly where geographic sectors can be organized for intra-zonal services (for example, Cape Cod, Massachusetts, and Orange County, California).

Key Implementation Issues

Several implementation issues are paramount in DAR services. These include financing, geography, grouping, and automation.

As the most personal of the transit modes, DAR has the lowest productivity potential and the highest cost. A general public DAR system can be very costly to support, particularly if immediate response service is provided. A related issue is the size of the service area for the DAR system. Travel time and distance of DAR trips directly affect the financing of these systems. Understandably, the general public DAR systems that survive seem to concentrate services within neighborhood or community zones.

In order to improve the productivity of an inherently inefficient mode, many operators try to promote group trips by developing contracts with human service agencies for services to nutrition sites, sheltered workshops, occupational training, and the like that can be scheduled well in advance. In essence, this moves the service from the least productive many-to-many configuration to a more productive many-to-one or many-to-few. Given a finite number of vehicles and travel patterns that create peak travel times, this laudable desire for productive use of public resources also constrains the capacity of the system to accommodate individual requests. In mature systems, this constraint generally levels demand for DAR services within a year or two of initiation. If the DAR service is not open to the general public and is being used to provide ADA paratransit, a "pattern or practice" of trip denials for ADA-eligible individuals because of capacity constraints can be the basis of a discrimination complaint.

The last key implementation issue is automation. Since the Haddonfield and Orange County experiments (noted above), where a minicomputer was required to power the routing and scheduling functions, state-of-the-art personal computers can do the job at low cost. The implementation issue now centers on whether to give the entire scheduling function to the computer or to retain some part of the decision-making with the human operator. Fielding (21) points out that there is a certain point (15 buses and 100 demands/hour) at which immediate response DAR scheduling simply exceeds the human decision-making capacity. As a result, the private sector has produced several computer software products that will either assist the scheduler in making the DAR scheduling decision or take control of the scheduling process entirely.

Early on, Nigel Wilson of MIT, widely credited with developing the original fully automated scheduling algorithm for DAR, foresaw the problems of keeping street networks up to date on a computer system as well as the benefits of retaining some decision-making capacity with the dispatcher and the driver of DAR systems. Wilson noted that "Where several stops are quite close together, the driver, knowing the local street pattern and the local situation with respect to congestion, is in a better position to decide on the optimal sequence of making those stops. I think a mix of computer and manual control techniques is desirable." (25) The issue of full control or a mix of computer-assisted and human decision-making in scheduling is resolving itself in the marketplace.

Two new technologies are also affecting the implementation of DAR systems. The now ubiquitous cellular telephone has found an application in some limited DAR services. In Norfolk, Virginia, the consumer may call the driver of the DAR vehicle for a particular zone through the vehicle's cellular phone (there

is only one vehicle per zone) and request a ride within that zone. Use of automatic vehicle location and monitoring (AVL/M) systems (based on the recently available Global Positioning System [GPS] satellites of the Department of Defense) may improve the productivity and response time of demand-responsive paratransit.

Service and Cost Information

The literature is not very current on operating statistics for general public DAR services—perhaps in response to the lack of resources in the 1980s to develop such systems. In a 1982 report (14), productivity for La Habra was listed at 3.8 passengers per vehicle-hour (1980), Ann Arbor was 5.6 (1977), and Santa Clara 5.0 (1975).

Reported Use and Effectiveness

Of the 309 respondents to the study survey, 90 indicated that they provided general public DAR service. Follow-up calls revealed, however, that these services were not typically used to replace traditional fixed-route services. It is likely that most of these general public DAR systems are open to the general public on a space-available basis to meet requirements of the FTA's Section 18 program.[7] No reliable listing of providers who have switched to general public DAR or rating of the effectiveness of this option is available from the survey.

SUBSCRIPTION BUS SERVICE

Subscription bus service is pre-arranged service designed to meet specific group or individual needs. Typically, this service is provided as part of a paratransit program; however, it can also be provided as part of a system's fixed-route service using accessible buses that are available off-peak or by using accessible spare fixed-route buses.

A subscription bus service can be provided with regular fixed-route buses, preferably ones that are accessible. Such a service could bring persons with disabilities to group programs such as sheltered workshops. Buses can be made available, for example, in a system with a peaking pattern where there are idle off-peak buses.

The subscription service differs only by degrees from a service route. The service route requires planning of the schedule and routing to accommodate programs and typical travel patterns of persons with disabilities. A subscription service requires specific pre-arrangement to serve groups or individuals.

---

[7]Programs funded by the USDOT under Section 18 of the Federal Transit Act of 1964, as amended, must be open to the general public. Many DAR systems, which serve primarily older persons and/or persons with disabilities, meet this requirement by advertising availability of the service to the general public on a space-available basis.

Rides might be arranged daily, weekly, or whatever is required to serve the target population. Typically, subscription services are not open to the general public. Because these services can be expected to change frequently, it would be difficult for the general public to learn of their availability.

Several transit authorities have developed subscription bus services using their fixed-route buses. For example, the Sacramento Regional Transit authority provided such service to 350 mentally retarded clients who attend sheltered workshops and vocational training programs (9). The programs adjusted their start and stop times to allow off-peak buses to be used. Sacramento also travel-trained 40 mentally retarded clients to take the subscription buses to the workshops and use regular buses on the return trips.

The City of Jackson Transportation Authority developed a subscription bus service with seven semi-fixed routes to take agency clients from care homes to services. The clientele for this service is very frail, so they might not be able to use public transit without the individual consideration available with the subscription service.[8]

At least two transit authorities provide subscription bus service to take senior citizens to shopping. Transit Windsor of Windsor, Ontario, provides a special subscription bus for seniors going to shopping on Tuesday and Wednesday. This service provides 70 trips per day of operation. The Worcester Regional Transit Authority of Worcester, Massachusetts, has been operating a "Shoppers Special" subscription bus service since 1975. This service operates one day per week in a particular sector of Worcester. Pickup times at senior housing projects are on a regular schedule, although the rest depends on phone requests.

Promoting Integration and the Appropriate Use of Fixed-Route and Paratransit Services

Although most subscription services are not open to the public, such services can help persons with disabilities develop confidence in the use of larger, fixed-route buses. As noted above, Sacramento combines subscription service with the use of regular route service to provide transportation to and from workshops.

Key Implementation Issues

If subscription services are to be helpful in integrating persons with disabilities onto general public transit, transit agencies must consider ways to encourage subscription service users to make further use of the system. Personnel accepting reservation requests and drivers could inform users of the availability and schedules of fixed-routes buses in the vicinity, which might be used at other times. Especially with smaller systems, drivers of nearby routes might take turns driving the subscription service so they could meet the passengers.

Shoppers Special subscription services can be a major convenience to persons with disabilities and elderly persons. This service is greatly enhanced with the addition of help (either paid or volunteer) to assist with groceries and packages.

Reported Use and Effectiveness

This option was not included in the study survey. It was identified as an option during the follow-up calls made to survey respondents. Effectiveness ratings and a listing of selected transit providers are, therefore, not available.

FLAG-STOP AND REQUEST-A-STOP SERVICE

Flag-stop service allows patrons to request a bus by waving it down anywhere along a route. Request-a-stop service allows a person on a bus to request to get off at any location along a route.

One way to reduce walk distances to and from bus stops is to allow more stop locations. Many rural and smaller urban areas, for example, have implemented flag-stop services, so that riders can board the bus at any location. The Merrimack Valley Transit Authority in Haverhill, Massachusetts, for example, reported that it allows flag stops throughout its fixed-route system.[9] Madison County Transit in Granite City, Illinois, also permits flag stops on its network of local service routes.[10]

A similar service, request-a-stop, allows individuals to get off a bus anywhere along the route where it is safe to do so. Such a service was recently implemented by the New Jersey Transit Corporation on a trial basis during late evening hours (26). Originally, the service was implemented to make travel safer by allowing riders to exit vehicles closer to their homes, not specifically to reduce walk distances for persons with disabilities, but it has provided this benefit.

Promoting Integration and Appropriate Use of Fixed-Route and Paratransit Services

Where travel distance to and from stops prevents the use of fixed-route systems for persons with disabilities, flag-stop and request-a-stop options can help reduce those distances, thus promoting greater use of fixed-route services.

Key Implementation Issues

In determining whether the use of flag-stop or request-a-stop options would make fixed routes a viable alternative for paratransit riders, transit agencies will have to consider whether the appropriate stop locations would be safe and accessible to the user. Because it may be difficult to know each location along a route, the transit agency may have to rely on a self-

---

[8]Garrett Erb, Jackson Transportation Authority, Jackson, Michigan.

[9]Patricia Monahan, Merrimack Valley Regional Transit Authority, Haverhill, Massachusetts.
[10]Todd Plesko, Madison County Transit, Granite City, Illinois.

certification by the user as to whether they can use a flag-stop location.

Although flag-stop and request-a-stop services help persons with disabilities who have problems traveling distances to and from bus stops, these services may not be helpful to persons with impaired vision. These customers may be better served by waiting for buses at a particular spot, and they may rely on a specific count of stops to determine their debarkation point. If flag stops are allowed, a system of fixed stops may still be required. Another solution is for the transit system to develop an identification card system, so that persons with vision impairments could indicate the buses they desire. The ADA requirement for on-board stop announcements is even more important to riders with vision impairments when a request-a-stop option is in place.

Another issue with flag stops is that they may be more difficult for persons with cognitive disabilities to use. Such customers may not know where to stand so that they will be safe when flagging a bus. The safety problem can be two-fold—the person with cognitive disability may be in an unsafe position, or the bus may find stopping unsafe. Although these issues can be addressed to some degree with travel training, experienced travel trainers feel that flag-stop systems make instruction more difficult.[11]

Despite these drawbacks, flag stops can work effectively for persons with cognitive disabilities in some systems. Madison County Transit, which operates more personalized service routes, indicated that it has many riders with mental disabilities who have been travel trained. The flag-stop system does not seem to be a problem for these customers.

Reported Use and Effectiveness

This option was not included in the study survey. It was identified as an option during follow-up calls made to survey respondents. Effectiveness ratings and a listing of selected transit providers are, therefore, not available.

LOW-FLOOR BUSES

A low-floor bus is one that has a floor between the front and rear doors sufficiently low so as to eliminate the need for steps in the vicinity of the doors or in the aisle between the doors. According to the International Union of Public Transport (UITP), the height of the floor above the street at the door should not exceed 320 mm (12.6 in.) (27). The 40-ft-long, low-floor buses available in North America have a floor that is 14 in. above the street; the height can be reduced to 10 or 11 in. by means of a kneeling feature.

A low-floor bus with a 14-in. floor height and a kneeling feature allows the step up from a 6-in. curb to be reduced to

4 or 5 in. ADA standards allow a ramp slope of 1:6 for heights in this range, so a ramp for wheelchairs would need to be only 24 to 30 in. long. Buses being purchased typically have 48-in. ramps.

By comparison, a conventional North American transit bus has a floor 30 to 35 in. above the street, with three steps inside the door, the first of which is 14 or 15 in. high. A kneeling feature reduces the height of the first step by 3 to 5 in. Access for wheelchair users and others who cannot climb steps is provided by a lift in the front or rear door.

In the 40-ft-long, low-floor buses in use in North American transit operations, the low-floor section extends only from the front door to the rear door, which is typically just rear of the center of the bus. Rear of the rear door, the aisle has a series of steps up to an elevated section over the engine and the rear axle. Buses of this type are available in North America from New Flyer Industries, Ltd. and Neoplan USA Corp. Buses of this type are now in service in Kitchener, Ontario; Calgary, Edmonton, and St. Albert, Alberta; Victoria, British Columbia; Ann Arbor, Michigan; and Champaign-Urbana, Illinois (28).

Figures 8 and 9 show New Flyer 40-ft-long buses built for and operated by the Port Authority of New York and New Jersey. Figure 8 shows passengers entering and exiting from a standard height curb. Figure 9 shows the bus being operated at a raised platform, which provides level entry for passengers.

The term "true low-floor" often refers to a bus in which the low floor extends the entire length of the vehicle. The only commonly used vehicle of this type in North American transit systems is the Orion II, built by Ontario Bus Industries in Canada and Bus Industries of America in the United States. The Orion II is available in 22-ft and 26-ft lengths. It uses a front-wheel drive and independent suspension rear wheels. The Orion II has a floor 12 in. above the street, which can be reduced by use of the kneeling feature to 8 in. at the front door and to 4 in. at the rear-facing door at the back of the vehicle. A prototype Orion VI 40-ft true low-floor bus was shown at the October 1993 International Public Transit Expo in New Orleans, Louisiana. A recently introduced true low-floor bus is the ELF Series 100, built by Thor Industries. The ELF Series 100 is built on a front-wheel-drive truck chassis. It has a floor 13 in. above street level and is available in 22-ft-, 25-ft-, and 28-ft-long versions. Thor Industries has also announced an ELF Series 200, a 30-ft-long true low-floor bus (29). Figures 10 and 11 show the Orion II and the ELF Model 125.

The low-floor concept has also been applied to light rail and commuter rail vehicles that serve low-platform stations. Light rail vehicles with a center section floor about 14 in. above the top of the rail are in use in several European cities, including Bern, Switzerland; Rome, Italy; Grenoble, France; Vienna, Austria; and Kassel, Germany (30). In the United States, the Tri-County Metropolitan Transit District of Oregon (Tri-Met), ordered 37 low-floor light rail vehicles from Siemens Duewag Corporation in June 1993, with delivery expected in September 1995 (31). In early 1994, the Massachusetts Bay Transportation Authority issued a request for proposals for 100 low-floor light rail vehicles similar in design to those operating in Grenoble (32).

---

[11]Catie Simpson, C. Simpson & Associates, Pleasanton, California.

Figure 8. New Flyer low-floor bus (photograph courtesy of New Flyer Industries).

Figure 9. New Flyer low-floor bus operated at a raised curb (photograph courtesy of New Flyer Industries).

Promoting Integration and Appropriate Use of Fixed-Route and Paratransit Services

Low-floor buses can promote use of fixed-route services by riders with disabilities as follows:

• Many passengers who cannot climb steps but who do not use a wheelchair will find it possible to step up the 4 or 5 in. to a low-floor bus in its kneeling position. These riders are permitted under ADA to ride in a standing position on lifts on conventional buses but may find riding a lift frightening and difficult.

• Wheelchair users can board by means of a short ramp instead of a lift. Because deploying the ramp is quicker and less obtrusive than deploying a lift, passengers in wheelchairs may feel less on display, less stigmatized, and less concerned about delaying other passengers. The disconcerting experience of riding a lift will no longer be a barrier.

• Boarding times for wheelchair riders should be significantly reduced. The cycle time for a wheelchair lift typically exceeds 1 min, compared to a few seconds for a short ramp. Many transit operators have used rear-door lifts because of the reliability and maintenance problems of front-door lifts. The opportunity to board wheelchair riders through the front door on a low-floor bus will save even more time for these operators; however, the time required for a passenger to maneuver to a tie-down location and tie down will not necessarily be reduced.

• The ramps should have lower maintenance costs than lifts. The ramps should also be less likely to fail causing loss of vehicle use and the need to rescue stranded passengers. Ramps can be easily deployed manually if an electrical or hydraulic failure occurs. Driver training will be simplified.

These differences may make it possible for passengers with disabilities to ride fixed-route buses for many trips for which they would otherwise require paratransit. The potential for co-ordinated service, such as paratransit feeder service, may also be enhanced because the number of passengers who can transfer to a fixed-route bus from a paratransit vehicle may be increased. Small low-floor buses are an essential ingredient

Figure 10. Orion II low-floor small bus (photograph courtesy of Bus Industries of America).

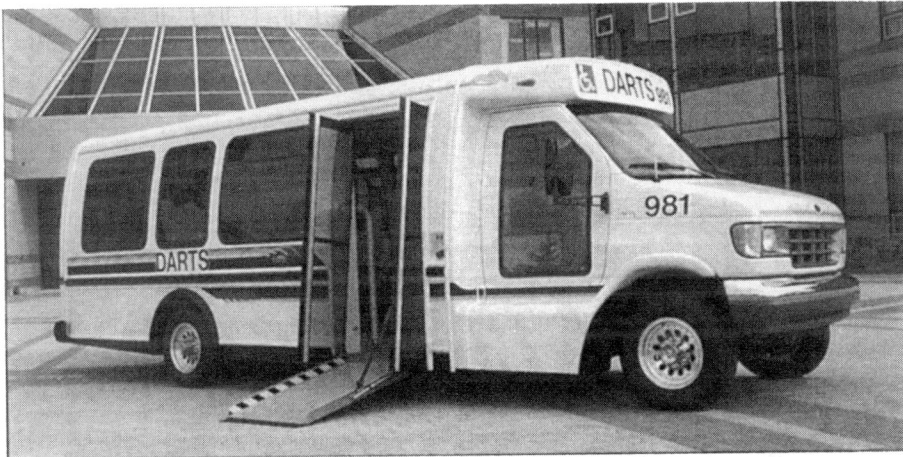

Figure 11. ELF Model 125 low-floor small bus (photograph courtesy of Thor Industries).

of service routes. Transit operators may be more inclined to encourage use of the fixed-route system by riders with disabilities because they will be less concerned about delays caused by lift operations or failures.

Other Benefits of Low-Floor Buses

Low-floor buses also have advantages from the point of view of the general public and transit operators completely apart from issues of accessibility. The following advantages are based on the experience of transit operators in Victoria,

British Columbia; Kitchener, Ontario; and Ann Arbor, Michigan:[12]

• Boarding and alighting are easier for all passengers, and dwell times are reduced, resulting in higher average operating speed.

• The interior of the bus has a roomier feel, partly because the amount of seating is reduced in most low-floor buses, but also because there is more interior headroom.

[12]Individuals and systems contacted were: Ray Williams and Michael Davis, BC Transit, Victoria, British Columbia; Chris White, Ann Arbor Transportation Authority, Ann Arbor, Michigan; and Wally Beck, Kitchener Transit, Kitchener, Ontario.

- Security problems in the rear of the bus are reduced because the driver has a clear view of the elevated rear section and because the rear seating is the most popular with most passengers.
- Ride quality is improved, particularly for standees, because the bus has a lower center of gravity.

Applicability and Implementation Issues

Applicability of current low-floor bus designs is limited by the following factors:

- Forty-ft-long low-floor buses typically have fewer seats than a 40-ft-long conventional bus because of the room taken up by the wheelwells. For example, in August 1993, the Chicago Transit Authority (CTA) ordered 40 low-floor buses with room for 37 seated passengers (33).[13] The conventional 40-ft-long buses used by the CTA have room for 45 seated passengers.
- Clearances between the bus undercarriage and the street are reduced. Typically, the greatest angle that can be driven over by current 40-ft-long low-floor buses is 9° at the front or back (the approach and departure angles) and 8° in the middle of the bus (the breakover angle). By comparison, most (though not all) standard 40-ft-long buses in North America have approach and departure angles of 10°. Newer low-floor bus designs are expected to have greater clearances (28).
- The shorter Orion IIs can negotiate steeper angles; however, one operator in Sonoma County, California, reports that these smaller buses are only appropriate for local service, because passengers find them scary at highway speeds, at least partially because of the low floor.[14]

North American transit operators who have purchased 40-ft-long low-floor buses have conducted demonstrations to gauge operating problems and public acceptance. Four such operators interviewed for this study (that is, Ann Arbor, Chicago, Kitchener, and Victoria) reported excellent public reaction to the demonstration buses. Until low-floor buses become commonplace, such public demonstrations will continue to be desirable.

As low-floor buses are added to a fleet, it will be important to plan to maximize the effectiveness and efficiency of a planned purchase of low-floor buses. For example, Calgary Transit formed an advisory committee that included user groups, hospitals, and transportation officials. The committee discusses and develops recommendations on route options, seating and securement positions, operational policies, promotional materials and public information programs, and evaluation of service (34).

The operators interviewed tested demonstration buses on various routes where clearances might be a concern and found no cases where clearances were a problem. Operators with particularly hilly service areas might find situations in which current designs would bottom out. Operators considering purchase of 40-ft-long low-floor buses should survey their routes, using a demonstration bus or other means, to determine if clearances will be a limiting factor.

The reduced seating on 40-ft-long low-floor buses suggests that they may not be appropriate for heavily used routes. On local routes where heavy loads occur only occasionally, the lack of seats may be compensated for by increased standing room, higher average operating speed because of faster boarding, and other advantages. At this time, low-floor buses are probably not appropriate for commuter or express service in which guaranteed seating is desirable. As development continues, designs with more seating are likely to become available.

Many transit managers have expressed concern about the safety of the step up to the rear seating area in low-floor buses. There is no quantitative information available on this point. None of the systems interviewed for this study had experienced passenger accidents related to the aisle steps.

Service and Cost Information

Prices for 40-ft-long conventional and low-floor buses appear to be comparable. For example, the Ann Arbor Transit Authority paid $198,000 per bus for 10 low-floor buses delivered in January 1993, compared to $185,000 per bus for an order of conventional buses purchased 4 years earlier.[15] Any price data must be viewed with caution, because manufacturers base prices on numerous factors, including desire to achieve visibility, the size of an order, the size of available backlogs, specific contract provisions, and the competitive situation.

Calgary Transit tested 22-passenger low-floor buses on a downtown shuttle route. A survey of passengers indicated a 19 percent increase in ridership and a 95 percent customer satisfaction score (34).

Kitchener Transit, which serves Kitchener and Waterloo, Ontario, conducted a test of boarding and alighting times on conventional buses and seven 40-ft-long New Flyer low-floor buses. The test showed a savings of 0.19 sec per boarding passenger and 0.33 sec per alighting passenger on the low-floor buses:[16]

	Alighting Time (Sec/Passenger)	Boarding Time (Sec/Passenger)
Low-Floor	1.16	2.23
Conventional	1.49	2.42

According to the General Manager of Kitchener Transit, the test results may have been influenced by the novelty of the low-floor buses at the time of the test, which caused many passengers to hesitate as they boarded the buses. He believes that the test results understate the savings on boarding times. Kitchener does not provide wheelchair-accessible service.

A study of boarding and alighting times on conventional and low-floor buses conducted by Levine and Torng in Ann Arbor

[13]Norm Santos and Jim Gebis, Chicago Transit Authority, Chicago, Illinois.
[14]Dave Knight, Sonoma County Transit, Santa Rosa, California.

[15]Chris White, Ann Arbor Transportation Authority, Ann Arbor, Michigan.
[16]Wally Beck, Kitchener Transit, Kitchener, Ontario.

also showed statistically significant savings in boarding and alighting times on low-floor buses (*35*):

	Alighting Time/ Passenger (Sec)		Boarding Time/ Passenger (Sec)	
	Front Door	Rear Door	No Fare	Cash Fare
Low-Floor	1.32	2.17	1.93	3.09
Conventional	2.55	2.67	2.76	3.57

Passengers receiving a transfer required 1.6 sec longer to board on the low-floor buses, apparently because of the placement of the transfer cutter.

Observation of two test boardings by wheelchair riders in Ann Arbor indicated that the time to enter or leave the bus (separate from securement) was slightly shorter on low-floor buses than conventional lift-equipped buses; however, the time needed for securement was much longer on the low-floor buses for two reasons: 1) the tie-down devices used in the low-floor buses took longer to operate; and 2) the distance from the front door ramp boarding location to the tie-down areas on the low-floor buses was longer than the distance from the rear-door lift boarding location to the tie-down areas on the conventional buses (*35*).

BC Transit is participating in a study commissioned by Transport Canada that will compare low-floor operations in Victoria with lift operations in Vancouver.

Reported Use and Effectiveness

Of the 309 respondents to the study survey, 46 indicated that they operate low-floor, fixed-route buses. The survey asked respondents to rate the effectiveness of each option employed on a scale of 1 to 5 (with 1 being "not effective" and 5 being "very effective"). Of the 16 respondents who completed the effectiveness rating portion of the survey, 13 reported that this option was moderately to very effective in promoting use of fixed-route service. Figure 12 shows the effectiveness rating given to this option by survey respondents.

Follow-up calls were made to the systems that reported relative success in using low-floor vehicles. Table B-6 in Appendix B provides information about 17 transit providers who use this equipment.

ACCESSIBLE TAXIS

An accessible taxi is a vehicle, operated in general public taxi service, that is accessible to all persons, including those who use wheelchairs and cannot transfer from the wheelchair to a seat in a taxi. Accessible taxis may be purchased by a public entity and leased to taxi companies or purchased directly by the taxi companies. Frequently, the public entity subsidizes use of taxis by eligible paratransit riders.

Accessible taxicabs may be low-profile vans with ramps, conventional vans with lifts, or modified taxis with a ramp and raised roof. The general concept of accessible taxis is to operate them in general public, non-subsidized service, increasing travel options for persons using wheelchairs. In a few cases, taxi companies have procured accessible vehicles and are operating them in regular service without any involvement of the public paratransit system. Primarily, however, public entities have become involved in procuring accessible taxis and contracting for their operation. Most accessible taxi programs in the U.S. and Canada are part of a publicly subsidized paratransit service. The public entities have found taxi service to be cost-effective in serving on-demand travel needs and off-peak, intermittent demand (such as late-night service).

Figures 13 and 14 show low-profile, ramp-equipped minivans operated by Yellow Cab of San Francisco and Yellow Cab of Benicia, California. As shown, vehicles can be designed to provide accessible access through either the side door, rear door, or both. Vehicles equipped with a rear door ramp are typically equipped with a rear axle kneeling device that lowers the floor height and decreases the slope of the ramp.

How accessible taxis are procured and used can be summarized as follows:

- Taxi companies procure accessible vehicles and use them in regular service with no subsidy. This variation was explored in Ottawa's Accessible Taxi Demonstration Project (*36*).
- Taxi companies procure vehicles and, under contract to a public entity, use them as part of a subsidized paratransit service and in regular service.
- A public entity procures the accessible taxis, leases them to the taxi companies, and taxi companies use the vehicles for both subsidized paratransit service under contract to the public entity and general public taxi service.

Promoting Integration and Appropriate Use of Fixed-Route and Paratransit Services

Accessible taxis can be a way to provide more effective paratransit service and integrate taxi service for persons with disabilities, including persons in wheelchairs. Historically, paratransit programs have used taxicabs because of cost-effectiveness and because of the immediate-response, 24-hour-a-day service offered by taxicabs. Conventional paratransit van service has an hourly cost regardless of how many riders are transported; it is cost-effective during peak times and for grouped trips. Taxi service is paid for, on the other hand, on a per-trip basis; if there are no trips, no costs are incurred. As a result, for demand-responsive trips that occur during off-peak, low-volume times of day, taxis are often the most cost-effective option for paratransit service. In urban areas with extensive taxi service, some programs have found that taxis are the most effective option for most trips.

34

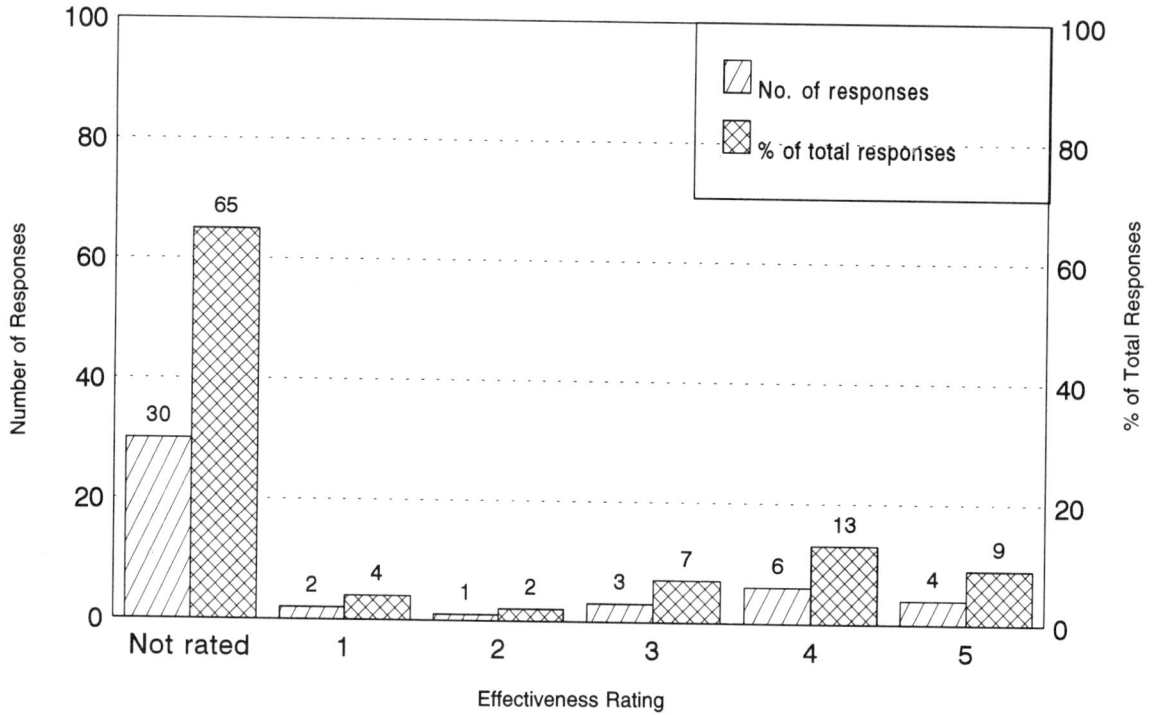

Figure 12. Reported effectiveness of low-floor buses. 1 = not effective; 5 = very effective.

Figure 13. Accessible taxi operated by Yellow Cab of San Francisco, California (photograph courtesy of Carmen Magana/S.F. Muni).

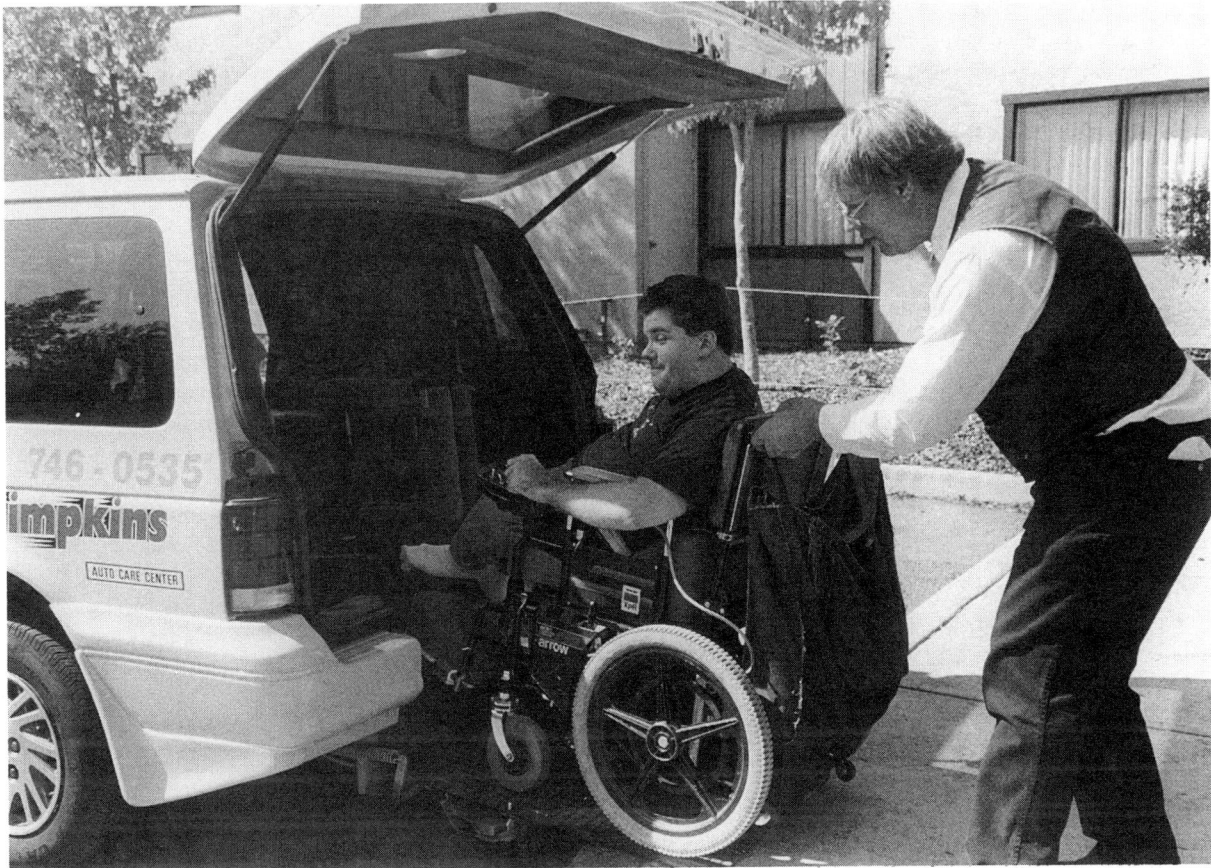

Figure 14. Accessible taxi operated by Yellow Cab of Benicia, California (photograph courtesy of John Metzler, Paratransit Program).

Without accessible taxicabs, programs using taxis have had to serve those passengers requiring use of a lift or ramp by means of lift-vans contracted on a per-trip basis from specialized van companies or by means of dedicated van service, usually operated directly by the paratransit program. The separate van service is often more expensive for the paratransit program than taxi service and sometimes provides a lower level of service for patrons than taxicabs.

With the establishment of accessible taxi programs, paratransit programs can extend taxi service to persons with disabilities who require a lift or ramp. In addition, accessible taxis are available for non-subsidized trips anytime, including hours when paratransit may not operate, and may be used by any wheelchair rider, regardless of eligibility for paratransit service.

Applicability to Particular Situations and Areas

Accessible taxi programs are implemented in areas with existing taxi service, usually where taxi companies have a history of being one component of paratransit services in a community. Accessible taxi programs work well in both large and small urban areas.

Key Implementation Issues

Capital Costs

Demonstration programs in Canada and Europe have indicated that supporting the ongoing operating costs of accessible taxi service is economically feasible for private companies (*36, 37, 38*). Assistance may be required, however, with the initial capital cost of accessible cabs. Typically, a ramp-equipped, low-profile minivan costs from $25,000 to $30,000. A new "taxi package" standard sedan may, on the other hand, cost only $15,000 to $18,000. Unless there is a significant amount of new business to be gained from the operation of accessible vehicles (for example, subsidized paratransit service), there may be little incentive for private companies to spend the additional $10,000 to $15,000 for accessible vehicles. Furthermore, many taxi companies, particularly smaller firms, purchase used vehicles that may cost $5,000 or less. The cost differential and economic disincentive in these cases is much greater.

Public entities interested in promoting private taxi accessibility may need to help purchase equipment. If vehicles are used as part of a public paratransit service, USDOT participation in such capital subsidies may also be considered. Current policies, which do not include private taxi systems in the definition of mass transit may not, however, permit federal participation in programs that support private taxi service for the general public.

Capital subsidies may not be necessary where taxi licenses carry a substantial value. In Boston, for example, where the market value of a taxi medallion is more than $70,000, the City was able to link the issuance of new medallions to requirements that a certain portion of larger fleets be wheelchair accessible.

Regulatory/Licensing

Depending on the licensing and regulatory climate for taxis in a locality, various issues can arise. For instance, in San Francisco, California, taxi companies would not relinquish existing conventional licenses for accessible licenses. Instead, the Police Commission had to be convinced to issue new licenses especially for accessible taxis.[17]

If the public entity is attempting to cover a large area with many cities, taxi companies may not be licensed to serve all cities. This situation can hamper the entity's ability to create an accessible taxi program. In the Los Angeles area, just such a situation exists; however, because LACMTA contracts with the taxi companies, they can lawfully travel in any jurisdiction as long as they are under contract for paratransit. The risk here is that another taxi company will spot a competitor in its area and report it to the police. Thus, LACMTA is developing a system where taxis can indicate by a sign in the window that they are on a contract trip and thus are not breaking any laws.[18]

Insurance

Also in Los Angeles, LACMTA requires taxi companies to comply with state laws in regard to insurance requirements. The companies claim that because their drivers are independent contractors, the companies are not subject to workers' compensation insurance requirements; however, this claim may be subject to argument in the future. In the City of Napa, the City's contract with the taxi companies requires them to obtain workers' compensation insurance or provide a legal opinion that they do not need it. One company chose to obtain the insurance; the other provided the legal opinion. The costs incurred for workers' compensation insurance may affect the taxi companies' ability to provide a cost-effective service.[19]

Liability coverage provided by taxi drivers and taxi companies is low by public transit industry standards. In Massachusetts, for instance, some taxi drivers claim that, as independent contractors, they need only purchase a minimum of liability insurance (about $20,000 to $40,000) in order to meet local requirements. Often, taxi companies may self-insure for colli-

sion coverage, and they may not have the capacity to maintain sufficient reserve accounts. Higher liability limits may be required if private taxi companies lease vehicles from public agencies or if they become involved in subsidized paratransit programs. Given typical insurance rates for taxi companies, this higher liability may be costly to obtain.

Vehicle Design

Some Canadian providers have identified problems with the general public's being able to recognize and accept accessible taxis as available and appropriate for public taxi service. This reluctance to use accessible taxis is particularly evident with a high-profile vehicle. In Canada, the GSM taxi, a vehicle that is accessible, low-profile, and durable is being developed. In the United States, ramped, low-floor, minivans are preferred over the standard lift-equipped paratransit van as most applicable to integrated, accessible taxi service. Public entities in the U.S. also report that acceptability by the general public is not as important an issue because accessible taxis are completely booked with travel requests from persons with disabilities. Also, as accessible taxis become more commonplace (more are procured and put into service), they will be accepted by the general public as integral to taxi service.

Vehicle Maintenance

When leasing accessible taxis to taxi companies, public entities include minimum maintenance requirements. Adherence to these requirements must be monitored regularly to ensure that the vehicles are being maintained properly. In some cases, entities require the taxi companies to submit reports indicating performance of vehicle maintenance. In others, spot checks ensure compliance (39).[20]

Maintenance costs for ramped minivans and other types of accessible taxis tend to be higher than for conventional taxis (40).[21] During the Ottawa demonstration, taxi companies bore extra costs for maintenance of new, 1988, raised-roof and low-floor accessible taxi designs. They also experienced interruptions in service because of downtime for maintenance. The Ottawa study concluded that incentives, such as capital subsidies, lower licensing fees, and availability of additional licenses, are necessary to make accessible taxi operations economically viable for the private sector (36).

It is unknown how low-floor minivans will perform in taxi service in the long term. The low-floor design is preferred for its profile, but it may compromise the durability of the vehicle. In Los Angeles, accessible taxis are accumulating as much as 8,000 to 10,000 mi per month.[22]

---

[17]Annette Williams, MUNI, San Francisco, California.
[18]Richard DeRock, Los Angeles County Metropolitan Transportation Authority, Los Angeles, California.
[19]Celinda Romaine, City of Napa, California.

[20]Richard DeRock, Los Angeles County Metropolitan Transportation Authority, Los Angeles, California; Celinda Romaine, City of Napa, California.
[21]Celinda Romaine, City of Napa, California; Marcia Kent, Benicia Yellow Cab, Benicia, California; Jim Bosso, Santa Cruz Transportation, Inc., Santa Cruz, California.
[22]Richard DeRock, Los Angeles County Metropolitan Transportation Authority, Los Angeles, California.

Taxi Driver Incentives

One area of concern mentioned in the literature is that taxi drivers perceive that they are doing more work for accessible taxi trips while getting the same fare as a conventional taxi trip (36). In Canada, it was reported that some taxi drivers keep the meter running during boarding and alighting thus compensating themselves.[23] If not specified as allowable in a contract, this practice would be considered discriminatory in the United States. Drivers may also receive, per a contractual agreement, a flat surcharge in addition to the meter fare for persons with disabilities who use wheelchairs (39). In other cases, the driver pays a lower lease or fee for the accessible vehicle because the taxi company is not depreciating it (it was provided to them by the public entity) (39). In addition, several areas indicated that accessible taxis are in such constant demand that drivers' total fares tend to be higher than when driving a conventional taxi (36, 40).[24] However, as discovered in the Ottawa accessible taxi demonstration, even though any loss of driver income may be offset by factors such as consistent demand during off-peak hours and longer distances, the drivers still perceive that they are experiencing a net loss of income when driving an accessible taxi. Drivers' interest and perceptions, in the context of the particular operating environment, must be addressed for accessible taxis to be successful (36).

Driver Training

Driver training, especially sensitivity training, is essential for a successful program. In some cases, the public entity provides the training. In others, the public entity has made driver training part of the taxi companies' contractual obligations. For example, the province of Quebec has implemented the "Training Course on Transporting Disabled Persons by Taxi" (developed by the Centre de formation professionelle pour l'industrie du taxi du Quebec) and is considering making the course a prerequisite for obtaining a taxi driver's permit (38). BC Transit in Vancouver contractually requires taxi companies participating in their Taxi Saver Program to ensure that drivers are properly trained. As a supplement to training, BC Transit has published *Transporting People with Disabilities, Tips for Taxi Drivers* in consultation with local transit advisory groups.[25]

A related issue, drug testing, may become a requirement for taxi drivers providing paratransit service under contract to a public entity. The expenses involved may increase the cost of service.[26]

Reported Use and Effectiveness

Of the 309 respondents to the study survey, 45 indicated that accessible taxis operate in their areas. Of the 13 respon-

dents who completed the effectiveness rating portion of the survey, 10 reported that this option was moderately to very effective in promoting integration of service. Figure 15 shows the effectiveness rating given to this option by survey respondents.

Follow-up calls were made to the systems that reported that accessible taxi programs were relatively effective in meeting the needs of customers with disabilities. Table B-7 in Appendix B provides information about selected transit providers who use this option.

AUTOMATED INFORMATION AND COMMUNICATION SYSTEMS

Automated information and communication systems use automated technology to enable and enhance communication with persons with disabilities. Devices have been developed to aid persons with hearing impairments in obtaining information directly from transit personnel or in obtaining information from announcements made in stations. Other devices assist persons with vision impairments by providing audible information.

Systems to Assist Persons With Hearing Impairments

Techniques and devices for assisting persons who are deaf and those with other hearing impairments to obtain information include the use of visual information and devices that enhance the ability to hear. These techniques and devices include hearing-aid-compatible/amplified telephones, automated speech recognition, electronic information signs, assistant listening devices, and emergency systems. These are discussed in the following paragraphs.

Hearing-Aid-Compatible/Amplified Telephones

In the past, all telephones were compatible with hearing aids. If a person with a hearing impairment had a hearing aid equipped with an induction coil and a t-switch, that hearing aid could be set so that the person could talk on the telephone; however, new phone technology that reduces the amount of energy produced by the phone made many phones incompatible with hearing aids. A 1982 law requires that all coin-operated and essential phones be compatible with hearing aids, however, full compatibility has yet to be achieved (41). Hearing-aid-compatible phones are essential in a noisy environment such as a transit station, and transit agencies should ensure that at least one such compatible phone is in each bank of phones.

[23]Bruce Chown, BC Transit, Vancouver, Canada.
[24]Jim Bosso, Santa Cruz Transportation, Inc., Santa Cruz, California.
[25]Bruce Chown, BC Transit, Vancouver, Canada.
[26]Richard DeRock, Los Angeles County Metropolitan Transportation Authority, Los Angeles, California.

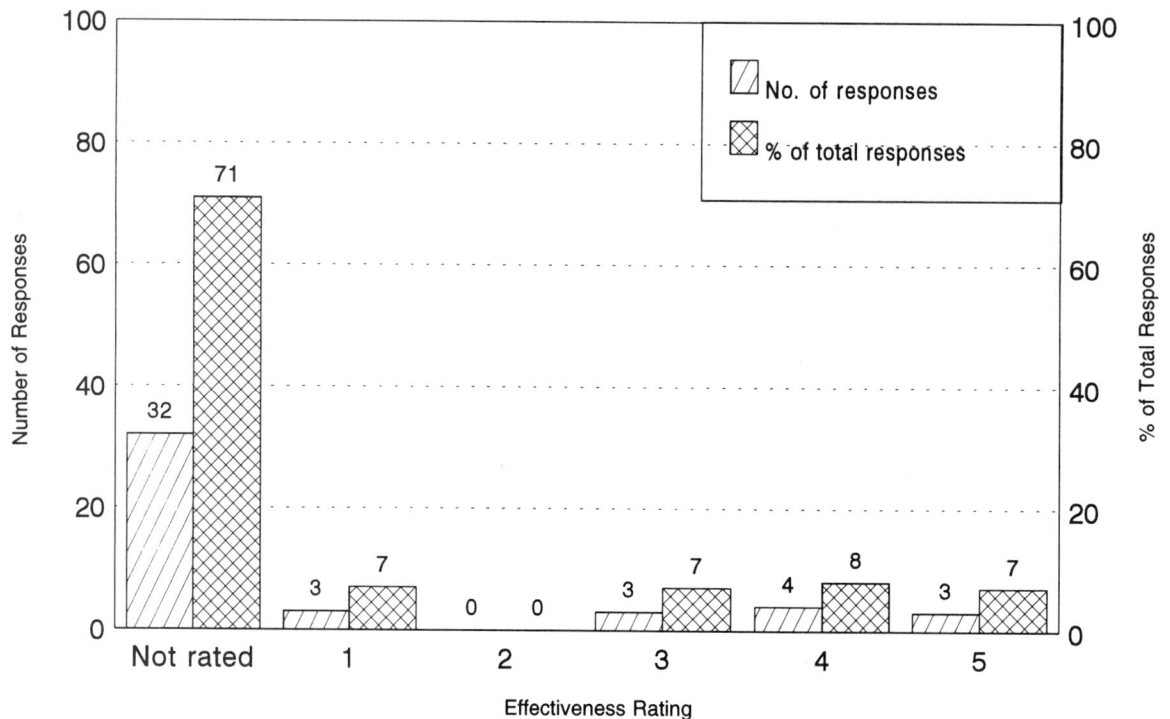

Figure 15.   Reported effectiveness of accessible taxi services. 1 = not effective; 5 = very effective.

Automated Speech Recognition

Automated speech recognition systems are computer systems that convert spoken words into text. These systems must learn different voices and will gradually learn vocabulary for the particular voices. Transit systems might use such a system at a ticket sales booth or information booth. The automated speech recognition system could interpret the transit attendant's words and present them in text form to a deaf person, who could respond using a computer keyboard.

Electronic Information Signs

These devices, which include electronic destination signs and variable information signs, can provide important information to persons with hearing disabilities inside vehicles, in stations, and at stops. In stations, electronic readerboards that scroll information or announcements are an excellent way to assist customers who have hearing impairments. These boards can be centrally controlled by a computer, which can update information instantly on selected boards. Video monitors can be used to make bus, train, or flight schedules continually available.

The Los Angeles Smart Traveler program provides pre-trip information on bus schedules and also on kiosks at several stations and malls. The light-emitting diode (LED) displays provide transit arrival information and are readable in sunlight. They are weatherproof and resistant to vandalism. They can be programmed and updated from a central location but are not yet triggered by the vehicles (*42*). The Transportation Development Centre of Canada has sponsored the development of Communicaid, an automated kiosk that provides information on such topics as flight arrivals and departures; location of amenities; and ground transportation for people with sight, speech, or hearing impairments. This kiosk has undergone a human factors evaluation that suggested improvements in the areas of glare reduction, monitor angle, seat height, and response controls (*43, 44*).

One example of an onboard system is the Visual Communication Network demonstrated on the Montreal Metro, shown in Figure 16. Electronic display panels have been installed in Metro cars. These display panels provide passenger information on electronic readerboards and through an audio system. Information provided includes the next station stop, available transfers, and emergency messages. This system also presents retail store promotions. The information is transmitted via a data radio network from control centers to receivers inside the cars. Passengers endorsed the system— with 72 percent rating the system from good to excellent (*45*).

With automatic vehicle location (AVL) systems, passenger information systems can report the actual schedule as opposed to the planned schedule. Halifax, Nova Scotia, uses video terminals in transit terminals and malls to show routes that stop at that location and the time that the next bus will arrive. Broward County Transit of Ft. Lauderdale, Florida, as well as transit providers in Toronto, Kitchener, and Guelph, Ontario, have installed viewers similar to monitors in airports but with sharper graphics. They present material on arrivals,

Figure 16. On-board electronic sign in Montreal Metro (photograph courtesy of Visual Communications Network: Telecite, Inc.).

departures, delays, and fares. Arrival and departure information is real-time and comes from sensors installed on the approach to the station (*42*).

Similar, but more extensive, systems are being implemented in Stockholm, Sweden, and in London, England. In Stockholm, each sheltered bus stop is being equipped with a computerized system that communicates next arrival information audibly and visually. In London, plans call for up to 4,000 bus stops to be equipped with electronic display boards that show next arrival information. The minutes to arrival are shown for the next three buses on a single route stop and up to seven buses at a multi-route stop (*46*).

Assistant Listening Devices

Several technologies provide assistance to persons with hearing impairments. Amplifiers can be used to convert public address (PA) announcements into FM or infrared signals. These signals can them be picked up by receivers on a person's headset. Unfortunately, such systems do not work well in noisy or crowded conditions (such as a transit station) and are expensive. Furthermore, few people own the receivers. There also is concern that different FM systems will interfere with one another. Still, some transit applications may be possible—one manufacturer has used an FM system successfully on tour buses, even when different buses were close to one another.

Another option is an induction loop system. This requires an induction loop to be installed along the entire perimeter of a room or waiting area. The loops connect easily to PA systems, and individuals can set their hearing aids to pick up the magnetic or induction field. These systems are relatively inexpensive but have limited use in transportation settings where there would be interference from metal in vehicles, electromagnetic fields, and the use of fluorescent lights (*47*). Successful examples of induction loop systems on buses can be found in Scandinavia and the Netherlands.

Emergency Systems

The need to communicate with those with hearing impairments must be considered in the design of emergency systems for transit. Where such systems now have alarms, the ADA Accessibility Guidelines require visual signals as well and that these signals meet certain requirements for visibility.

Systems to Assist Persons With Vision Impairments

Techniques for assisting persons who are blind or who have low vision to obtain information include the use of devices that provide verbal information on routes, schedules, fares, stops, and so forth. Technologies that use human speech are becoming common, particularly with telephone voice-mail systems and menu systems for obtaining information. Technologies useful for transit include talking bus stops and signs, talking buses and trains, telecommunication systems, auditory maps, and auditory pathways. These are discussed in the following paragraphs.

Talking Bus Stops and Signs

The technology of talking signs has been demonstrated with talking elevators, which have been used for some time. Most experimentation with this technology for transit has been done in England. In the town of Weston-Super-Marc, Electronic Speech Information Equipment (ELSIE) was demonstrated. In this demonstration, nine bus stops were equipped with a system that uses digital speech. A box mounted on the bus stop or within a bus shelter clicks so that a person who is blind can locate the box. When the person pushes the button on the box, a voice announces the route numbers and timetable information for all buses using the stop and also the arrival time of the next bus. The system includes a bus identification system that detects arriving buses approximately 600 ft ahead of the bus stop. The system was well received by persons with visual impairments, the elderly, and visitors *(41)*.

In London, England, talking bus stop technology is being implemented at 100 bus stops on one route. When a passenger pushes a button, the system announces the arrival times of the next three buses at the stop and any delays *(42)*.

Another promising technology is that of the talking sign. Talking signs emit infrared signals that can be converted to audible information by a pocket-sized unit carried by individuals with vision impairments. This technology provides audible information only when the signal is received by the appropriate unit and, thus, is quiet at other times. Another advantage is that the infrared signal is directional, thus serving to guide the customer to the sign. As illustrated by Figure 17, signage can be programmed to indicate "Exit," "Elevator," "Escalator," "Men's Room," "Ladies' Room," and in general, to provide the same information as visual signs provide for a person without vision impairments. Talking signs have been installed by Bay Area Rapid Transit in San Francisco, California. Figure 18 shows a passenger using the hand-held receiver to locate the exit at the Market Street station.

Talking Buses and Trains

Voice enunciator systems can be used to provide automatic stop announcements in a clear, human voice. In Vancouver, British Columbia, the unmanned SkyTrain system uses a digitized voice message to provide next stop and destination information *(46)*. In Salem, Oregon, four buses are equipped with voice enunciators. These buses announce stops at major intersections and provide information to passengers on local retailer promotions. The system runs on a timer activated by a button pressed by the driver. The LYNX bus system in Orange, Osceola, and Seminole Counties, Florida, also has equipped nearly 50 buses with enunciator systems that announce every stop *(42)*. Durham Area Transit Authority in North Carolina is testing a talking bus system that is a voice messaging system that announces stops. Systems have also been developed that will broadcast the bus route number and destination to people waiting at the stop. Figure 19 illustrates how talking bus technology works. The location of buses is tracked by a satellite global positioning system (GPS) or other vehicle location technology. Recorded messages are then activated as buses approach stops. As shown in Figure 19, voice announcements can be made inside the bus and outside to waiting customers. Messages can also be displayed on internal and external signs for customers with hearing impairments.

A new development is the use of a GPS on buses to identify their location and signal the appropriate voice announcement. Several such systems were demonstrated at the 1993 New Orleans Expo of the American Public Transit Association.

Telecommunication Systems

Many transit systems are using computerized speech along with a transit information system to provide travel information to passengers. These systems allow customers to use touch telephones to request schedules, fares, and, in some cases, trip planning information. These systems are not necessarily designed for persons with disabilities; however, they allow persons with vision impairments improved access to verbal information (that is, these systems are likely to be available on a 24-hour basis, and usually they reduce the incidence of receiving a busy signal).

An example of such a system is the Bus Line System developed for Expo 86 by Oracle Communications as part of the Transport Canada-funded Integrated Transportation Information System (ITIS) project. This system provides general transit information, bus schedules, and trip planning information. The

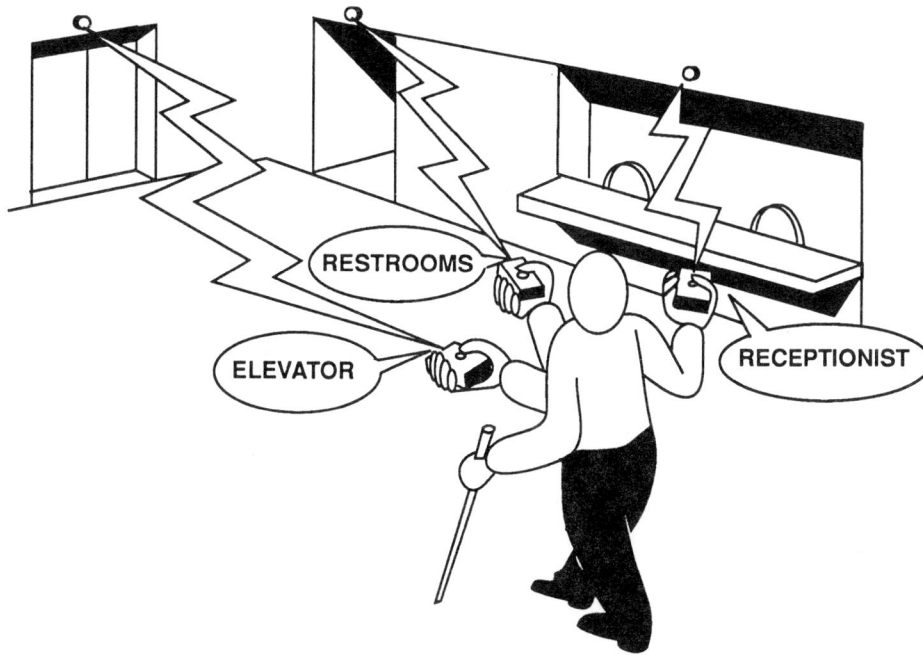

Figure 17. Illustration of talking sign technology.

Handyline system was developed at the same time and used computer-generated speech to assist in communicating with customers of the BC Transit's HandyDART paratransit system (*48*). The Handyline system offered information about the system, allowed customers to cancel pre-booked trips, and provided booking capability. Although the Handyline system was used successfully by customers of HandyDART, around 30 percent of the users were confused by the menus, had difficulty using a telephone, or could not access the information for various reasons. To increase usage, more marketing and instructional exercises are probably required (*43*).

An important consideration in the design and use of these systems, particularly for transit systems subject to the requirements of the ADA, is access to the information provided by persons who cannot use standard telephones. Similar system information and assistance should be able to be accessed by individuals using telecommunications devices for the deaf (TDDs).

Auditory Maps

Although no known auditory maps exist in transit facilities, such maps would probably be very helpful for persons with vision impairments. Tapes could be produced describing a particular route from a specific origin to a destination describing a transit system, rail line, or station area (*41*).

Map displays in stations or at key transfer points could include a verbal description activated by a person pressing a button. The location of the button could be signaled by a particular sound, such as a clicking noise.

Auditory Pathways

An auditory pathway is created by a series of speakers, positioned along a pathway, that broadcast directional instructions to blind persons following the pathway. The user would signal the speaker system by pressing a button at the start of the pathway, such as a transit station entrance. The person's progress along the pathway would be determined by a sensor on the speakers that would detect something worn by the person.

Research, on using auditory pathways in noisy environments like a transit station, showed that persons with vision impairments could follow the auditory pathways and that the speakers were the most useful when placed wherever a change in direction was required. A concern is that the system would interfere with PA announcements in stations (*41*).

Systems to Assist Persons With Cognitive Impairments

Although many technologies and policies exist that can help persons with visual or hearing impairments use public transit, there is much less available for persons with cognitive disabilities. Training and individual attention are key to helping these customers. In addition, transit agencies need to design materials such as maps, brochures, and timetables to be as straightforward and understandable as possible.

Research with 81 persons with cognitive impairments indicated that using symbols along with short text explanation is the best way to increase understanding of signage for most people (*49*). Uniform use of visual and audio signals, as well as color coding can help a person who has been trained to

Figure 18. BART passenger using talking sign receiver to locate exit (photograph courtesy of Smith-Kettlewell Eye Research Institute and Talking Signs, Inc.).

recognize the correct bus or train. Training, along with high auditory quality, can help persons recognize special announcements. In addition, training is needed to help the person look for landmarks, listen to announcements, and identify the correct stop. The mechanism for notifying a driver of the wish to disembark should also be uniform. Likewise, training is needed to help a person determine how to exit a station (50).

In the design of passenger information systems, it is recommended that such systems be designed for a broad range of users. Designing for the average user will make such information unusable for many. Designing for persons in the 95th or 98th percentile, however, will allow many customers with vi-

sual, hearing, or cognitive disabilities to use the systems (43, 44). Research has been undertaken to aid designers of customer information materials, including electronic information systems, to make their systems more understandable to those with cognitive disabilities (51).

Promoting Integration and Appropriate Use of Fixed-Route and Paratransit Services

These automated devices provide information to persons with hearing or seeing disabilities in order to promote their

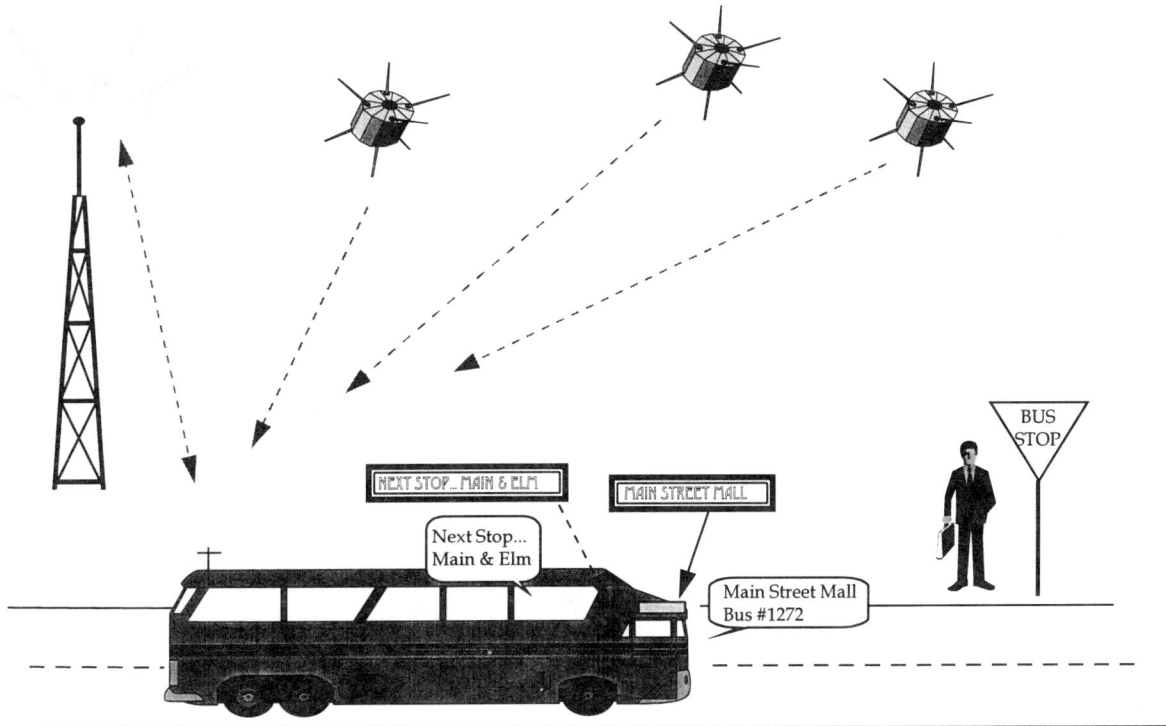

Figure 19.   Illustration of talking bus system.

independent use of fixed-route transit systems. Communication and information are especially important for new system users, and often visitors without disabilities have difficulty using unfamiliar transit systems. Careful design of visual and auditory systems to explain transit routes, schedules, fares, stops, and real-time arrival information to those with visual and hearing disabilities will probably lead to better information systems for those without disabilities.

Research on systems developed in Canada indicates that a system "designed to enhance information for the general public has the additional benefit of reducing barriers for people with disabilities. On the other hand, systems designed solely for the use of persons with disabilities, with no particular application for the general public, are less acceptable to either group." (44)

Key Implementation Issues

A major implementation issue with these systems is ensuring that they are updated when changes occur. Inaccurate information could be dangerous. For example, an auditory pathway could lead a person who has vision impairments to an area under construction, if the messages are not updated. System maintenance may also be an issue, but more experience will be needed to understand maintenance requirements. Finally, the transit system must develop emergency evacuation plans that can be communicated to persons with visual, hearing, and cognitive disabilities. Transit personnel and customers will need to be trained in the emergency procedures.

Reported Use and Effectiveness

Of the 309 respondents to the study survey, 43 indicated that they have audio/visual systems to assist persons with disabilities. The survey asked respondents to rate the effectiveness of each option employed on a scale of 1 to 5 (with 1 being "not effective" and 5 being "very effective"). Of the nine respondents who completed the effectiveness rating portion of the survey, three reported that this option was moderately to very effective in promoting use of fixed-route service. Figure 20 shows the effectiveness rating given to this option by survey respondents. Table B-10 in Appendix B lists those transit properties that indicated that some form of audiovisual system was in use. Because the survey did not ask for the type of system used and because this option or enhancement was not targeted for follow-up calls, more detailed information is not provided.

TRAVEL TRAINING AND FACILITATED TRAVEL

Travel training teaches people with disabilities the skills and confidence needed to use public transportation effectively. Travel training is most often applied to travel by fixed-route transit but can be applied to paratransit services. Facilitated travel provides ongoing assistance, usually a travel monitor or companion,

44

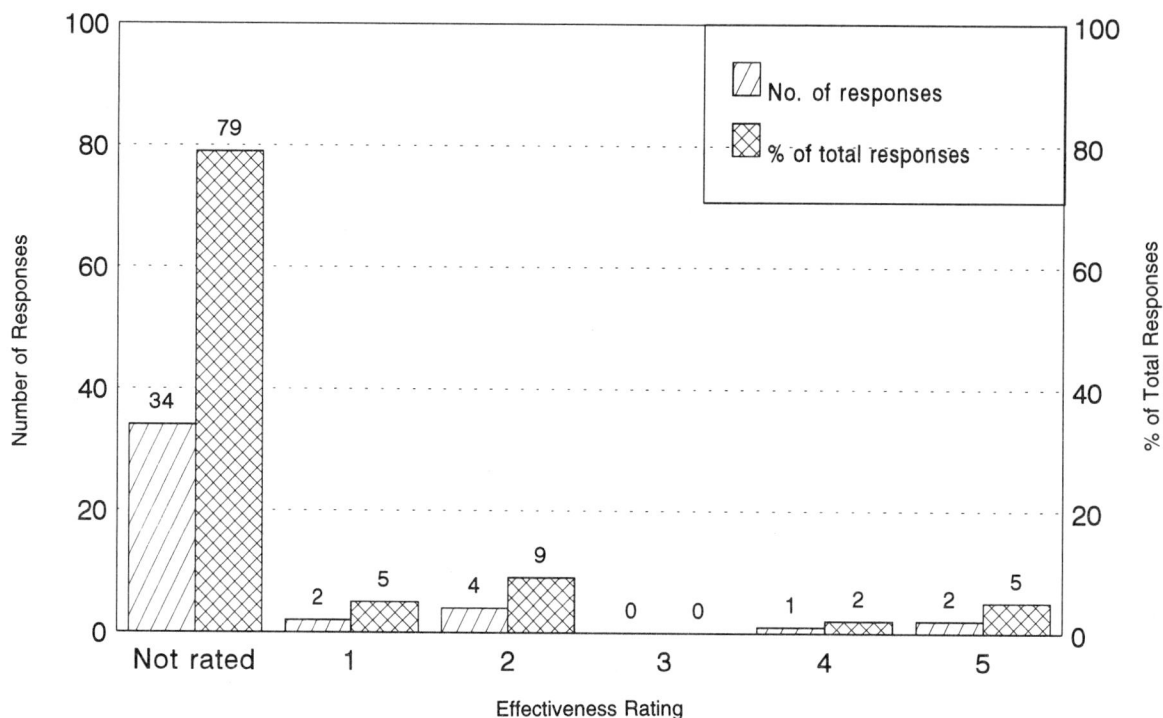

Figure 20. *Reported effectiveness of audio/visual systems. 1 = not effective; 5 = very effective.*

to enable people with disabilities, usually mental, to travel by fixed-route transit.

For many years, human service agencies have provided "mobility training" to clients. This training assisted individuals in negotiating their environment. The earliest examples of this type of training assisted persons with vision impairments. Use of transit may sometimes have been one of the skills taught. It was typically not, however, the focus of the training. More recently, training programs have been developed that focus on using transportation services. "Travel training" is the term used to describe this service. Travel training, particularly one-on-one "destination training" for individuals with cognitive disabilities, sometimes includes instruction in general mobility skills. More typically, specific training in using public transit is provided to individuals who have some degree of personal mobility.

Travel training can take various forms, the best of which depends on the nature and degree of an individual's disability. Different types of travel training (for example, destination, general use, and peer training; facilitated travel; and bus buddies) are discussed in the following paragraphs (*52, 53*).

Destination Training

For many people with developmental disabilities, and some with physical or mental impairments, training is provided to use the fixed-route system to travel to a daily destination. Training is usually provided by professional instructors on a one-

on-one basis, with the training program tailored to the needs of each student. In some cases, people who live in a group situation and attend the same program are trained as a group. Programs of this type often include a formal assessment of the needs and capabilities of each student, a formal program of instruction based on standard curricula, and a formal assessment of training progress. Students typically have various other people responsible for their care, often including parents and personnel of human service agencies. Trainers must coordinate closely with these caretakers, because their support is essential to the effectiveness of the training.

The skills taught in destination training include finding the way to and from the transit stop, recognizing the bus stop, recognizing the correct vehicle, how to pay the fare, appropriate behavior on board the vehicle, recognizing the correct place to alight, signalling the driver where to stop, and how to deal with unexpected situations.

General Use Training

Many individuals with physical disabilities and few or no mental limitations can learn to use transit services in general. Training may be provided by professional instructors, using a formal process as described for destination training, or by volunteer peer guides. Training is usually provided on a tailored one-on-one basis. Group demonstrations are also used to familiarize potential riders with transit equipment, especially how to get on and off a lift-equipped bus and secure a wheelchair using the tie-down devices available on the bus.

The skills taught in general use training will vary widely depending on a person's disability and personal history. For people with visual impairments, learning routes and schedules and how to obtain information, route finding, and determining the right vehicle and the right place to alight will be important. For wheelchair users, use of accessibility equipment will be important. For people with no prior transit experience, general familiarity and confidence building will be important. Learning what to do when things go wrong is an important element of all travel training and may extend to evacuation techniques.

Peer Training

Training by volunteer peers, sometimes called peer guides, can be particularly effective for people with physical disabilities and for the elderly. Many people with physical disabilities have overcome fear of using public transportation and have gained significant knowledge of how to access the system. This knowledge may include techniques highly specific to particular disabilities. Those who are new to the system may find it easier to learn from a person who has a disability similar to theirs. They are encouraged by the example of the peer, which helps them to overcome their own fears. As suggested by this description, a successful peer training program will depend heavily on appropriate matching of trainees and peer trainers.

Senior citizens are particularly receptive to learning from a person who they feel is understanding and attuned to their situation. Many have difficulty using the system because of increasing vision problems, slower reaction times, and increasing frailty but do not think of themselves as disabled. Many senior citizens have no prior experience riding transit. Achieving general familiarity with the system and overcoming fear of it can often be most effectively accomplished by riding with another elderly person. A program in Worcester, Massachusetts, has targeted senior citizens living in particular neighborhoods or housing complexes as peer trainers for other senior citizens in the same neighborhood or housing complex.

Cerenio Management Group in San Francisco, California, has sought to combine the advantages of peer training and training by professionals. This program has established a certification program specifically targeted at training people with disabilities in how to provide travel training and how to provide sensitivity training for transit personnel (54).

Facilitated Travel

Facilitated travel is a technique that has been applied to individuals with developmental disabilities who may not be able to learn to ride transit independently but who can ride with some supervision and assistance. Attendants or monitors ride buses with the program participants between home and work or training. The attendants ensure safe travel by the riders with disabilities and supervise behavior if necessary. Attendants may also be present at major transfer points to facilitate the safe movement of riders from one bus to another. The San Andreas Regional Center in San Jose, California, has been operating a facilitated travel program since July 1992 with

funding from the Santa Clara County Transit District. Some participants have graduated from escorted service to fully independent transit travel (55, 56).

A closely related idea is the Natural Helping Network, developed by People Accessing Community Transportation (PACT) in Bridgeport, Connecticut. In conjunction with a peer guide program, "natural helpers" are identified with whom disabled riders would normally come into contact during a regular daily trip (57).

Bus Buddies

Bus buddies provide a form of personalized, facilitated travel. A bus buddy is a volunteer who is paired with a disabled rider to provide long-term learning assistance or continuing transportation assistance for riders who may not be able to learn to ride transit on their own. Examples of people for whom continuing assistance may be appropriate would include some people with serious memory, balance, vision, orientation, or learning disabilities. The Bus Buddy program of the Handicapped Action Committee of Victoria, British Columbia, has provided learning assistance for as long as a year to develop independent transit riding ability (58).

In a Project ACTION demonstration, the Paralyzed Veterans of America, Buckeye Chapter, in Euclid, Ohio, trained people with disabilities to act as "travel buddies." In this case, the buddy was a form of peer trainer (59).

Promoting Integration and Appropriate Use of Fixed-Route and Paratransit Services

Travel training and related concepts reduce dependence on paratransit services by enabling people with disabilities to ride fixed-route transit for some or all of their travel needs. For those people who can learn general transit riding skills, travel training provides increased independence and greater mobility overall, regardless of whether they were paratransit riders before their training. For people with cognitive and developmental disabilities, travel training appears to be primarily effective with respect to repeated daily trips, which are also those that consume the greatest amount of paratransit resources. For such riders, travel training may not greatly expand their travel options, but it does integrate them more into the mainstream of everyday life.

In the context of the ADA, travel training is particularly relevant for people who are conditionally ADA paratransit eligible and for senior citizens who have been riding paratransit but who are not ADA paratransit eligible. Under the ADA, certain people may be eligible for some trips but not for others, depending on factors such as terrain, weather, the availability of accessible transit services, the accessibility of sidewalks, and variations in the health or condition of the individual. Screening on the basis of these criteria is known as trip-by-trip eligibility screening. Travel training, in conjunction with a trip-by-trip eligibility screening, should be particularly effective in reducing dependence on paratransit. Paratransit can be provided

46

to individuals who are travel trained for only those trips they cannot make by fixed-route.

In practice, trip-by-trip screening, particularly for infrequent trips, can be difficult and costly to implement. Many systems have chosen not to implement trip-by-trip screening and allow individuals (determined conditionally eligible) to use the paratransit service on an honor system—that is, riders determine their ability to use fixed-route service for a given trip. Because travel training is often provided for repetitive trips, screening trips based on this factor should be less difficult. Even if trip screening for travel training skills is not employed, a travel training program can encourage eligible individuals to use fixed-route services.

Travel training supports other innovations, especially service routes and paratransit feeder service, by increasing the pool of riders who can use them. Travel training would also be effective in conjunction with a fare incentive program. Deep discounts in fixed-route fares can be helpful in recruiting paratransit riders for travel training programs.

Applicability and Implementation Issues

Travel training is applicable to nearly every transit system, although certain conditions increase the benefits to be derived. Where the same organization is responsible for fixed-route transit and paratransit (as is the case throughout the United States under the ADA), incentives and motivation for a travel training program should be strong. Factors that increase the potential benefits and effectiveness of travel training include the following:

• A high degree of accessibility on the fixed-route system, including accessible vehicles, stops, and stations (Accessible vehicles are particularly helpful to riders who use wheelchairs. Other aspects of accessibility, however, such as signage, will be helpful to people with cognitive and developmental disabilities.)
• An effective program of training transit personnel to be sensitive to the needs of riders with disabilities
• A high degree of accessibility in the built environment, including sidewalks near transit stops (For some systems that serve areas without sidewalks, the applicability of travel training for people who use wheelchairs may be limited.)
• A good working relationship with the community of those with disabilities in developing the travel training program
• A good working relationship with human service agencies who can provide training or act as resources to design a program.

Transit operators considering establishing a travel training program can choose from three primary arrangements as follows:

• Refer potential trainees to human service agencies that provide training suited to their needs
• Contract with one or more organizations or individuals with the experience needed to train individuals with various disabilities

• Provide training directly.

The appropriate relationship with human service agencies may depend on the extent to which the transit operator is providing paratransit service for human service agency clients.

A key factor in a travel training program is the method of recruitment. Working through networks that already provide various services to senior citizens and people with disabilities is probably the best way of recruiting trainees who are not already receiving paratransit services. Travel training can be linked to the eligibility screening process for paratransit service. Applicants who are judged capable of learning to ride transit may be offered travel training.

The cost of travel training can vary considerably. Training in a group setting or by volunteers has minimal costs. Many people with severe disabilities, however, will require at least several days of one-on-one training with a professional trainer at a cost of several hundred to a thousand dollars. Even at such costs, the investment for each individual will be rapidly recouped if the training significantly reduces that person's paratransit riding (53).

Several transit providers (see Table B-8 in Appendix B) offer free passes or coupons to human service agencies providing travel training for clients. Although the cost to the transit provider is marginal, this incentive is often enough to gain the cooperation of local agencies.

A common problem is overcoming the resistance of parents, guardians, and direct care human service providers who are often reluctant to allow the individuals for whom they are responsible to be trained or to travel independently after being trained (60). If travel training programs are not detailed, thorough, and offered with consistent quality, this reluctance may be well founded. Providing high-quality, professional training developed in cooperation with parents, guardians, and agencies can help to overcome potential resistance.

Service and Cost Information

The most extensive travel training programs have historically been those aimed at people with developmental disabilities and have been provided by human service agencies. Organizations serving people with visual impairments also have been active in providing mobility training, not limited to use of transit. With the advent of the ADA and the general trend toward transit agencies' assuming responsibility for paratransit services, transit operators have expressed greater interest in travel training, and training for senior citizens and people with physical disabilities has received more attention. For the most part, transit agencies have limited their training activities to transit riding skills rather than general orientation and mobility training.

During 1991, Project ACTION funded five demonstrations of travel training (59, 61). These demonstrations generally reported positive results. For example, a project in Austin, Texas, trained 59 persons with disabilities to use fixed-route buses. A follow-up survey, administered 30 days after training was completed, found that 81 percent of those trained continued to use fixed-route bus service as their primary means of transportation. Projects in Euclid, Ohio, and San Antonio, Texas, reported increases in lift usage on accessible, fixed-route buses. A project in Reno, Nevada, found that trainees' field-tested ability to use fixed-route transit improved significantly and that, for 48 percent of trainees, accessible, fixed-route buses became their primary mode of transportation. The Reno project found, however, that travel training did not result in decreased paratransit usage. Those trainees who were also paratransit riders continued using paratransit for their regular trips and used fixed-route transit for discretionary trips, especially in good weather. The Reno program did not use a strict screening for paratransit eligibility and also had paratransit fares equal to the discounted fixed-route fare. These results suggest that travel training will be most effective at reducing paratransit ridership when combined with trip-by-trip eligibility screening and some difference between paratransit and discounted fixed-route fares.

Madison County, Illinois, reduced paratransit ridership from about 12,000 to about 7,000 passengers monthly over a 2-year period by means of a coordinated program involving travel training, introduction of an extensive service route network, and facilitating trips requiring a transfer from paratransit to a fixed-route bus (7).

Reported Use and Effectiveness

The use of travel training to encourage use of fixed-route service appears to be fairly widespread in the transit industry. Of the 309 respondents to the study survey, 135 indicated that

travel training programs were in operation in their area. Of the 80 respondents who completed the effectiveness rating portion of the survey, 71 reported that this option was moderately to very effective in promoting use of fixed-route service. Figure 21 shows the effectiveness rating given to this option by survey respondents. A high percentage of systems indicated that travel training was very effective.

Follow-up calls were made to the systems that reported that travel training programs were relatively effective in meeting the needs of customers with disabilities. Table B-8 in Appendix B provides information about selected transit providers who use this option.

FARE INCENTIVE PROGRAMS

Fare incentive programs offer fare reductions that exceed the federal half-fare requirement and are designed to encourage paratransit-eligible individuals to use fixed-route rather than paratransit service.

Paratransit-eligible individuals who can use fixed-route transit for at least some of their trips often have very little incentive to use fixed-route service when the alternative is door-to-door service. The appeal of paratransit service has become strengthened by the increasingly user-friendly, ADA-compliant service. For many individuals, door-to-door service with limited advance notice requirements and no capacity constraints has more

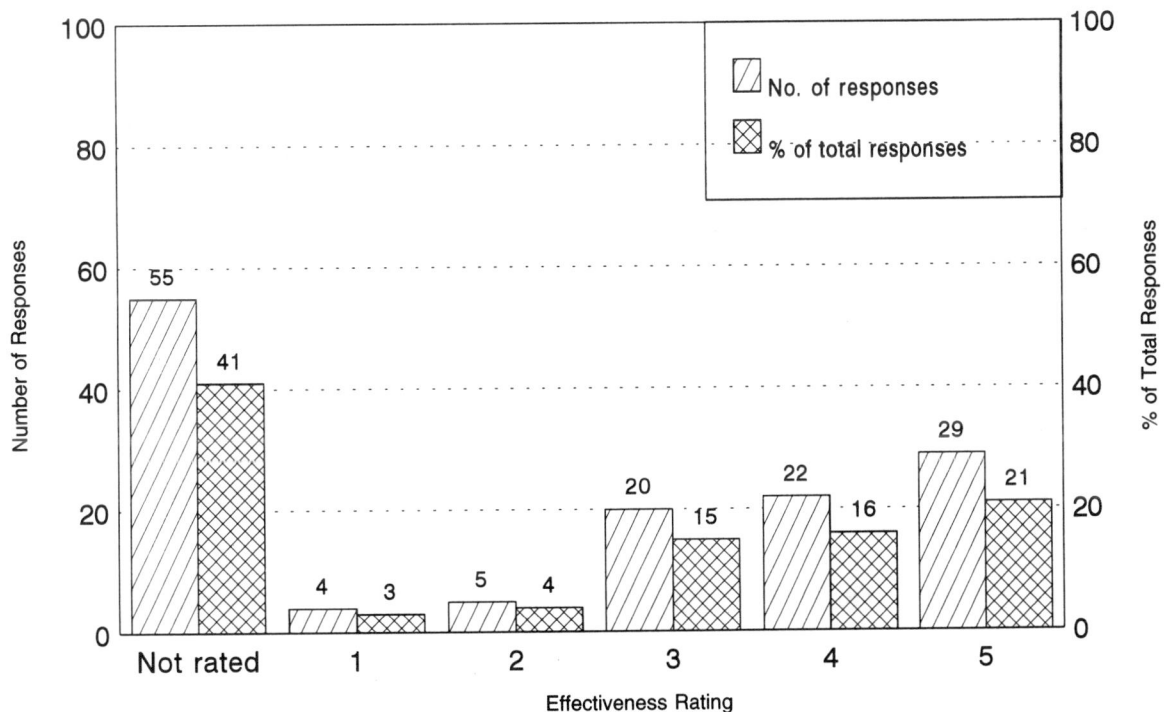

Figure 21. Reported effectiveness of travel training programs. 1 = not effective; 5 = not effective.

appeal than waiting for a bus or a train that may not stop close to one's trip origin and may have extended headways.

Several transit systems use fiscal mechanisms to encourage individuals who can do so to choose fixed-route service. This fiscal approach may be adopted as an alternative to the regulatory approach available to U.S. transit agencies through the ADA regulations. The regulatory approach enables agencies to choose between relying on persons in categories 2 and 3 to use fixed-route service when they can or implementing costly trip-by-trip eligibility screening procedures to ensure the appropriate use of paratransit service. Even agencies that implement trip-by-trip screening will have to rely heavily on riders' self-assessment of their abilities, so fare incentives will still have a role.

Because of the limited average income of people with disabilities, financial incentives have a strong potential for encouraging people to use fixed-route service.

Fare incentive programs can take several different forms, including the following:

• Agencies can embark on promotional campaigns that encourage individuals to use fixed-route service by making it available free of charge for a limited time. In Bridgeport, Connecticut, a May 1993 promotional campaign to draw people with disabilities onto fixed-route service adopted a three-pronged approach: free fares on fixed-route service, a substantial paratransit fare increase, and a comprehensive travel training program. The month-long campaign was considered so successful that the free-fare program was extended through 1993 and 1994.[27]

• Fare incentives may also be applied to accessible taxi programs. In Vancouver, British Columbia, BC Transit introduced a Taxi Saver Program, in 1991, that entitles paratransit users to purchase half-price taxi coupons. In 1992, clients made 6,000 trips monthly, at a cost to the transit agency of $7.80 per trip. This compares favorably with the $17.00 per trip on HandyDART, the paratransit program. BC Transit reports that the program is becoming increasingly popular with Handy-DART users, although no figures regarding diversion from the paratransit system are available (62).

• Free fare for paratransit-eligible individuals may also originate as part of a broad fare incentive program for the general riding population. In Austin, Texas, when a 15-month free-fare pilot program was discontinued in January 1991, because of problems with vandalism, it was decided to maintain free fares for people who are paratransit eligible, to discourage them from reverting to paratransit usage. In July 1993, there were 5,000 wheelchair boardings on the fixed-route service. The program has exceeded the most optimistic projections.[28]

• Free-fare programs, originally implemented for practical reasons, may be retained because of financial benefits. For example, the Niagara Frontier Transit System in Buffalo, New York, has been allowing wheelchair users to travel free on the

system's bus and light rail service since 1988 for two reasons. First, it was deemed impractical for the bus driver to have to leave his or her seat to go to the rear door entrance to collect a fare. Second, the ticket vending machines in the rail system were too high for wheelchair users to access. Because of pressure from the community of those with disabilities, new vending machines have been installed, but fares for wheelchair users are still voluntary (63).[29]

• The Tulsa Transit System in Oklahoma adopted a free-fare program concurrent with a major revamping of the fixed-route system to make it accessible. The Transit System's board of trustees felt that if a substantial amount of money was being invested in expanding the accessibility of the fleet, incentives should be provided to ensure that the wheelchair lifts would be used frequently (64).[30]

• The Metropolitan Transit Authority of Harris County (Houston, Texas) recently implemented a fixed-route, free-fare program for their MetroLift patrons. Between April and December 1993, approximately 3,000 out of 24,000 MetroLift clients received the Metro Freedom Passports, which entitle them to ride fixed-route buses at no charge. This represents a substantial percentage, given that only one-quarter of the Metro buses were fully accessible (65). In a survey of MetroLift clients who had received Freedom Passports, Metro found that about 10 percent had become new riders of the fixed-route services. Just over two-fifths of the Freedom Passport holders had already been riding the regular routes. The remaining Freedom Passport holders surveyed had not yet tried the fixed-route services.

Promoting Integration and Appropriate Use of Fixed-Route and Paratransit Services

The primary goals of fare incentive programs are to mainstream people with disabilities while substantially reducing the operating costs of transporting riders with disabilities. By structuring fares so as to promote use of fixed-route rather than paratransit service, individuals who can use fixed-route service will be encouraged to do so.

Key Implementation Issues

Following are issues that should be considered in the development of fare incentive programs:

• On most transit systems, some of those who have disabilities but who are not paratransit eligible may be required to continue paying half-fare on the fixed-route system. Those persons have an incentive to attempt to become paratransit eligible in order to travel for free. To avoid inappropriate eligibility approvals, transit systems will need to strengthen eligibility screening procedures and ensure that only the targeted population rides free on the transit system.

---

[27]Kimberlee Kelly-Morton, Greater Bridgeport Transit District, Bridgeport, Connecticut.
[28]Nancy Crowther, Austin-Capital Metropolitan Transportation Authority, Austin, Texas.

[29]Sherry Kolke, Niagara Frontier Transit Authority, Buffalo, New York.
[30]Becky Hefley, Tulsa Transit, Tulsa, Oklahoma.

• Although all systems consulted in this study report substantial cost-savings because of the fare incentive programs, administrative costs, particularly with regard to the tightening of paratransit eligibility screening procedures, must be considered when determining cost-effectiveness. Declines in half-fare ridership concurrent with the implementation of free-fare programs may signal problems with the program.

• Fares can be either free or deeply discounted beyond the federally required half-fare discount for senior citizens and people with disabilities. Transit systems should consider whether a partial discount would be enough of an incentive to cause people to ride on fixed-route service instead of paratransit.

• In evaluating the success of the free-fare programs described above, one should consider the stringency of existing eligibility screening procedures. If these have historically been lax, one may assume that many paratransit riders should have been riding fixed-route transit in the first place. Although this does not detract from the success these programs have experienced in diverting riders onto fixed-route service, systems that replicate these programs may prove less successful if they have traditionally employed stringent eligibility screening procedures.

• Free-fare programs may be prohibited by local regulatory limitations. For example, the CTA is prohibited by Chicago's city charter from allowing non-employees to ride transit free of charge.[31]

Service and Cost Information

There is no detailed information in the literature regarding the cost of fare incentive programs. Given that the farebox recovery ratio for fixed-route systems typically ranges from 20 percent to 40 percent of total operating cost, reduced fare programs can have a significant cost if applied broadly to populations using fixed-route service. If carefully targeted to paratransit riders or potential paratransit riders, costs can be marginal while savings are significant. With excess capacity available on fixed-route vehicles, the marginal cost of transporting additional riders is likely to be small compared to the average cost of a paratransit trip.

Information obtained from several transit providers as part of the follow-up to the industry survey suggests that cost-savings can indeed be significant. The Greater Bridgeport Transit District, which, since May of 1993, has provided free fares to persons determined ADA paratransit eligible has seen use of fixed-route buses by persons eligible for the program increase from 150 trips in the first month (May of 1993) to over 5,500 trips in September of 1993.[32] This program was supplemented by a major marketing campaign, and the Transit District provides travel training and trip planning services as well. Still, ridership increases have been significant and appear to be related, to a large degree, to the introduction of free fares. As noted above, similar increases in fixed-route ridership have been documented in Austin, Texas.

Reported Use and Effectiveness

Of the 309 respondents to the study survey, 153 indicated that they use fare incentives to encourage riders to use fixed-route service when possible. Follow-up calls revealed, however, that most of these providers considered standard half-fare programs or the setting of paratransit fares higher than fixed-route fares to be "fare incentive programs." Even these standard reduced fare efforts and fare policies were reported to be effective in encouraging fixed-route use. The survey asked respondents to rate the effectiveness of each option employed on a scale of 1 to 5 (with 1 being "not effective" and 5 being "very effective"). Of the 65 respondents who completed the effectiveness rating portion of the survey, 54 reported that this option was moderately to very effective. Figure 22 shows the effectiveness rating given to this option by survey respondents.

Table B-9 in Appendix B provides information about fare incentive programs at selected transit agencies. Program design varies greatly from free-fare to half-fare programs that have been extended to all hours.

FARE SIMPLIFICATION MECHANISMS

Fare simplification mechanisms include vouchers, ID cards, passes, and other methods used by transit agencies to assist people with disabilities who would otherwise have problems using standard fare collection mechanisms.

Some people with disabilities are prevented or discouraged from using fixed-route buses by manual impairments that prevent them from handling money. Some individuals have created alternative means for making the money accessible to the driver, such as pinning a bill onto an item of clothing. For security and liability reasons, however, many systems prohibit drivers from handling money and prefer to use automatic fare collection systems.

To address the coin handling problem, some systems provide coupons, vouchers, cards, or passes for people to produce or wear in a spot visible to the driver. Many systems have adopted fraud prevention measures to ensure that these fare substitutes are not used by ineligible persons.

Advanced technology is poised to transform radically the array of options available to transit systems in encouraging individuals with manual impairments to use the system. Two recent reports described how "smart cards" can simplify fare collection and provided an overview of the use of this technology in the United States and Canada (*42, 66*).

Information Management International, Inc., an information systems consulting firm, is under contract to the Department of Health and Human Services (DHHS) to develop an electronic ID card system to enable trip tracking for reimbursement purposes.[33] Because the initial target population is DHHS service recipients with disabilities, simultaneously with the trip

---

[31]Manuel De Alba, Regional Transportation Authority, Chicago, Illinois.
[32]Kimberlee Kelly-Morton, Greater Bridgeport Transit District, Bridgeport, Connecticut.

[33]Promotional material provided by Information Management International (IMI), Inc., and conversations with Robert Tannenhaus of IMI.

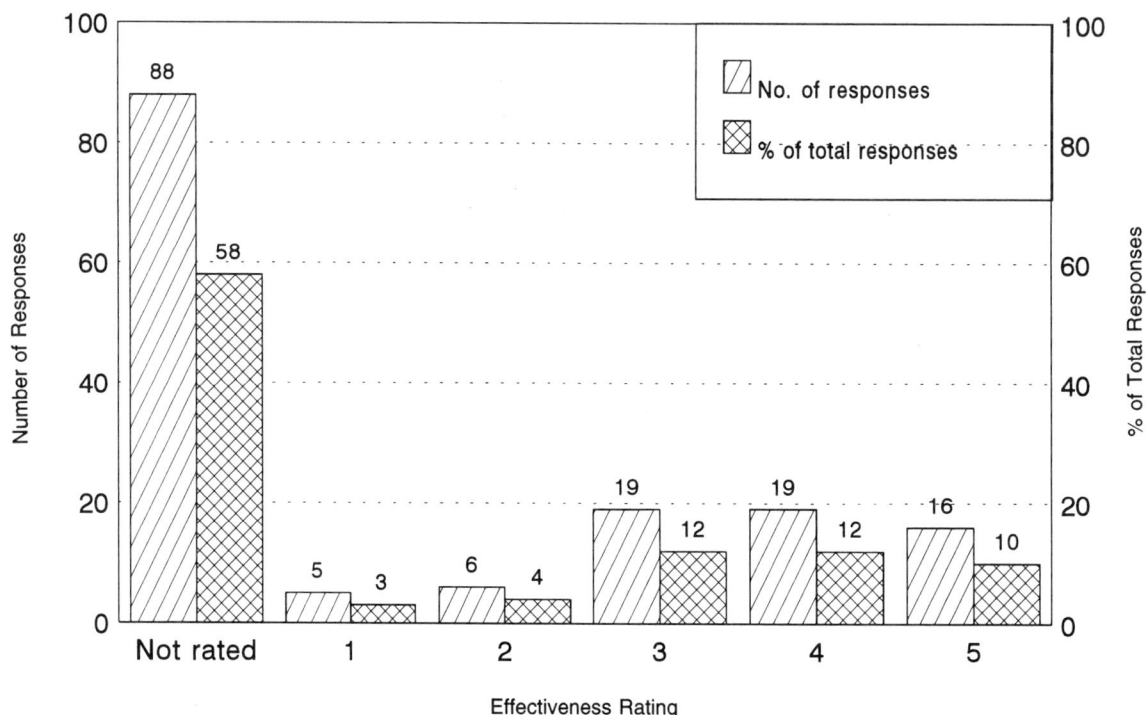

Figure 22. Reported effectiveness of fare incentive programs. 1 = not effective; 5 = very effective.

tracking features, the firm is developing technology that will include smart cards in braille, have a chain or band for attaching to one's clothing, and can be read through radio signals even if the person's hand is shaking. Variations include proximity cards and contactless cards, neither of which require any handling by the rider. The cards can hold comprehensive data on the person's capabilities and assistance needs, regular trip origins and destinations, and which vehicles the driver may need to coordinate with for transfer trips.

The three-phase project is expected to be completed and ready for commercial implementation in 1995. Operational and cost information is not available.

Reported Use and Effectiveness

The use of passes and vouchers is fairly common in the transit industry. Of the 309 respondents to the study survey, 115 indicated that they have mechanisms that simplify fare collection for persons with disabilities. The survey asked respondents to rate the effectiveness of each option employed on a scale of 1 to 5 (with 1 being "not effective" and 5 being "very effective"). Of the 34 respondents who completed the effectiveness rating portion of the survey, 29 reported that this option was moderately to very effective in promoting use of fixed-route service. Only five providers reported that it was less than moderately effective. Figure 23 shows the effectiveness rating given to this option by survey respondents.

Table B-11 in Appendix B lists those transit properties that indicated that they have simplified fare collection that is effective in promoting use of the fixed-route system.

MARKETING PROGRAMS

Marketing programs are promotional and information dissemination programs designed to increase ridership by persons with disabilities on general public transit systems. Programs may consist of general campaigns, including published brochures and materials; use of paid or free print, TV, or radio media; direct mail; and/or special promotions such as "ride free" days. Marketing programs may also include personal appearances by transit personnel before meetings of community groups and social service agencies and discussions of transit personnel with individual users.

Because transit systems in the past were inaccessible, many persons with disabilities have never used public transit. Others may not be familiar with recent changes, such as improved driver training or stop announcements, that make the system more usable. Marketing programs are, therefore, key to any effort to increase the use of public transit systems by persons with disabilities.

A complete marketing effort might include the following:

• Seeking the assistance and advice of the community of those with disabilities through advisory group representatives or other persons able to guide the effort

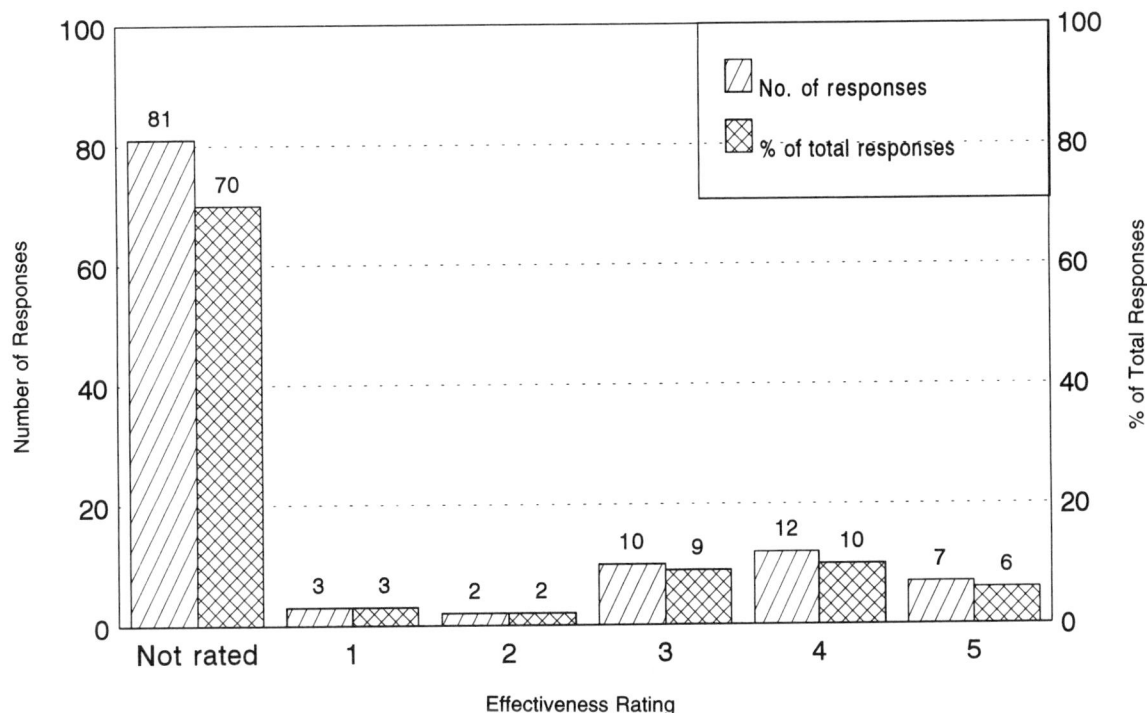

Figure 23. Reported effectiveness of fare simplification programs. 1 = not effective; 5 = very effective.

• Defining the potential users as specifically as possible and the goals and measures of effectiveness of the marketing campaign

• Determining a cost-effective approach to reaching the target population, including the types of media to be used and the allocation of staff resources

• Developing materials to be used for the marketing campaign, including printed materials, materials in accessible formats, and scripts for radio, TV, or public appearances

• Pre-testing the materials on representatives of the targeted groups and then revising and producing information and promotional material aimed at the target group

• Providing internal education and training to transit agency staff so that they are informed about the campaign and the services it promotes

• Implementing the campaign

• Evaluating the effectiveness of the campaign against the goals and measures of effectiveness.

Few marketing campaigns actually include all of the preceding measures—campaigns often use only one or a few of them. Marketing campaigns are often used to provide information about new paratransit services or newly accessible fixed-route services.

Marketing programs designed to increase use of fixed-route systems by persons with disabilities can be very targeted campaigns. They can be aimed at those specific individuals who are registered as ADA eligible for paratransit services and at human service agencies providing services to persons with disabilities. Marketing campaigns can be conducted on a very personal basis where the drivers, telephone operators, and dispatchers get involved in promoting the fixed-route system.

Marketing programs to promote the use of fixed-route transit should stress the advantage of the fixed-route system for persons with disabilities. In particular, fixed-route systems do not require day-ahead planning, so more spontaneous travel is feasible. In many systems, the fixed-route transit fare may be half that of the paratransit system. Promotions can be used whereby paratransit users are provided with a temporary free pass for the fixed-route system.

Promoting Integration and Appropriate Use of Fixed-Route and Paratransit Services

A marketing campaign should be part of any program to increase use by ADA-eligible persons of fixed-route transit systems. Marketing campaigns are appropriate when a fixed-route system receives accessible buses, when routes become accessible, or when new services become available. Marketing campaigns are necessary to promote "call-a-lift" bus service where a person needing a lift bus can request the previous day a lift bus to be used on his or her route. Marketing campaigns are needed to provide information on available services, to assure potential users that the system will welcome them, and to inform the general public that persons with disabilities will be riding more frequently.

Applicability to Particular Situations and Areas

No matter the size of the community in which a marketing campaign is implemented, there is reason to consider a very personal approach. Because the campaign is an effort to persuade people to switch use from the specialized paratransit service to a general public service, the initial target population is often well-defined. This group could, therefore, be reached with such devices as direct mail or with personal contact through the paratransit service providers. Presentations to social service agencies and community groups can also be effective.

In areas where paratransit service users are only a fraction of the potential users who may be ADA eligible, a broader campaign may be required in addition to one targeted at existing paratransit registrants. A broader campaign may also enhance public opinion regarding the use of fixed-route transit by persons with disabilities. For example, in Omaha, Nebraska, the League of Human Dignity hired a professional advertising agency to develop a comprehensive marketing campaign to introduce new lift bus service (67). The logo and slogan, "The Lift Lets Everyone Ride," appeared everywhere, including on decals, posters, bus shelters, and promotional brochures. Public service announcements were broadcast widely. The result was an increase in local support and awareness of accessible transportation in Omaha.

Key Implementation Issues

Marketing campaigns should ensure that staff are well informed about the services to be promoted. For example, the Sacramento Regional Transit District began an important marketing campaign aimed at the general public by explaining all changes to the telephone operators and the bus and light rail supervisors and dispatchers (68). In developing the Project ACTION-sponsored marketing, outreach, and training project, A Lift to Freedom, the Baltimore Mass Transit Administration (MTA) provided training sessions at each bus division. "Operators receive information on service delivery, as well as demonstrations and practice in lift operation and securing various common wheelchairs. A panel of consumers, with various disabilities, share their expectations and experiences of using MTA transit services (69)."

Marketing campaigns should involve representatives of persons with disabilities. Such representatives can help guide the presentation of material so that it is appropriate for the intended audiences. They also can be helpful in convincing parents, agencies, and persons with disabilities to try something new. In the Cleveland area in the late 1980s, the Transportation Coalition for Disabled Riders undertook an aggressive marketing and training program to encourage the use of accessible, fixed-route bus services (70). This group aimed the marketing efforts at persons with disabilities and the general public. The group feared that current bus commuters would not appreciate any delays caused by the use of lifts on the fixed-route system. Agencies were asked to run promotional articles about the service in their newsletters, and the transit authority advertised the new service in the press and on buses.

Marketing efforts must be targeted at particular groups, and different strategies may be required depending on the group. As an example, a recent paper by Mary Kihl, "Marketing Rural Transit Among Senior Populations," (71) pointed out that se-

nior citizens fell into several distinct lifestyle groups, and each group chose different media; therefore, an appeal to each group needed to be tailored to the group's perception of their level of independence and their needs. Capital Metro of Austin, Texas, placed advertisements promoting their service to senior citizens and individuals with mobility-impairments in publications targeting those populations. In addition, they included senior citizens and persons with disabilities in advertisements aimed at the public at large. In this way, they aimed their advertisements at those independent of the social service network as well as those who can be targeted (72).

Marketing programs to promote the use of fixed-route transit among persons with disabilities should include some training for the target group in how to use the fixed-route system. The Project ACTION program in Omaha, Nebraska, provided classroom training to 103 persons with disabilities in eight sessions. The program included how to use lift-equipped buses, self advocacy, and travel safety tips. In Cleveland, Ohio, consumer training initially offered a "pit stop" incentive to wheelchair users by offering free wheelchair repair and maintenance. Training in the use of lift buses was offered at the same time. In addition, training was provided to school-age children with disabilities.

Another approach to outreach and training was used by Madison County Transit. The paratransit provider, the Agency for Community Transit (ACT), met with parents, counsellors, and client groups to advertise new fixed-route service. The most effective effort, however, occurred when ACT personnel met with individuals with disabilities on the street to show each person how the service would work. The individualized coaching continued until the person was confident enough to continue the trip without a coach (7).

As required by the ADA, any marketing program should ensure that materials are provided in accessible formats. In particular, large print and tape should be provided as an alternative for any printed text, and braille or tactile maps can be very helpful. Many systems have developed information in accessible formats. The Metropolitan Transportation Authority (of New York City) has announced that braille and tactile maps are available free of charge (73). The Southwest Ohio Regional Transit Authority has developed bus schedules in large print and tone-pulse audiotape format (74).

Service and Cost Information

Although there is little information on the budget requirements for establishing a marketing program to promote the use of fixed-route transit by persons with disabilities, some information is available through the Project ACTION demonstration program. Profiles for recent projects from 1991 to 1992 showed that funding levels ranged from $42,000 to $151,169. Each of these projects involved outreach, marketing, and training for persons with disabilities. The more expensive projects either involved identifying (through surveys) persons with disabilities or using a professional advertising firm to develop the ad campaign.

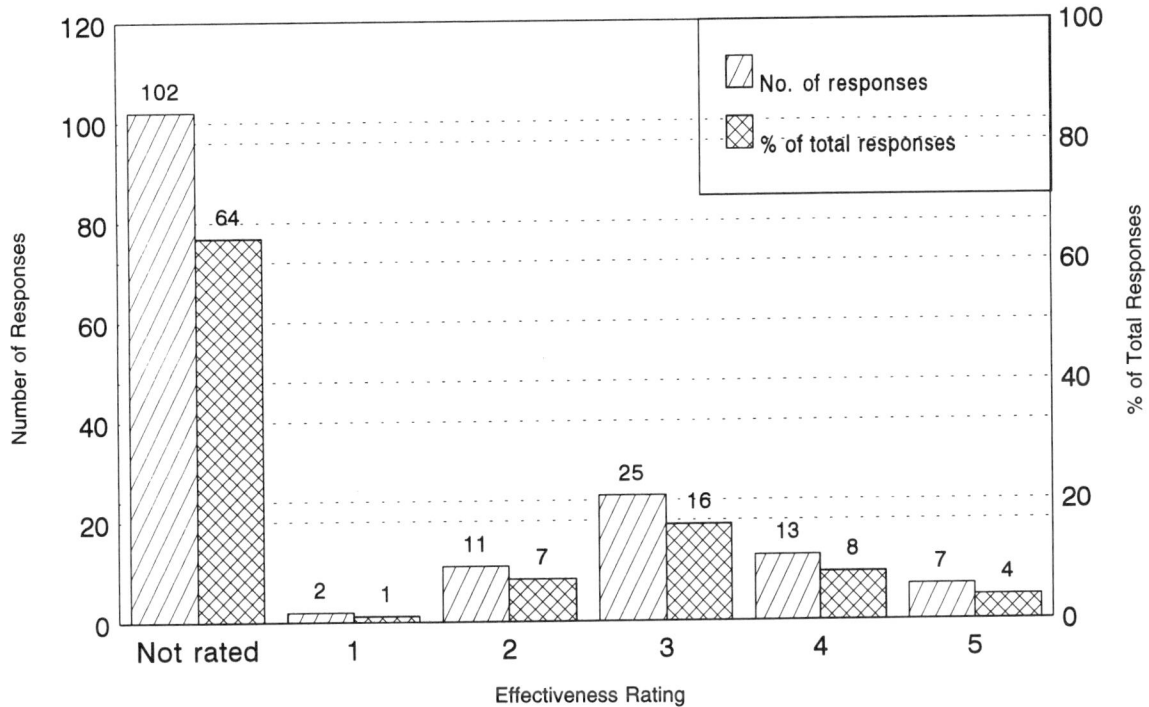

Figure 24. Reported effectiveness of marketing programs. 1 = not effective; 5 = very effective.

Reported Use and Effectiveness

Of the 309 respondents to the study survey, 160 indicated that they have marketing programs that target persons with disabilities. The survey asked respondents to rate the effectiveness of each option employed on a scale of 1 to 5 (with 1 being "not effective" and 5 being "very effective"). Of the 58 respondents who completed the effectiveness rating portion of the survey, 45 reported that this option was moderately to very effective in promoting use of fixed-route service. Figure 24 shows the effectiveness rating given to this option by survey respondents.

Table B-12 in Appendix B lists those transit properties that indicated that their marketing efforts were particularly effective in promoting use of fixed-route services and/or appropriate use of paratransit services.

TRIP PLANNING SERVICES

Trip planning services provide personalized assistance in developing an itinerary for a given trip that a customer wishes to make. Trip planning offers more assistance than is typically provided by general customer information programs and may include information not only about routes and schedules, but bus stop locations, accessible paths of travel, vehicle and equipment operation, driver assistance, and other service information to acquaint riders and potential riders with all aspects of a planned trip by transit.

Many individuals with disabilities, particularly those who have had a disability since birth, have never used fixed-route public transit. Architectural barriers and service policies in the transit industry have either made it impossible for these persons to use mainline service or have directed them to paratransit programs. Some individuals who have attempted to use fixed-route services may have had unfavorable experiences because accessible equipment malfunctioned or they may have encountered insensitive employees.

Aggressive marketing programs are important in encouraging use of fixed-route service when this mode is appropriate. Once the accessibility of the transit system has been improved, individuals with disabilities need to be made aware that travel on the fixed-route system is possible. Marketing efforts alone may not, however, provide enough information to make potential customers feel comfortable with the system and confident enough to attempt to travel on a fixed route. Trip planning services can help to address this issue.

Typically, trip planning services are developed by identifying and marketing a telephone number that riders can call for assistance. Often, this number is separate from any general customer information service that may already be provided. Although it may be desirable to integrate such services at some level, the detail about accessibility that calltakers must be trained to provide may require that separate personnel be used.

Trip planning staff can be housed with general information service programs, but a separate phone line may be used. It is also possible to locate trip planning services in an administrative office that has oversight responsibility for, and is therefore familiar with, all types of accessible service within the agency.

As part of an aggressive campaign to promote fixed-route service use, the Greater Bridgeport Transit District in Bridgeport, Connecticut, provides trip planning services to persons with disabilities in their area. Administrative staff who are responsible for general ADA implementation provide this service. Trip planning is augmented by an extensive marketing effort and a fare incentive program that provides free fixed-route rides to persons determined to be ADA paratransit eligible. The overall effort has resulted in an increase in fixed-route ridership by ADA-paratransit-eligible persons from approximately 300 trips monthly to over 20,000 trips monthly (75).[34]

Trip planning services can provide a wide range of information and assistance. In addition to route, schedule, and fare information, callers can be given directions to the closest bus stop or information about the accessibility of bus stops. For customers who have never used a fixed-route bus, information about lift operation, securement systems, and the level of driver assistance that can be expected is important. Specific inquiries about possible problems with particular types of mobility aids or other problems the customer may have encountered or be concerned about can also be addressed.

If a particular trip would be difficult or impossible using a fixed-route system, operators also can provide information about alternative modes and services, such as paratransit service or service routes. Information about other service enhancements that may be available (such as feeder service; route deviation; on-call, accessible bus programs; travel training; and so forth) can be explained.

Promoting Integration and Appropriate Use of Fixed-Route and Paratransit Services

Offering personal assistance in planning travel on the fixed-route system can encourage persons unfamiliar with or apprehensive about using fixed-route service to try this mode. By allowing individuals to make their travel plans and needs known to the system in advance, trip planning services not only provide riders with important information and an added sense of security but allow transit providers to double-check access equipment and to prepare to offer quality service to first-time riders.

Applicability to Particular Situations and Areas

Although trip planning services can be used in any public transit system, they may be particularly appropriate in the following situations:

• In systems introducing accessible, fixed-route service for the first time

---

[34]Kimberlee Kelly-Morton, Greater Bridgeport Transit District, Bridgeport, Connecticut.

• In areas where the fixed-route system is extensive and complex

• In areas that have had problems providing accessible transit service and where riders are likely to distrust the reliability of the service.

Key Implementation Issues

Operator Training and Knowledge

Personnel who take calls and arrange travel itineraries need to have a working knowledge of all system features and options, including routes and schedules, equipment operation, levels of driver assistance, and other service policies. They also should be familiar with different types of disabilities and the functional capabilities associated with each. Persons with disabilities who have used the fixed-route system and are aware of potential problems should be involved in program development and employee training. Employing such persons to offer the service may be beneficial.

Coordination with Fixed-Route and Paratransit Operations

Because calltakers assigned to trip planning service are likely to receive requests for particular assistance, effective communication with operating departments and agencies is important. Arrangements should be made to allow calltakers to contact key operating staff. This communication is vital to ensure that arrangements for assistance are, in fact, made and to alert operating staff to particular customer needs.

Placement of the Service Within the Agency

Consideration must be given to the most appropriate location of this service within the agency. Decision factors include staff capabilities, interdepartmental communication, and integration with existing public information offices and the ability to use any available computerized information systems that these offices may have.

Accessibility of Information and Communications Provided

Arrangements must be made to ensure that telephone lines and other information and communications are available to persons with hearing and speech impairments. Trip planning phone lines should be equipped with TDDs and staff must be trained to use this equipment. Any voice messaging systems used should be compatible with the TDD equipment selected.

Identifying Access Needs

If transit providers offer general customer information services, regardless of whether or not trip planning services for persons with disabilities are included, consideration must be given to identifying callers who need particular information about the accessibility features of the system. Callers may not always identify themselves as persons with disabilities. Customers may have seen marketing material advertising accessible services and not realize that only certain buses and routes are accessible; consequently, they may not realize that specific information about system access should be requested. This is a particularly important issue if trip planning services are combined with general customer information programs. Because the service is specifically advertised to assist persons with disabilities, callers are more likely to assume that operators are aware of their particular needs. Staff assigned to the service should be instructed to make appropriate inquiries.

Transit providers may want to consider advertising a separate trip planning number, even if staff functions are combined with general customer information programs. It may also be desirable to ask all callers whether they are seeking general service information or trip planning assistance at the outset. Such a question could be made part of an automated telephone system. If done in this way, the accessibility of this communication to callers using TDDs must be considered.

Reported Use and Effectiveness

This option was not included in the study survey. It was identified as an option during follow-up calls to survey respondents. Effectiveness ratings and a listing of selected transit providers are, therefore, not available.

FIXED-ROUTE PLANNING

Fixed-route planning refers to the many operational options for increasing the use of the existing fixed-route network by persons with disabilities. Planning for such enhancements can be made part of the existing service planning process. The only difference is that there would be a concerted effort to define, analyze, and implement changes in fixed-route operation to encourage use by individuals with disabilities.

There are operational options for enhancing the use of existing fixed-route services by individuals with disabilities. These options can be implemented inexpensively and can be planned as part of the standard service planning process for fixed-route services. These options include small route changes and schedule changes to existing routes.

Transit agencies often get requests to divert bus service to serve housing complexes for senior citizens and persons with disabilities, special service programs, and so forth. The convenience that such diversion would add to travel for the groups requesting them must be weighed against the inconvenience to those riders who would lose more direct service. In particular,

diversions that may not be economical or fair if run all day may be desirable in off-peak hours.

In addition to looking at small route changes, the service planning process could consider how schedules could be changed slightly to accommodate group services for persons with disabilities, such as service to sheltered workshops. Such changes would be similar to the types of schedule adjustments often made to accommodate school schedules. A related option is to encourage social service programs to adjust their schedules so that clients can take regular fixed-route services.

In addition to schedule changes to accommodate groups, transit agencies may need to update schedules periodically to reflect the extra time needed for increased lift boardings. They should also consider adding time to the schedule if needed to allow riders to be seated once they have boarded the bus. Drivers need to be trained to provide this courtesy as well.

Grays Harbor Transportation Authority of Hoquiam, Washington, is an example of a transit system trying to accommodate persons with disabilities with fixed-route adjustments. They adjusted their routes to accommodate group homes and workshops and timed their service to arrive at workshop shifts.[35]

Promoting Integration and Appropriate Use of Fixed-Route and Paratransit Services

Small changes in service, either with route location or with schedule changes, can increase the likelihood that persons with disabilities will be able to use fixed-route service. Because there is no requirement for advanced reservations on the fixed-route service, conveniently located and scheduled routes can offer a higher level of service than paratransit, which may require day-in-advance reservations.

Key Implementation Issues

The convenience that small changes in routes and schedules would add to travel for the groups requesting them must be weighed against the inconvenience to those riders who would lose more direct service. Often transit agencies have service standards that guide planning for such requests. Given the requirements of the ADA and the cost and social incentives for encouraging persons who are ADA paratransit eligible to use fixed-route services, transit agencies may wish to reexamine and revise their service standards to encourage persons with disabilities to use the most cost-effective mode.

Reported Use and Effectiveness

This option was not included in the study survey. It was identified as an option during follow-up calls to survey respondents. Effectiveness ratings and a listing of selected transit providers are, therefore, not available.

---

[35]Dave Rostedt, Grays Harbor Transportation Authority, Hoquiam, Washington.

56

ACCESSIBLE BUS STOP PROGRAMS

An accessible bus stop program is a proactive program, in coordination with procurement of accessible transit vehicles, to make bus stops accessible to and usable by persons with disabilities. The program usually includes a partnership with the local government for street and sidewalk improvements and a community education/outreach component.

As defined by the ADA, an accessible bus stop consists of a level boarding area or pad measuring at least 8 by 5 ft and an accessible path so that riders can get to and from the stop (76). If a shelter is provided (it is not required), it must have an opening at least 32 in. wide, be at least 80 in. tall, and include a minimum clear floor area of 30 by 48 in. A diagram detailing ADA-accessible bus stop dimensions is provided as Figure 25. Another equally important aspect to bus stop accessibility is that the stop be "information/communication accessible" for those people with hearing or vision impairments. This informational accessibility may be as straightforward as clear

signage and having operators call out their route when arriving at a multiple route stop. It can also involve use of automated systems such as the ones described previously in the Automated Information and Communication Systems section.

This description of accessible bus stops focuses on physical access, usually involving use of a wheelchair. For most transit systems that have an accessible bus stop program, the following criteria (which are broader than the ADA definition) are used to determine accessibility of a stop:

• The wheelchair lift (or other boarding assistance device) on the bus can be deployed safely.
• There is a boarding/alighting area that is safe from hazards (for example, ditches and traffic).
• There is a path that can be used by persons using wheelchairs to get to and from the stop.

The ADA does not require public entities to retrofit existing bus stops to conform with the ADA standards. It does require, however, that all new bus stops conform with accessibility standards. The ADA also requires public transit entities to deploy wheelchair lifts at any bus stop unless conditions at the stop prevent use of it by all passengers or unless the lift cannot be deployed without damaging it. Although curb cuts or ramps may not be required beyond the immediate area of a bus stop

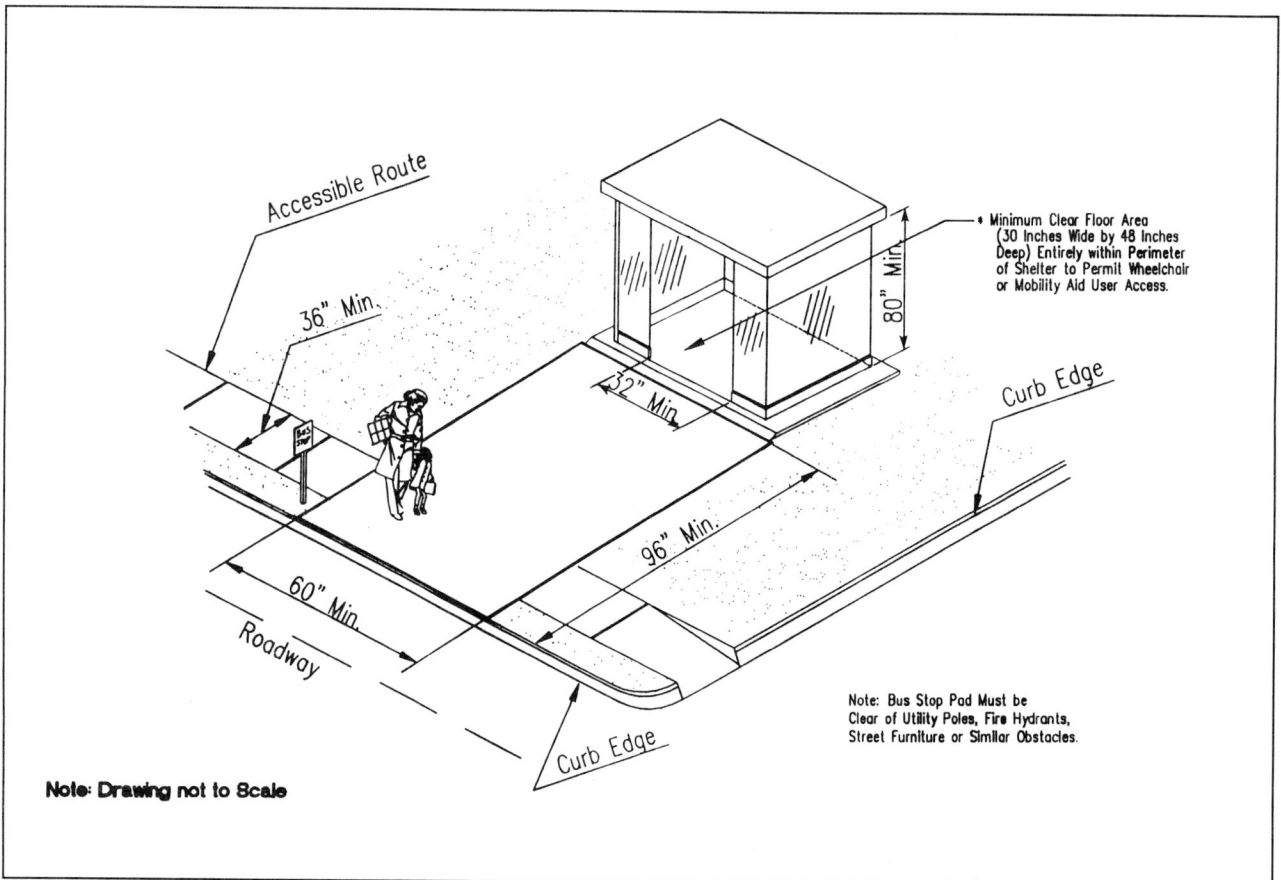

Figure 25.   Diagram of a bus stop designed to ADAAG standards (Source: CGA Consulting Services, et al.) (77).

for the stop to be considered accessible, many public entities have coordinated bus stop accessibility with broader curb cut programs.

Development of an accessible bus stop program goes hand-in-hand with procurement of accessible buses and designation of accessible fixed-routes. Most public entities that have an accessible bus stop program have been procuring accessible rolling stock for many years and have an ultimate goal of making all bus stops accessible. This approach, which exceeds ADA requirements, usually has the following components:

- Inventory of bus stops
- Accessible stop guidelines and prioritization system
- Identification mechanism
- Community outreach/education
- Bus operator training.

These components are discussed in more detail in the following sections.

Inventory of Bus Stops

The programs researched had all developed (or were developing) bus stop inventories. These inventories varied in sophistication.[36] In some cases, the inventory consisted of a simple listing of stops and an indication of whether they are accessible or non-accessible. In another case, the bus stops were included in a systemwide database, which enabled access to additional information such as why a certain stop was designated non-accessible. This same database also can match the bus stops in the system with various community centers, group homes, and other locations that might be popular destinations for persons with disabilities. The Virginia Department of Rail and Public Transit has developed a guide for inventorying bus stops (77).

Guidelines and Prioritization

Usually, these transit operators have developed standards for what constitutes an accessible stop. These standards are consistent with, and usually exceed, federal requirements. When a shelter is appropriate, a standard accessible design is used. A boarding pad size, from 8 by 5 ft to 10 by 10 ft, is specified. All new bus stops are constructed to these standards.

Various methods are used to prioritize retrofitting of existing stops to make them accessible. Some systems will designate a specific route as accessible, and, at the same time, begin work on making the stops on that route accessible. Others are working on a method to link major attractors to bus stop accessibility records so as to prioritize destination locations for accessibility. By sending notices out to these attractor locations, they hope to get additional information about origin locations and so prioritize those for accessibility as well. Other prioritization

systems are based primarily on community input from an advisory committee.

Community Education—Outreach and Identification Mechanisms

Community education and outreach were mentioned by survey respondents as essential components of their programs. Often community involvement is informal, with people calling in about the accessibility of a particular stop. This is valuable information for planners who may have no way of knowing what stops are important to persons with disabilities in "origin" areas such as residential areas. In other cases, community participation may be formalized with a committee providing input on the most effective ways to use available money.

Another component of community education/outreach is identification of accessible stops. Transit systems that have implemented accessible bus stop programs have attempted to make stop identification straightforward for riders and drivers. Some have developed decals or stickers to be affixed to bus stop signs. The international symbol of access is used to identify accessible stops. A red symbol with a slash through it is being used in some areas to indicate non-accessible stops. These transit operators are also finding a need to develop "accessible but not recommended," "accessible with caution," or "accessible for standees only" stickers for stops where the lift may be deployed but the surrounding terrain may be hazardous in some way. This type of sticker is especially helpful for those riders who use the lift as standees. Safety issues and the use of these stickers are discussed under Key Implementation Issues in this section

Bus Operator Training

Transit operators are finding that they need to train bus operators in understanding the identification mechanisms and the requirements of the ADA in order to ensure passenger safety and ADA compliance. Some transit operators felt that passenger safety and ADA compliance are sometimes at odds in situations where the lift can be deployed but the surrounding terrain is not accessible. This issue is discussed in more detail.

Promoting Integration and Appropriate Use of Fixed-Route and Paratransit Services

Accessible bus stop programs promote use of fixed-route services by enabling individuals with mobility impairments to more easily get to, board, and exit buses. Implemented in coordination with procurement of accessible vehicles, these programs enable those who might otherwise be ADA paratransit eligible to use general public fixed-route transit for some or all trips. If curb cuts exist or are added in conjunction with accessible bus stop programs, access for all transit users, as well as all pedestrians, is improved. These programs are also a key link between the community and the transit system.

[36]Individuals and systems contacted included: Micki Kaplan, Lane Transit District, Eugene, Oregon; Elizabeth Morgan, Metro, Seattle, Washington; Annette Williams, MUNI, San Francisco, California; and Nancy Crowther, CMTA, Austin, Texas.

Applicability to Particular Situations and Areas

Implementation of accessible bus stops programs is universally applicable. In areas where a significant number of fixed-route buses are accessible, a proactive accessible bus stop program may have higher priority than in an area where procurement of accessible buses is just beginning.

Key Implementation Issues

For the most part, transit systems that were contacted could make the modifications needed to build new stops that are accessible and to modify existing stops to be accessible (either by relocating the stop or modifying it in its current location). Two problems were, however, cited by several systems—the lack of control over access to the bus stop itself and safety.

Control

Transit systems, except those operated by local government entities such as cities and counties, do not control when and where curb cuts are built or when other road work that might hinder access to a bus stop is performed. Terrain is another factor that cannot be controlled. The transit operators that were the subject of research on this option all had developed working relationships with jurisdictions responsible for curb cuts. In one case, the city government agreed to allow the transit operator to fund and implement curb cuts. In another, an established relationship had been developed with the local government's traffic engineering department so that the transit operator was able to provide input to the city's planning process for curb cuts. A factor that has assisted with efforts to provide curb cuts is a Department of Justice regulation that requires cities and towns to prepare "transition plans" and to include a timetable for providing curb cuts in these plans (78).

To compensate for this lack of control of streets and sidewalks, transit systems have taken various actions. In one area where there are few curb cuts, a temporary arrangement can be for people with disabilities to flag down a bus at a nearby accessible location (for example, a driveway) if the bus stop is not accessible. Other terrain issues are often overcome by moving the stop altogether. One area of particular difficulty, however, is when bus stops are in areas under federal or state jurisdiction (for example, a state highway) that may not have basic amenities such as sidewalks. Getting appropriate changes made in cases such as this can take considerable time.

Safety

The ADA requires that operators "permit a passenger who uses a lift to disembark from a vehicle at any designated stop, unless the lift cannot be deployed, the lift will be damaged if it is deployed, or temporary conditions at the stop, not under control of the entity, preclude the safe use of the stop by *all* passengers" (79, emphasis added). Transit operators subject to the ADA and who participated in this study felt that implemen-

tation of this provision is difficult. They know of conditions that exist, that are out of their control, that make a particular bus stop unsafe for persons with certain types of disabilities and/or persons using certain types of mobility aids. The conditions might involve the terrain, lack of sidewalk improvements, weather (for example, heat, ice, and snow), or lack of an accessible path after alighting. In these cases, operators are implementing identification mechanisms (see above) that warn passengers that the lift can be deployed but that the area around the stop may be difficult to access or unsafe. In keeping with basic quality customer service, bus drivers also should alert riders to any unsafe conditions that might exist.

Reported Use and Effectiveness

Of the 309 respondents to the study survey, 63 indicated that they have accessible bus stop programs. The survey asked respondents to rate the effectiveness of each option employed on a scale of 1 to 5 (with 1 being "not effective" and 5 being "very effective"). Of the 19 respondents who completed the effectiveness rating portion of the survey, 16 reported that this option was moderately to very effective in promoting use of fixed-route service. Only three providers reported that it was less than moderately effective. Figure 26 shows the effectiveness rating given to this option by survey respondents.

Table B-13 in Appendix B lists those transit properties that indicated that they have implemented accessible bus stop programs.

BUS IDENTIFIER SYSTEMS

Bus identifier systems are simple, manual systems that can be used by persons with vision impairments and others to hail buses that they wish to use.

Persons with vision impairments face challenges identifying and boarding vehicles that they need to use, locating designated bus stops, and distinguishing bus stop signs from other streetside hardware. Once at a bus stop, certain riders must rely on drivers to recognize that they are in fact waiting to board the bus if they cannot distinguish between buses and other heavy-duty vehicles. If the stop is served by more than one route, riders with vision impairments must be sure that they board the correct bus. Busy transfer stations pose a particular problem given that several vehicles may be at the station at any given time. Fixed-route systems in rural areas that operate as flag-stop services without designated stops also are particularly difficult for customers with vision impairments to use.

Identifying and hailing correct buses can be problematic to other riders as well. Older persons and persons with ambulatory disabilities may not always be able to travel to designated stops in time, especially in areas where there may be a considerable distance between stops. To assist such persons, many transit providers permit riders to flag buses between stops. Drivers

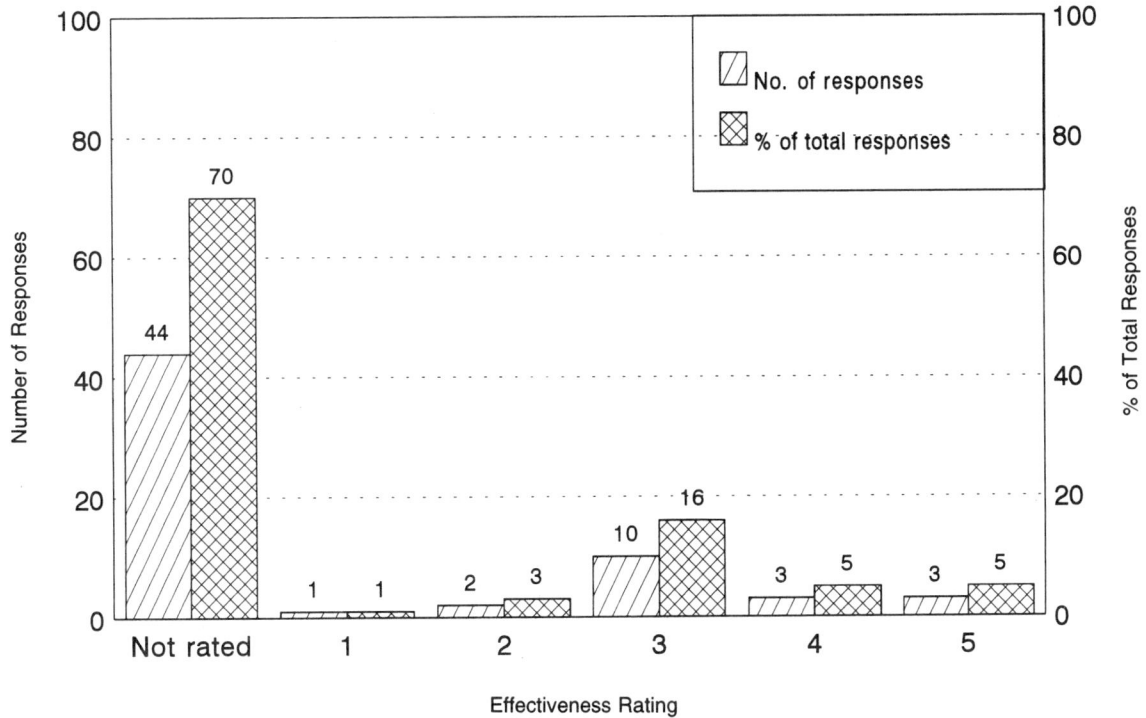

Figure 26. Reported effectiveness of accessible bus stop programs. 1 = effective; 5 = very effective.

may not, however, recognize customers who are attempting to hail their buses. Unsure of the exact bus number, passengers may also hail the wrong bus.

Many strategies can be used to assist riders with identifying and hailing appropriate vehicles. Improved vehicle signage can assist many individuals with poor vision. In the United States and Canada, signage standards have been developed and implemented. The ADA contains signage requirements that must be followed by all U.S. transportation companies and agencies. The Ontario Ministry of Transportation has developed improved accessibility standards, including signage standards, as part of its Easier Access Program.

Driver training is also important to the solution. Drivers should be trained to recognize mobility aids that would indicate that customers have vision impairments (e.g., a long white cane or a harnessed guide dog). Having drivers identify the bus and its major destinations to waiting and boarding riders can also be helpful to those who are not easily identified as having vision impairments (as well as to the general public).

Emerging technologies also offer promise in this area. These include talking buses, which provide automated announcements inside and outside the vehicle and which can be triggered when doors are opened or by transmitters at bus stops; talking bus stops, which receive signals from approaching buses and provide vehicle and route information to waiting passengers; and digital locator/paging systems, which can be used by particular customers to receive information about bus or bus stop locations or to signal approaching vehicles. The Automated Information and Communications Systems section in this chapter contains more detailed information about these technologies.

Although new technologies are likely to address this need in the long run, several simple, manual systems (developed by transit providers) can be used (80). Perhaps the first recorded approach was the "red mit" system developed by transit providers in Michigan. A bright red mitten was worn by riders wishing to hail local buses. The mitten provided a common, visible identifier that allowed drivers to better recognize passengers. Other signaling systems that use standard identifiers have also been employed. Such simple signaling systems can be effective in small systems with limited route structures. Their obvious limitation is that they cannot be used to distinguish between different buses operating on common route segments or serving common stops.

Bus identifier kits have been developed to offer a somewhat more thorough method of bus identification and hailing. Using these kits, riders can prepare a hand-held sign that gives the number of the bus that they want to use. By holding this sign along a route, at a bus stop, or at a busy terminal, they can identify themselves as passengers and alert drivers and employees to their particular travel needs.

Bus identifier kits typically contain a set of numbered cards and a clear plastic pouch designed to hold an appropriate number of cards. To assist users in assembling the desired bus number, the back of the cards have braille numbers or raised lettering. Cards should be designed with a bright background and can have different colored backgrounds to help employees identify different rider needs. The system developed by Seattle Metro, for example, uses black lettering on a white background for riders with vision impairments. Kits that use black lettering on a yellow background are provided to riders who are deaf-blind. The Seattle system uses 4-in.-high cards. For conve-

60

Figure 27. Example of a bus identifier kit.

nience, the plastic pouch has separate compartments for each letter and can be folded (it measures 3 by 4 in. when folded). Figure 27 illustrates Seattle's bus identifier kit.[37]

Some bus identifier kits allow passengers to signal general travel needs as well as specific bus/route numbers. Chatham Area Transit in Savannah, Georgia, includes a single "BUS" card in its kit that can be used when it does not matter exactly which bus is needed (*81*). BC Transit in Vancouver, British Columbia, uses a "LIFT" card to alert drivers that the passenger will need to use the lift to board the bus.[38]

Kits can also be developed by binding together sets of cards that can be independently arranged to create bus numbers. Although this type of number booklet is self-contained, it may not, however, be designed to be folded and may, therefore, be more cumbersome to carry.

Promoting Integration and Appropriate Use of Fixed-Route and Paratransit Services

By allowing individuals with disabilities to identify vehicles more easily and effectively, bus identifier kits eliminate a barrier to the use of fixed-route programs. Although they enable persons to use mainline service, such identification (ID) kits require individuals to identify themselves visibly. Several systems have reported that certain riders prefer not to make their disability known in this way. Other riders reportedly decline to take advantage of this system for this reason. In the long run, as information and communication technology improves, this manual system will likely be replaced by talking buses, talking bus stops, and other forms of automated communication. In the interim, ID kits can be provided to riders who wish to use them.

Use of this system need not be limited to riders with disabilities. One system contacted during this study, the Mid Mon Valley Transit Authority in Charleroi, Pennsylvania, reported that ID kits are made available to the general public and provide welcome assistance to riders who are unfamiliar with the system.[39]

Applicability to Particular Situations and Areas

Bus identifier programs are usable in bus systems of all sizes. Simple signaling systems (for example, red mit programs) are

applicable in smaller systems. Bus identifier kits are applicable in systems with more complex route structures.

Some method of vehicle/passenger identification must be developed by public transit providers in the United States. Section 37.167 (c) of the USDOT regulations implementing the ADA requires that public entities operating fixed-route service develop some system or method of communication to be used at all stops served by more than one route. These systems must permit riders with vision impairments and other disabilities to identify vehicles or to allow vehicle operators to identify passengers seeking to ride on their vehicle.

Key Implementation Issues

Employee Training

Successful use of bus ID systems requires that information about the system be included in driver training programs. Information should also be added to any driver manuals or operating instructions distributed to employees.

Customer Acceptance

Several of the systems contacted indicated that persons with disabilities preferred not to be visibly identified. This issue might be addressed by advertising bus ID systems for use by the general public (for riders unfamiliar with the system as well as for persons with disabilities).

Involvement of Disability Organizations

Bus ID systems should be developed and implemented with the involvement of individuals with disabilities and local disability organizations. It is likely that systems will receive little use if they are developed internally and made available with little outreach and community involvement. The system needs to be designed in a format acceptable to potential users and its availability needs to be advertised with the help of local agencies and advocacy groups.

Reported Use and Effectiveness

Of the 309 respondents to the study survey, 25 indicated that they have bus identifier systems available. The survey asked respondents to rate the effectiveness of each option employed on a scale of 1 to 5 (with 1 being "not effective" and 5 being "very effective"). Of the 12 respondents who completed the effectiveness rating portion of the survey, 7 reported that this option was moderately to very effective in promoting use of fixed-route service. Figure 28 shows the effectiveness rating given to this option by survey respondents.

Table B-14 in Appendix B lists those transit properties that indicated that they have developed bus identifier systems.

---

[37]Karen Rosenzweig, Metro, Seattle, Washington.
[38]Bruce Chown, BC Transit, Vancouver, Canada.
[39]Nancy Qualk, Mid Mon Valley Transit Authority, Charleroi, Pennsylvania.

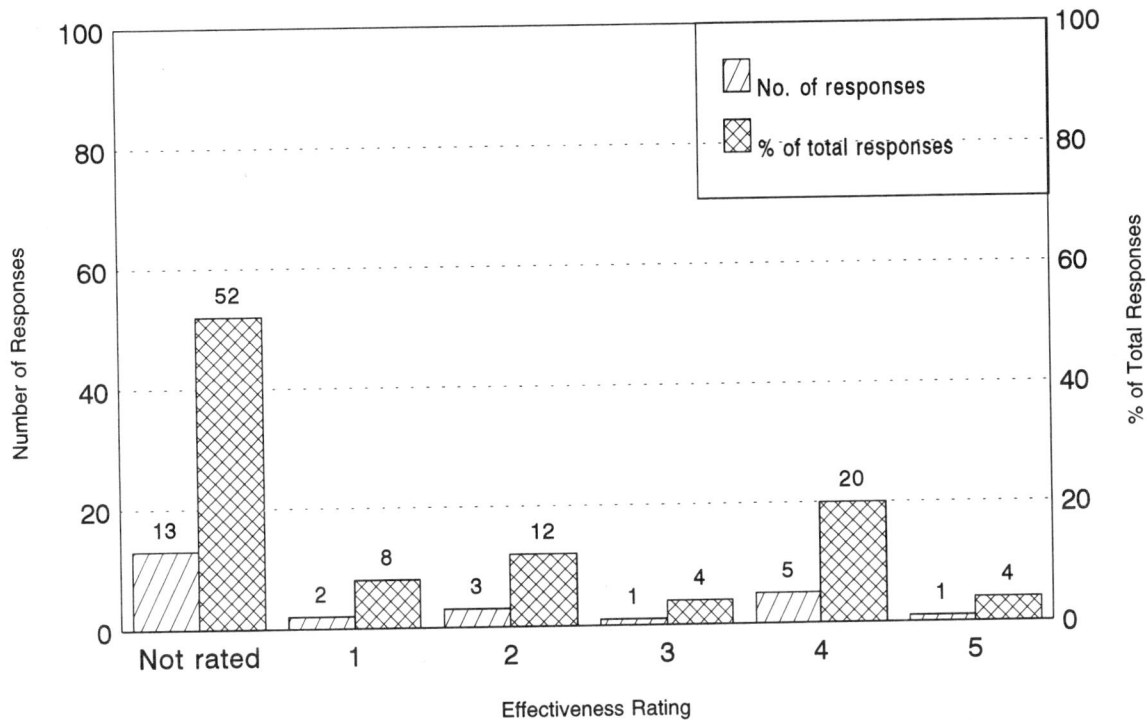

Figure 28. Reported effectiveness of bus identifier systems. 1 = not effective; 5 = very effective.

DESTINATION CARD PROGRAMS

Destination card programs permit passengers to alert vehicle operators to their travel plans so that appropriate assistance can be provided.

Certain persons with disabilities may have difficulty recognizing their desired destination and exiting the bus at the correct stop. This includes individuals with cognitive disabilities who cannot understand or remember detailed directions, those with hearing impairments who may not be served by verbal stop announcements, and persons with speech impairments who would otherwise rely on verbal communications with the driver to obtain travel assistance. Destination card programs address these needs. Basically, destination cards are small forms, filled out by riders or persons assisting riders, that contain information about the passenger's desired destination. Typically, a form contains a description of the actual destination (for example, 260 Main Street) as well as the stop at which the rider wishes to get off (for example, the corner of Main and Elm Streets). The card can also contain the number of the route to be traveled to ensure that the rider has boarded the correct bus.

Upon boarding a fixed-route vehicle, the rider hands a completed card to the operator. The card alerts the operator to the

rider's desired destination. Cards are kept by the operator to serve as a reminder once the destination is reached.

For convenience, destination cards are sometimes designed in two parts with information about the first part of the trip on one portion and the return trip on a separate part. Individuals can then complete both sections before beginning their trip.

Figure 29 is an example of the destination cards used by Metro in Seattle, Washington.[40]

Promoting Integration and Appropriate Use of Fixed-Route and Paratransit Services

Destination card programs are an enhancement of fixed-route service that can eliminate communication barriers that may be preventing certain persons with disabilities from using mainline service. They enhance the interaction between drivers and customers. They also reinforce other operating procedures, such as stop announcements, to further ensure that individuals receive the information they need to navigate the system.

Applicability and Implementation Issues

Destination card programs can be used in any transit system. Similar to bus ID systems, they may be particularly useful in areas with larger, complex, fixed-route services. Destination

---

[40]Karen Rosenzweig, Metro, Seattle, Washington.

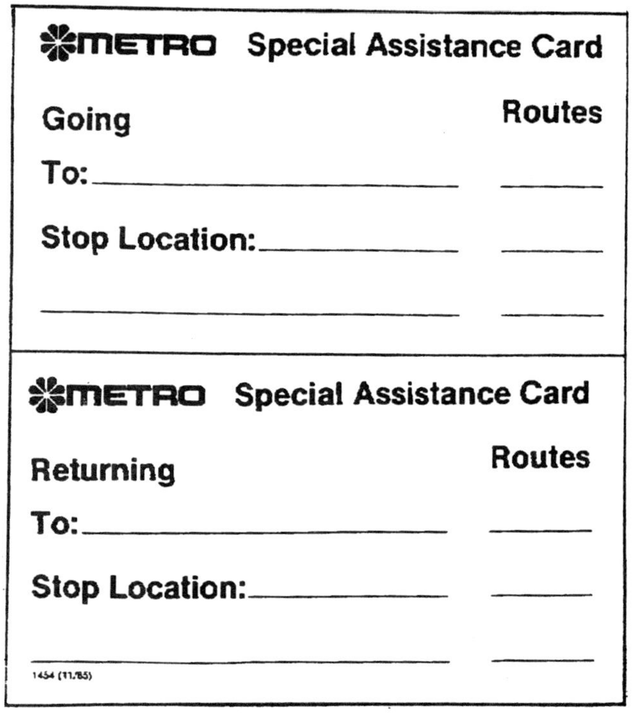
METRO Special Assistance Card

Going To: ____ Routes ____

Stop Location: ____

METRO Special Assistance Card

Returning To: ____ Routes ____

Stop Location: ____

1454 (11/85)

Figure 29. Example of destination cards.

card programs can also be used effectively in conjunction with travel training programs.

Implementation issues for this enhancement, which are similar to those for bus identifier systems, include employee training and the involvement of organizations representing people with disabilities. These are discussed in the following paragraphs.

Employee Training

Successful use of destination card systems requires that information about the system be included in driver training programs. Information should also be added to any driver manuals or operating instructions distributed to employees.

Involvement of Disability Organizations

The development and implementation of a destination card system should be done with the involvement of individuals with disabilities and local disability organizations. It is likely that systems will receive little use if they are developed internally and made available with little outreach and community involvement. The system must be designed in a format acceptable to potential users and its availability must be advertised with the help of local agencies and advocacy groups.

Reported Use and Effectiveness

Of the 309 respondents to the study survey, 18 indicated that they have destination card programs available. The survey asked respondents to rate the effectiveness of each option employed on a scale of 1 to 5 (with 1 being "not effective" and 5 being "very effective"). Of the five respondents who completed the effectiveness rating portion of the survey, three reported that this option was moderately to very effective in promoting use of fixed-route service. Figure 30 shows the effectiveness rating given to this option by survey respondents.

Table B-15 in Appendix B lists those transit properties that indicated that they have developed destination card programs.

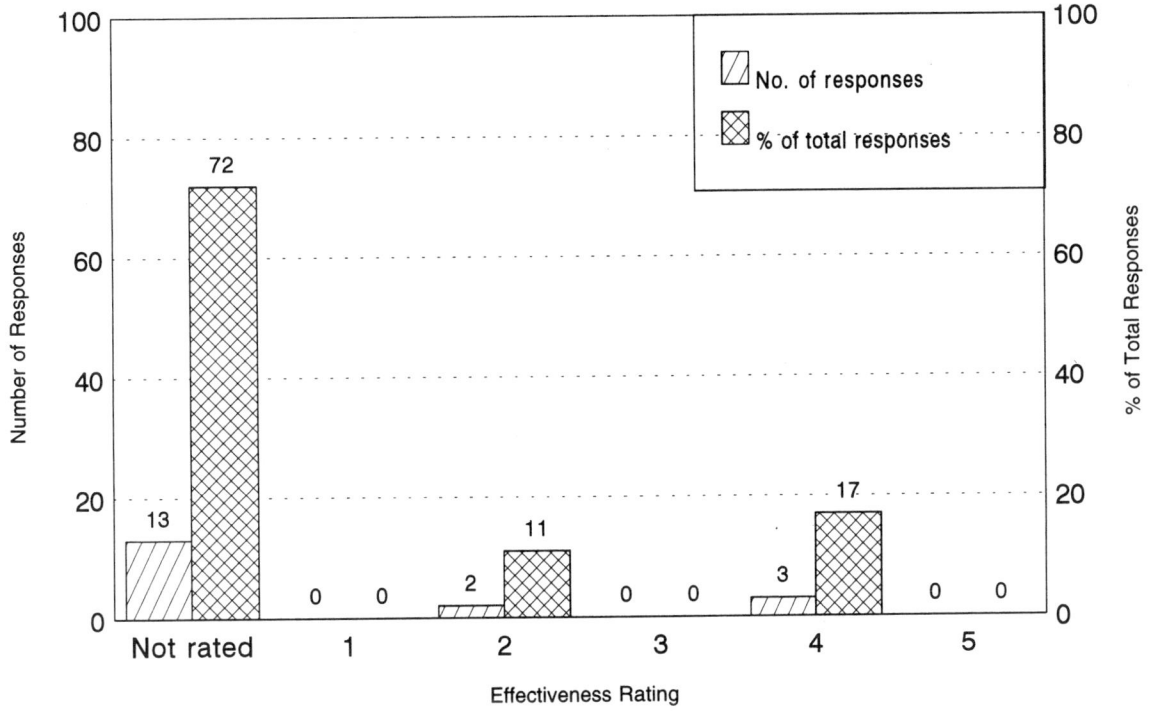

Figure 30. *Reported effectiveness of destination card programs. 1 = not effective; 5 = very effective.*

REFERENCES

1. EG&G Dynatrend and Crain & Associates, Inc., *Evaluating Transit Operations for Individuals with Disabilities*, Transit Cooperative Research Program, Transportation Research Board, Washington, D.C. (1995).

2. EG&G Dynatrend et al., "Implementation of the Complementary Paratransit Provisions of the Americans with Disabilities Act of 1994 (ADA), First Year Experience," Volpe National Transportation Systems Center, Cambridge, Massachusetts (Feb. 1993).

3. Norrbom, C. E. and Stahl, A. "Service Routes in Boras," Mobility and Transport for Elderly and Disabled Persons, 5th International Conference Proceedings, Gordon and Breach Science Publishers, Philadelphia, Pennsylvania (1991) pp. 721-730.

4. "Community Bus Experience in Metropolitan Toronto," Toronto Transit Commission, Service Planning Department (Feb. 1992).

5. "Introducing S.C.A.T. in the Park, Breaking Down the Barriers," Alberta Transportation and Utilities (Nov. 1992).

6. Regiec, A., "Accessible Community Bus Service," City of Winnipeg Transit System, City of Winnipeg, Canada (May 13, 1993).

7. "Small Buses and Service Routes," Madison County Transit, Granite City, Illinois (Apr. 1992) pp. 1-9.

8. McLary, J. J., Stahl, A. and Persich, S., "Implementation of Service Routes in the United States," *Transportation Research Record 1378*, Transportation Research Board, Washington, D.C. (Apr. 1993).

9. Starks, J. K., "Overview of the Transportation Demand of Mentally Retarded Persons," *Transportation Research Record 1098*, Transportation Research Board, Washington, D.C. (Jun. 11, 1993).

10. Thatcher, R. H. and Gaffney, J. K., *ADA Paratransit Handbook*, Federal Transit Administration, Washington, D.C. (Sep. 1991) pp. 6-8 and Appendix G.

11. 49 CFR Part 37, "Transportation for Individuals with Disabilities; Final Rule," *Federal Register* (Sep. 6, 1991).

12. "You Can Get There From Here," Massachusetts Bay Transportation Authority, Boston, Massachusetts, undated service brochure.

13. Falcocchio, J.L. and Cantilli, E. J., *Transportation and the Disadvantaged*, D.C. Heath and Company, Lexington, Massachusetts (1974).

14. Multisystems, Inc., *General Community Paratransit Services in Urban Areas*, U.S. Department of Transportation, Washington, D.C. (Jan. 1982).

15. Harman, L. J. and Roblin, R. [Eds.], Student Workbook, Rural and Small Urban Transit Manager's Workshop, U.S. Department of Transportation, Washington, D.C. (Mar. 1981).

16. "Paratransit: State-of-the-Art Overview," U.S. Department of Transportation, Washington, D.C. (Mar. 1981).

17. 49 CFR Part 37, "Transportation for Individuals with Disabilities; Final Rule," *Federal Register* (Sep. 6, 1991) Appendix D, p. 45733.

18. "System Changes Fixed Routes to Variation of Demand-Response," *Metro Magazine*, (Jul./Aug. 1993).

19. "Feeder Service to Mass Transit Proposal," New York City Department of Transportation, internal memorandum (Jan. 10, 1991).

20. "ADA Complementary Paratransit Plan," Chelan-Douglas Public Transportation Benefit Area, Wenatchee, Washington (1992).

21. Fielding, G. J., and Shilling, D. R., "Dial-A-Ride: Opportunity for Managerial Control," *TRB Special Report 147*, National Research Council, Washington, D.C. (1974).

22. "ADA Complementary Paratransit Plan," Cape Cod Regional Transit Authority (Jan. 1993).

23. MANOP Services Ltd., "Paratransit in Canada—A Review," final report prepared for the Transportation Development Centre, Transport Canada, TP6015E (rev. May 1986).

24. Tidewater Regional Transit District, "Direct Transfer Paratransit Service," (Sep. 1992).

25. Wilson, N, "Automation in Dispatching Demand-Responsive Vehicles," *TRB Special Report 147*, National Research Council, Washington, D.C. (1974).

26. "Request-A-Stop Brings Newark Riders Closer to Destinations," *Passenger Transport*, APTA, Washington, D.C. (Dec. 14, 1992) p. 5.

27. Schneider, W. and Brechbuel, A., "Defining the Low-Floor Bus: Its Advantages and Disadvantages," Public Transport '91, Study of Buses, Report No. 5, International Union of Public Transport, 49th International Congress.

28. Giuliani, C. I., Francis, G. A. and King, R. D., "Status of Low-Floor Transit Bus Development," Battelle, Federal Transit Administration, Office of Technical Assistance and Safety, *Report No. FTA-OH-0060-92-1* (May 1992).

29. "Low Floor is Quickly Becoming the Only Way to Go," Canadian Urban Transit Association Forum (Oct. 1993).

30. von Rohr, J., "Low-Floor Light Rail Vehicle Development in Europe," *Transportation Research Record 1361*, Transportation Research Board, Washington, D.C. (1992).

31. "Portland's Tri-Met to Buy Low-Floor Light Rail Cars," *Passenger Transport*, APTA, Washington, D.C. (Jun. 7, 1993).

32. "Boston Moves on Purchase of 100 Low-Floor Streetcars," *Passenger Transport*, APTA, Washington, D.C. (Mar. 21, 1994).

33. "Chicago Focuses ADA Plan on Accessible Transportation Options," *Passenger Transport*, APTA, Washington, D.C. (Oct. 19, 1992).

34. Twaddle, J., "Calgary to Expand Accessibility with Low-Floor Buses," *Passenger Transport*, APTA, Washington, D.C. (Jun. 7, 1993).

35. Levine, J. C. and Torng, G., "Dwell Time Effects of the Low Floor Bus Design," paper for presentation at the 1994 Annual Meeting of the Transportation Research Board.

36. ABT Associates of Canada, Ottawa Accessible Taxi Demonstration Project, Transportation Technology and Energy Branch, Ministry of Transportation of Ontario, Downsview, Ontario, Canada (Jun. 1992).

37. European Conference of Ministers of Transport, "Access to Taxis," Organization for Economic Cooperation and Development, Paris, France (Jun. 1992).

38. Smith, T., "Lessons Learned from Canadian R & D and Demonstrations," Transportation Development Centre (1992).

39. Cerenio Management Group, "Description of Ramped Taxi Demonstration Project," (Jan. 1993).

40. "Evaluation of the Accessible Taxi Demonstration Program," Santa Cruz Transportation, Inc. (Oct. 5, 1988).

41. Coburn, N., Martin, C., Thompson, R., and Norstrom D., *Guidelines for Improvements to Transit Accessibility for People with Disabilities*, Federal Transit Administration, U.S. Department of Transportation, DOT-T-93-04 (Sep. 1992).

42. Schweiger, C., Kihl M., and Label, L., Advanced Public Transportation Systems: The State of the Art, Update '94, Volpe National Transportation Systems Center, Cambridge, Massachusetts (Jan. 1994).

43. Geehan, T., "Evaluation of HandyLine: Vancouver's Automated Paratransit Information System," prepared by TransVision Consultants for BC Transit and the Transportation Development Centre, TP 11656E (Mar. 1993).

44. Geehan, T., "User Acceptance of Advanced Traveller Information Systems for Elderly & Disabled Travellers in Canada." (No date).

45. "Montreal Metro Inaugurates Visual Communication Network," *Passenger Transport*, APTA, Washington, D.C. (Jun. 21, 1993) p. 8.

46. Hunter-Zaworski, K., "Audio-Visual Communication Systems to Improve Transit Accessibility," Transportation Research Institute of Oregon State University, Federal Transit Administration (Jan. 1, 1994).

47. Bettger, G. and Pearson, T., "Accommodating Deaf and Hard-of-Hearing Persons on Public Transportation Systems in Massachusetts," *Transportation Research Record 1209*, Transportation Research Board, Washington, D.C. (1989).

48. Chown, B. and Geehan, T., "The Canadian Approach to Transportation for Persons with Disabilities." (No date).

49. Velche, D., "Access to Signage Information and Use of Transportation Systems by Mentally Disabled People," Mobility and Transport for Elderly and Disabled Persons, Proceedings of the 6th International Conference, French National Institute for Transport and Safety Research (1992).

50. Hunter-Zaworski, K. and Hron, M., "Improving Bus Accessibility Systems for Persons with Sensory and Cognitive Impairments, Final Report," Transportation Research Institute of Oregon State University, Federal Transit Administration, *FTA-OR-11-0007-93-1* (Aug. 1993).

51. Block, W. and Hoyt, R., "Modifications Menu for System-Wide Map and Timetable Design," Kennedy Center, Inc., Bridgeport, Connecticut (Feb. 1992).

52. Simpson, C., "An Overview of Travel Training Models," Appendix G of *ADA Paratransit Handbook*, Federal Transit Administration (Sep. 1991).

53. Simpson, C., "Mobility Training, Disability Awareness and Sensitivity Training," paper for the 13th National Conference on Accessible Transportation and Mobility, Tampa, Florida (Oct. 1992).

54. Cerenio, V. and Soper, C., "Travel Training Avenue to Public Transit," *Transportation Research Record 1378*, Transportation Research Board, Washington, D.C. (Apr. 1993).

55. "San Andreas Regional Center Facilitated Transit," *PTI Journal* (Mar./Apr. 1993).

56. "Facilitated Transportation Pilot Program," undated staff paper from Santa Clara County Transportation Agency.

57. Bloch, W., "The Natural Helping Network—An Innovation in Travel Training," Project ACTION Update, Spring 1992.

58. Neubauer, J., "The Bus Buddy Program of the Handicapped Action Committee of Victoria, British Columbia, Canada," Mobility and Transport for Elderly and Disabled Persons (conference proceedings), Gordon and Breach (May 1989).

59. Project ACTION, "Demonstration Project Profile, Training for Transit Users with Disabilities," abstracts of projects in Salt Lake City, Bridgeport, Euclid (Ohio), Reno, and San Antonio, National Easter Seal Society, Washington, D.C. (No date).

60. "Parents Hesitant about Travel-Train Premise Programs," *TD Safety Report* (Jul. 28, 1993).

61. Project ACTION, Combined Research Results, National Easter Seal Society, Washington, D.C. (No date).

62. Chown, B., "The Canadian Approach to Transportation for Persons with Disabilities," *BC Transit*, Vancouver, British Columbia, Canada (1993).

63. "ADA Complementary Paratransit Plan," Niagara Frontier Transit Authority, Buffalo, New York (1992).

64. "Tulsa Transit to Make All Routes Accessible This Month," *Passenger Transport*, APTA, Washington, D.C. (Oct. 19, 1992).

65. "Free Regular Houston Bus Service Is Available to MetroLift Riders," *Passenger Transport*, APTA, Washington, D.C. (Jan. 10, 1994).

66. Roberts, G. D. and Wong, J. D. E., "Assessment of the Potential Application of 'Smart Cards' in the Passenger Travel Industry," (Jan. 1988).

67. Gorham, P., "The Lift Lets Everyone Ride," Project ACTION Update, Project ACTION, National Easter Seal Society, Washington, D.C. (Spring 1992) p. 5.

68. Blymyer, R. W., "Successful Marketing Begins with Operations," California Transit Association, Sacramento, California (Aug. 1993) p. 49.

69. Simon, R., "A Lift to Freedom—A Model for Change," Project ACTION Update, Project ACTION, National Easter Seal Society, Washington, D.C. (Fall 1991) pp. 7-8.

66

70. "Cleveland Coalition for Disabled Riders Markets Lift-Equipped Buses and Trains Drivers," Project ACTION Update, Project ACTION, National Easter Seal Society, Washington, D.C. (Fall 1990) p. 4.

71. Kihl, M., "Marketing Rural Transit Among Senior Populations," *Transportation Research Record 1338*, Transportation Research Board, Washington, D.C. (1992) pp. 60-64.

72. Goldman, H. J., "Increasing Mobility-Impaired Ridership on Mainline Service," *Passenger Transport*, APTA, Washington, D.C. (Apr. 22, 1991) p. 5.

73. "New York Intros Braille Maps," *Passenger Transport*, APTA, Washington, D.C. (May 24, 1993) p. 9.

74. "ADA Helps Open Doors to Cincinnati's Metro Buses," *Passenger Transport*, APTA, Washington, D.C. (Nov. 2, 1992) p. 7.

75. "E&D Newsletter," Greater Bridgeport Transit District (Apr. 1993).

76. Appendix A, Section 10.2, 49 CFR Part 37, *Federal Register* (Sep. 6, 1991).

77. CGA Consulting Services et. al., "Bus Stop Accessibility: A Guide for Virginia Transit Systems for Complying with the Americans with Disabilities Act of 1990," Virginia Department of Rail and Public Transit (Jul. 1, 1992).

78. Section 35.150, 28 CFR Part 35, *Federal Register* (Jul. 26, 1991).

79. Section 37.167(g), 49 CFR Part 37, *Federal Register* (Sep. 6, 1991) p. 45640.

80. Community Council, Inc., "Bus Hailing System for Passengers with Vision Disabilities, A Survey of 16 Peer Cities," Regional Transportation Authority of Phoenix, Phoenix, Arizona (Apr. 1, 1992).

81. "Chatham Offers Signaling Kit to Assist Riders with Disabilities," *Passenger Transport*, APTA, Washington, D.C. (Jul. 5, 1993).

ADDITIONAL SOURCES OF INFORMATION

The following additional sources of information, not cited above, were used to develop this report.

SERVICE ROUTES/COMMUNITY BUS

Hoey, W. F., "Dial-A-Ride in the Context of Demand-Responsive Transportation: A Critical Appraisal," *Transportation Research Record 608*, Transportation Research Board, Washington, D.C. (1976) pp. 11-15.

ON-CALL ACCESSIBLE FIXED ROUTE BUS SERVICE

"Office of Transportation Access (OTA) Report," Minutes of the Access Advisory Committee to the Massachusetts Bay Transportation Authority (MBTA), Boston, Massachusetts (Sep. 23, 1993).

Jon Roth, Southeastern Pennsylvania Transportation Authority, Philadelphia, Pennsylvania.

FEEDER SERVICE

"Direct Transfer Paratransit Service," Tidewater Transit District, Norfolk, Virginia (Sep. 1992).

Jeff Becker, Tidewater Transit District, Norfolk, Virginia.

John Nelson, Prince George's County Department of Public Works and Transportation, Maryland.

"RVTD Valley Feeder Service," Rogue Valley Transportation District, Medford, Oregon, undated.

Doug Pilant, Rogue Valley Transportation District, Medford, Oregon.

Transport Canada, *Dial-a-Bus Manual*, Volume II (Mar. 1974).

ADA Complementary Paratransit Plan, Greater Cleveland Regional Transit Authority (Jan. 22, 1992).

Central Transportation Planning Staff, "Special Needs Transportation Evaluation: Analysis of the User Survey," Metropolitan Area Planning Council, Boston, Massachusetts (Jan. 1986).

"OC Transpo Strives to Meet the Needs of all Riders," *Passenger Transport*, APTA, Washington, D.C. (Nov. 18, 1991).

MANOP Services, Ltd., "Paratransit in Canad—A Review," Transportation Development Centre (May 1986).

Michael Davis, Manager of Victoria Planning, BC Transit, Vancouver, British Columbia, Canada.

New Jersey Transit, "Vehicle to Vehicle Transfer Program," Project ACTION profile.

Henry Nicholson, Monmouth County Director of Transportation, Freehold, New Jersey.

Sheila Barberini, City of Phoenix Transportation Department, Phoenix, Arizona.

GENERAL PUBLIC DIAL-A-RIDE

"Previous Experience with Demand-Responsive Bus Service," Appendix B, Dial-A-Bus Project Report, Massachusetts Institute of Technology Urban Systems Laboratory, Cambridge, Massachusetts (May 1970).

Transport Canada, *Dial-a-Bus Manual*, Volume II (Mar. 1974).

"Demand-Responsive Transportation," *TRB Special Report 147*, National Research Council, Washington, D.C. (1974).

Multisystems, Inc., "Paratransit: Options for the Future — An Overview," U.S. Department of Transportation (Dec. 1982).

LOW-FLOOR BUSES

BC Transit and Coplan, *Transportation Needs of the Elderly and Disabled in the Victoria Region 1986-2001* (Sep. 1990).

BC Transit, "Accessibility—The Low Floor Bus Concept", undated.

Beck, W. T., "Low Floor Buses in Kitchener: Operations Perspective," paper presented at the Canadian Urban Transit Association Fall Conference, Laval, Quebec (Nov. 1992).

TransVision Consultants, "Accessible Transit Buses: Development & Implementation in Canada," technical memorandum prepared for Transportation Development Centre, Transport Canada (Jan. 1994).

Shanley, J., "Orion II Bus Demonstration, Final Report," Central New York Regional Transportation Authority, *Urban Mass Transportation Administration Report No. UMTA-NY-03-0182-89-1* (Feb. 1989).

Goodwin, B., "Low Floors and Improved Layouts: Trends in European Bus Design," *Urban Transport International*, Landor Publishing Limited, London (Jan. 1991).

68

"Low Floor Buses Enter Service in Ann Arbor," *Passenger Transport*, APTA, Washington, D.C. (Mar. 1, 1993).

ACCESSIBLE TAXIS

MANOP Services, Ltd., "Paratransit in Canada—A Review," Transportation Development Centre (rev. May 1986).

Rick Boxer, Nevada Taxi Board, Nevada, (702) 486-6532.

AUTOMATED INFORMATION AND COMMUNICATION SYSTEMS

Besette, R. and Carter, D., *Directory of User Information Systems in Public Transit*, Direction des Communications, Ministére des Transports du Quebec, Montréal, Québec (1992).

Deaton, J. and Parasuraman, R., "Sensory and Cognitive Vigilance: Effects of Age on Performance and Subjective Workload," *Human Performance*, Volume 6, Number 1 (1993) pp. 71-97.

Martin, M., Williges B., and Williges R., "Improving the Design of Telephone-Based Information Systems," in Proceedings of the Human Factors Society 34th Annual Meeting, Santa Monica, California (1990) pp. 198-202.

Moreyne, M., "Integrated Communication, Information and Security Systems (ICISS) for Visually and Hearing Impaired Persons," prepared by Télécité for the Transportation Development Centre, TP 11265E, Montreal, Quebec (Jan. 1992).

Richesin, C., Grace, G., Lantkow, M., and Gillies, T., "Access Needs of Blind and Visually Impaired Travellers in Transportation Terminals: A Study and Design Guidelines," a report by the Canadian National Institute for the Blind for the Transportation Development Centre, Montreal, Quebec (Dec. 1987).

Rutenberg, U., "Communicaid II: Development of a Prototype Information System for Sensory and Speech-Impaired Persons in Transportation Terminals," prepared by Rutenberg Design Inc. for the Transportation Development Centre, TP 11307E, Montreal, Quebec (Mar. 1992).

Rutenberg, U. and Heron, R., "Development of Information and Communication Devices for Sensory Impaired Travellers," Proceedings of the 6th International Conference on Mobility and Transport for Elderly and Disabled Persons, Lyon, France (Jun. 1992) pp. 538-542.

Suen, L. and Geehan, T., "Transportation Technologies for Improving Independence in Canada," *Transportation Research Record 1378*, Transportation Research Board, Washington, D.C. (Apr. 1993).

TRAVEL TRAINING AND FACILITATED TRAVEL

"Shifting Gears Saves Money, Augments Service," *Community Transportation Reporter* (Jul. 1993).

Towner, C., "Training the Transportation Handicapped to Use Public Transit," Third International Conference on Mobility and Transport of Elderly and Handicapped Persons, Conference Proceedings, *USDOT Report # DOT-I-85-07* (Oct. 1984).

FARE INCENTIVE PROGRAMS

Mario Garcia, Metro-Dade County Transit, Miami, Florida.

FARE SIMPLIFICATION MECHANISMS

Suen, L. and Geehan, T., "Transportation Technologies for Improving Independence in Canada," *Transportation Research Record 1378*, Transportation Research Board, Washington, D.C. (Apr. 1993).

"Hands-Free Fare Payment—Even Smarter," *Community Transportation Reporter* (Jul. 1992).

Korach, R., "Southern California Pulls out all Stops to Serve Disabled Community," *Passenger Transport*, APTA, Washington, D.C. (Jul. 8, 1985).

Ognibene, P., "Role of Automated Identification and Fare Collection in Paratransit," *Passenger Transport*, APTA, Washington, D.C. (Jul. 13, 1992).

Schweiger, C. L., Kihl, M., and Labell, L. N., "Advanced Public Transportation Systems: The State of the Art, Update '94," *FTA-MA-Z6-0007-94-1* (Jan. 1994).

MARKETING PROGRAMS

"Local Demonstration Program, Phase I 1991-1992," Project Profiles, Project ACTION, National Easter Seal Society, Washington, D.C. (1992).

"Outreach and Marketing: Increasing Ridership on Fixed-Route Transportation," Project ACTION Update, Project ACTION, National Easter Seal Society, Washington, D.C. (Winter 1993) p. 2.

Pederson, C., "Parkrose Targeted Marketing Campaign Pass Incentive Program," *Transportation Research Record 1209*, Transportation Research Board, Washington, D.C. (1989) pp. 65-72.

BUS IDENTIFIER SYSTEMS

EG&G Dynatrend and Katherine McGuinness and Associates, Inc., ADA Resource Packet, prepared for the Washington State Department of Transportation (Mar. 6, 1992).

DESTINATION CARD PROGRAMS

EG&G Dynatrend and Katherine McGuinness and Associates,
Inc., ADA Resource Packet, prepared for the Washington State
Department of Transportation (Mar. 6, 1992).

APPENDIX A

SURVEY FORM

Innovative Fixed Route and Paratransit Service Options and Enhancements
Information Request

Name of Transit Agency: _____

City: _____ State/Province: _____

Contact Person: _____

Phone #: (___) _____

1. Please indicate if you "Tried but Discontinued", are "Presently Using", "Will be Implementing", or "Are Considering" each of the following service options and enhancements. A brief description of each option/enhancement is enclosed.

Service Option/Enhancement	Tried but Discontinued	Presently Using	Will be Implementing	Are Considering
"On-call" Bus or "Call-a-Lift" Bus				
Feeder Services				
Employee Training				
Service Routes/Community Bus Program				
Route Deviation				
Point Deviation				
Marketing Programs				
Travel Training				
Facilitated Transportation				
Fare Incentive Programs				
Accessible Taxis				
Low-floor Fixed Route Buses				
Corridor Paratransit				
General Public Dial-a-ride				
Bus identifier Kits				
Destination Card Systems				
Audio/Visual Displays and Systems				
Simplified Fare Collection				
Accessible Bus Stop Programs				

2. Please describe below any other innovative service design options or service enhancements, not listed on the previous page, which you have tried, are using, or plan to implement.

_____
_____
_____
_____

3. If you indicated above that any of the service options/enhancements have been or are being used, please list below those which you feel have been most effective in getting paratransit customers or potential paratransit customers to use fixed route services. For each, indicate on a scale from 1 to 5 how effective you feel the option has been   (1 = not effective; 5 = very effective)

Option/Enhancement Tried or Being Used	Effectiveness
_____	_____
_____	_____
_____	_____
_____	_____
_____	_____
_____	_____

Please return this form in the enclosed self-addressed envelope or FAX it to:

Mr. Russell H. Thatcher
EG&G Dynatrend
(617) 270-4999

*   *   *   THANK YOU   *   *   *

Description of Service Options/Enhancements

"On-call" Accessible Fixed Route Bus Service: Also known as "Call-A-Lift-Bus", this service allows persons with disabilities to call in advance and request that an accessible **fixed route** bus be used on a route that they plan to use at a time when they will be traveling.

Feeder Service: Uses one mode of transportation to support and "feed" into another type of service. Typically, paratransit service is used to transport individuals with disabilities to the nearest fixed route that they are able to use and/or to take them from a fixed route stop/station to their destination.

Employee Training: Training in disability awareness, customer relations and "sensitivity", passenger assistance techniques, and other skills that enable employees to more appropriately assist and serve persons with disabilities.

Service Routes/Community Bus Service: Service routes, also known as community bus service, are fixed routes designed to reduce the distances that elderly persons and persons with disabilities must travel to get to and from bus stops. Typically, smaller vehicles are used, neighborhood streets rather than main arterials are served, and drivers provide more assistance than in conventional fixed route programs. While routes are designed to better meet the needs of persons with disabilities and elderly persons, they are open to the public. They can be operated as conventional fixed routes, as feeders to arterial routes, or can include a "route deviation" option.

Route Deviation: In route deviation systems, vehicles operate along a fixed route and follow a fixed schedule. Vehicles can deviate from the set schedule, however, if a request is made by a rider. After deviating from the route, vehicles return to the same point to continue their run.

Point Deviation: In point deviation systems, specific stops (pickup and drop-off "points") are established. Vehicles arrive at these designated points on a set schedule. There is no set route between these points, however, and vehicles operate in a door-to-door or curb-to-curb mode as required to meet passenger needs.

Marketing Programs: Programs targeted specifically to persons with disabilities to encourage or facilitate use of the fixed route system or to improve understanding of the appropriate use of paratransit versus fixed route service. Can include service brochures, "How to" guides, community access guides, or "micro-marketing" efforts that focus on particular user groups and utilize non-traditional media to better reach the target population.

Travel Training: Also known as Mobility Training, this alternative provides potential riders with the skills and information needed to use the fixed route service independently. Instruction can focus on use of the lift or other access features, route planning, landmark identification, street crossing safety, emergency procedures, stranger safety awareness, appropriate behavior, or any combination of these. Training can be specific to a particular route or trip or can be designed to develop more general system use skills. Training can be provided by "peers" (individuals with disabilities or elderly persons who know and use the system) or by human service agency or transit agency staff or contractors.

Facilitated Transportation: Facilitated transportation programs provide attendant(s) on vehicles or at transfer points to assist individuals in using the fixed route service. Typically, these programs assist individuals who are more developmentally disabled and cannot independently use the system even with travel training.

Fare Incentive Programs: These programs offer reduced fares on an ongoing basis or as special promotions to encourage individuals to use fixed route rather than paratransit service.

Accessible Taxis: Typically, ramp-equipped minivans or other accessible vehicles are operated as general public taxicabs. Accessible vehicles are not segregated from the rest of the fleet but serve persons with and without disabilities. Standard meter rates or zonal rates are used for all riders.

Low-Floor Fixed Route Buses: Ramp-equipped vehicles, typically with a finished floor height of fifteen inches (375 millimeters) or less used in conventional fixed route operation, route deviation service, or on service routes.

General Public Demand Responsive Service: Door-to-door or curb-to-curb service provided to the general public as well as to persons with disabilities.

Bus Identifier Kits: Highly visible cards that can be held by persons with disabilities to let drivers know that they are waiting for a bus and to identify the bus/route number that they need.

Destination Card Systems: Cards that are typically used by persons with hearing impairments or persons with developmental disabilities. The cards identify the desired destination, stop number, and connecting route numbers for a particular trip and are handed to drivers or other transit personnel so that appropriate assistance can be provided.

Audio/Visual Displays and Systems: On-board or wayside systems that provide audio and/or visual information to riders. Can include video monitors, LED displays, audio pathways, signage targeted to particular needs, "talking buses", "talking bus stops", or other systems.

Simplified Fare Collection: Includes vouchers, IDs, passes, and other fare collection programs targeted specifically to persons with disabilities who may have difficulty with the standard fare collection system.

Accessible Bus Stop Programs: Proactive programs which identify specific bus stops used by persons with disabilities and add needed accessibility features to enable individuals to more easily use the stops and the fixed route service.

APPENDIX B

SELECTED TRANSIT PROVIDERS PRESENTLY USING SERVICE OPTIONS/ENHANCEMENTS

This appendix contains detailed information about transit providers that reported that they are presently using various service options and enhancements. The information was obtained from a survey of transit providers in Canada and the United States using the survey instrument shown in Appendix A. For certain options, additional information was obtained through follow-up telephone calls to providers who responded to the survey.

Tables B-1 through B-9 provide detailed information for the options that were the focus of follow-up calls.

Tables B-10 through B-15 summarize survey information about option/enhancements that were not the subject of follow-up calls. They provide a listing of transit agencies that reported using each option/enhancement. The tables are presented herein in the format provided by the research agency.

Table B-1. Selected Transit Providers Presently Using Service Routes

Agency Name	City State/Province	Total Population	Service Area (mi.²)	Fixed Route Fleet Size	% FR Fleet Accessible	Paratransit Trips/Year	Serv. Route Effectiveness	Date Serv. Routes Implem.	Peak/ Off-Peak	# Former PT Trips Served	Serv. Routes General Info
AJAX Transit	Ajax, Ontario	60000	NA	27	0	27000	5	Sept., 1992	All times	15% decrease	M-F, 9:30-5:30; 82-86 passengers per day; supplements Fixed route; decreased paratransit trips by 15%; 100 pax/day; no deviation; can flag bus anywhere on route
Broward County Transit	Pompano Beach, Florida	1200000	410	200	50	NA	4	1991	NA	NA	small buses operated by 7 cities in the county; local routes deviate when schedule allows; feed into regional routes
Cornwall Transit	Cornwall, Ontario	48000	NA	29	0	8000	4	Feb., 1993	NA	0	serves senior housing, shopping centers, medical centers; 5.0 trips/veh-hr (greater than local paratransit - 2.5); no decrease in PT trips observed.
Lakeland Area Mass Transit District	Lakeland, Florida	110000	60	21	62	62000	3	April, 1991	NA	NA	special service on Saturdays only; will also deviate from routes; open to general public; "Red Carpet Service"
Madison County Transit	Granite City, Illinois	227000	390	78	81	85000	5	June, 1989	All times	5000/mo.	replaced as well as supplemented prior fixed route; coordinated w/ travel training; paratransit decreased from 12000/mo to 7000/mo (42% decrease)
Madison Metro Transit System	Madison, Wisconsin	240000	100	170	25	150000	4	April, 1992	All times	NA	no deviations; supplement program w/ travel training; less than 10 paratransit trips per day moved to service route
OC Transpo	Ottawa, Ontario	600000	225	828	1	700000	3	May, 1992	All times	NA	one route presently; will be expanding in 1994; expansion will include route deviation; also do travel training; 20% of service route riders are registered for paratransit

Table B-1. Selected Transit Providers Presently Using Service Routes (Continued)

Agency Name	City State/Province	Total Population	Service Area (mi.²)	Fixed Route Fleet Size	% FR Fleet Accessible	Paratransit Trips/Year	Serv. Route Effectiveness	Date Serv. Routes Implem.	Peak/ Off-Peak	# Former PT Trips Served	Serv. Routes General Info
Pecos Trails Transit	Roswell, New Mexico	45000	29	9	100	13000	5	1993	All times	100/day	4 service routes; city is long and narrow; 100 riders/day who otherwise would be on paratransit; also do travel training; 30% of riders are persons with disabilities
Regional Transit Board	Minneapolis/St. Paul, Minnesota	2050000	1100	900	9	1500000	NA	1989	All times	NA	2 circulators (one a new route, one replaced a traditional fixed route); anchored by shopping centers, senior centers and senior housing; 10 buses; 1500 trips/day; 5-10 wheelchair users per day
Richmond Hill Transit	Richmond Hill, Ontario	82000	NA	21	0	11000	5	March, 1993	NA	NA	supplements fixed route; low-floor buses used; open to general public; costs are: $13/trip paratransit; $5/trip service routes; 60% of paratransit trips switched but paratransit filled w/ unmet demand

"Serv. Route Effectiveness" = effectiveness rating provided in survey
"Peak/Off-Peak" = hours the service is provided (e.g., at all times, off-peak only, etc.)

"Date Serv. Routes Implem." = date the program was implemented
"# Former PT Trips Served" = paratransit trips diverted to service routes
NA = not available

Table B-2. Selected Transit Providers Presently Using On-Call Accessible Fixed Route Bus Service

Agency Name	City State/Province	Total Population	Service Area (mi.²)	Fixed Route Fleet Size	% FR Fleet Accessible	Paratransit Trips/Year	On-Call Effectiveness	Date On-Call Implemented	% FR Access when Implem.	On-Call Requests/ Month	On-Call General Info.
Ann Arbor Transportation Authority	Ann Arbor, Michigan	180000	71	57	NA	337000	3	1985	33	NA	trips requested day before are guaranteed; same day done if possible; used program to identify and designate fully accessible routes
Broward County Transit	Pompano, Florida Beach	1200000	410	200	50	NA	3	Sept., 1993	50	NA	call day ahead
Central Oklahoma Transportation & Parking Authority	Oklahoma City, Oklahoma	900000	500	89	10	24546	5	1992	10	4	24 hour notice required; usually used for express service
City Utilities of Springfield	Springfield, Missouri	90000	NA	29	50	18000	4	April, 1992	50	80	call day before; 3-4 regular riders; use to assign accessible buses to routes
Fayetteville Area System of Transit	Fayetteville North Carolina	82000	42	20	30	NA	4	1993	30	12	next day notice required
Greater Attleboro-Taunton Regional Transit Authority	Attleboro, Massachusetts	100000	80	13	100	220000	3	March, 1991	50	7	now not used as system is 100% accessible; used to require 1 day advance notice
Grays Harbor Transportation Authority	Hoquiam, Washington	65400	2000	38	28	69000	2	1992	28	8	24 hour notice requested; will attempt to accommodate if less
Housatonic Area Regional Transit District	Danbury, Connecticut	64000	NA	21	50	66000	4	1989	67	15	
Jefferson Transit	Port Townsend, Washington	21000	3000	14	71	12000	4	1993	71	3	calls only required prior to bus leaving the garage

Table B-2. Selected Transit Providers Presently Using On-Call Accessible Fixed Route Bus Service (Continued)

Agency Name	City State/Province	Total Population	Service Area (mi.²)	Fixed Route Fleet Size	% FR Fleet Accessible	Paratransit Trips/Year	On-Call Effectiveness	Date On-Call Implemented	% FR Access when Implem.	On-Call Requests/Month	On-Call General Info.
Lowell Regional Transit Authority	Lowell, Massachusetts	200000	67	35	80	90000	5	1992	80	30	2 hour notice required
Massachusetts Bay Transportation Authority	Boston, Massachusetts	2775000	891	1171	50	406000	NA	1986	20	500	calls required by 1 p.m. on day before; program operated out of 8 garages; calls received at central admin. office; send requested bus and next bus on route.
Merrimack Valley Regional Transit Authority	Haverhill, Massachusetts	281000	325	45	91	130000	NA	1987	91	NA	primarily to allow people to ensure that bus on route will be accessible; almost 100% accessible; can occasionally be an inaccessible bus in service
Mid Mon Valley Transit Authority	Charleroi, Pennsylvania	68000	NA	19	75	0	4	1987	50	10	24 hour notice required
Municipal Transit Administration	Clinton, Iowa	29000	NA	9	67	4800	5	1992	22	8	24 hr notice requested; can do with 1/2 hour notice
Ottumwa Transit Authority	Ottumwa, Iowa	25000	50	7	86	4200	2	1992	86	NA	600-700 lift usages per month; use program to also have riders call to be sure lift is on route and working as buses are older (1981s/1982s)
Red Rose Transit Authority	Lancaster, Pennsylvania	250000	NA	41	NA	28000	5	1990	7	25	24 hour notice required
Rogue Valley Transportation District	Medford, Oregon	111000	158	26	74	48000	4	Oct., 1991	47	150	4 hours advance notice required

Table B-2. Selected Transit Providers Presently Using On-Call Accessible Fixed Route Bus Service (Continued)

Agency Name	City State/Province	Total Population	Service Area (mi.²)	Fixed Route Fleet Size	% FR Fleet Accessible	Paratransit Trips/Year	On-Call Effectiveness	Date On-Call Implemented	% FR Access when Implem.	On-Call Requests/ Month	On-Call General Info.
Southeastern Pennsylvania Transportation Authority	Philadelphia, Pennsylvania	4200000	1164	1400	15	NA	NA	NA	15	300	"Suburban On-Call" used only in suburban areas; requests taken 1-7 days in advance; send bus requested as well as next bus on route; use paratransit to backup; use program to identify routes for 100% accessibility
Transit Authority of North Kentucky	Ft. Wright, Kentucky	208000	84	97	50	32000	5	March, 1992	13	100	require 1 day advance notice; in beginning had to sometimes turn down requests (only 13% of busses accessible); average 5 calls per day
Westmoreland Transit	Greensburg, Pennsylvania	179000	NA	22	54	180	4	NA	NA	NA	not a true on-call; variation: riders call in advance to make sure lift on route is working (result of past problems with lifts); usually 10 calls/mo.

"On-Call Effectiveness" = effectiveness rating provided in survey

"% FR Access when Implemented" = % of the fixed route fleet that was accessible when the program was started

"On-Call Requests/Month" = number of calls received per month for accessible vehicles

"Date On-Call Implemented" = date the program was implemented

NA = not available

Table B-3. Selected Transit Providers Presently Operating Route Deviation Services

Agency Name	City State/Province	Total Population	Service Area (mi.²)	Fixed Route Fleet Size	% FR Fleet Accessible	Paratransit Trips/Year	Route Dev. Effectiveness	Date Route Dev. Implem.	Deviate for Gen. Public?	# of Dev. Requests/Mo.	Route Dev. General Info.
BC Transit	Vancouver, British Columbia	1600000	1125	950	29	800000	NA	1991	NA	NA	1 hour headways; used in suburban community; very limited use; use 25' buses
CART, Inc.	Idaho Falls, Idaho	65000	20000	NA	NA	200000	5	1986	Yes	6000	3 interconnected loop routes; will deviate up to 3 blocks; coordinated with paratransit; 1 hour headways (38 min. w/ 22 minute layover to accommodate deviations.
City of Astoria Transit	Astoria, Oregon	9980	5.7	1	100	0	5	Feb., 1993	No	150	circular route; will deviate up to 3/4 of a mile; only for individuals with disabilities; 6 trips per day served by deviation
CityLink Abilene	Abilene, Texas	106000	NA	13	100	25200	5	1991	Yes	150	deviate to specific sites; deviations only if possible; calls accepted anytime before bus passes; coordinated w/ paratransit-will dispatch vans if not possible; 1 hour headways

Table B-3. Selected Transit Providers Presently Operating Route Deviation Services (Continued)

Agency Name	City State/Province	Total Population	Service Area (mi.?)	Fixed Route Fleet Size	% FR Fleet Accessible	Paratransit Trips/Year	Route Dev. Effectiveness	Date Route Dev. Implem.	Deviate for Gen. Public?	# of Dev. Requests/Mo.	Route Dev. General Info.
Fairmont Marion County Transit Authority	Fairmont, West Virginia	45000	NA	21	18	1500	5	1993	No	25	for ADA eligible persons; 24 hour notice (will try if less); deviate up to 3/4 mile; 30 min. headways; deviations done for entire system (routes from 3-20 miles in length); coord. w/ paratransit (90% on fixed route though)
Greater Attleboro-Taunton Regional Transit Authority	Attleboro, Massachusetts	100000	80	13	100	220000	NA	NA	NA	NA	worked deviations into regular schedule as agency clients were travel trained; site specific, not general deviation program
Grays Harbor Transportation Authority	Hoquiam, Washington	65400	2000	38	28	69000	NA	1975	NA	100	deviate over ten miles of fixed route; deviate five times daily
Housatonic Area Regional Transit District	Danbury, Connecticut	64000	NA	21	50	66000	4	1983	Yes	NA	preselected locations for deviations; schedule notes "on request only"; 1-2 hrs. notice required; deviations in some locations only at certain times; pulse system w/ 5 min layover
Indiana County Transit Authority	Indiana, Pennsylvania	90000	830	9	100	NA	4	1982	Yes	220	deviate in rural areas only; deviate for general public; 54 trips/week; 1 hour headways

Table B-3. Selected Transit Providers Presently Operating Route Deviation Services (Continued)

Agency Name	City State/Province	Total Population	Service Area (mi.?)	Fixed Route Fleet Size	% FR Fleet Accessible	Paratransit Trips/Year	Route Dev. Effectiveness	Date Route Dev. Implem.	Deviate for Gen. Public?	# of Dev. Requests/Mo.	Route Dev. General Info.
Jefferson Transit	Port Townsend, Washington	21000	3000	14	71	12000	2	June, 1993	Yes	1	deviate over 260 miles of routes (19% of total system); only 2 requests in first 4 months
Lakeland Area Mass Transit District	Lakeland, Florida	110000	60	21	0.62	62000	3	April, 1991	Yes	NA	Route deviation done in conjunction w/ Saturday service route program - "Red Carpet Service"; dev. up to 2 blocks; general public can request
Lane Transit District	Eugene, Oregon	180000	76	77	100	75000	NA	1975	NA	30	only prearranged deviations; not on-call; started in 1970's; 30 locations where deviations are allowed (many on daily basis); try to accommodate groups if facility near route
Madison County Transit	Granite City, Illinois	227000	390	78	81	85000	4	Sept., 1993	Yes	10	rural community, 2 hr headway; deviate at ends of route; ask for day ahead notice, but will try same day; also do prescheduled deviations on other routes if possible

81

Table B-3. Selected Transit Providers Presently Operating Route Deviation Services (Continued)

Agency Name	City State/Province	Total Population	Service Area (mi.²)	Fixed Route Fleet Size	% FR Fleet Accessible	Paratransit Trips/Year	Route Dev. Effectiveness	Date Route Dev. Implem.	Deviate for Gen. Public?	# of Dev. Requests/Mo.	Route Dev. General Info.
Marquette County Transit Authority	Marquette, Michigan	70000	1864	27	100	NA	4	1985	Yes	NA	deviate in rural area in AM/PM only; vehicle operates as demand-response in AM and picks up passengers to take them to urban area, makes designated stops in urban area; returns same way
Miami Valley Regional Transit Authority	Dayton, Ohio	600000	458	258	100	121000	1	April, 1993	NA	NA	deviate on two routes during designated hours; on 44 miles of routes; requires 24 hours notice; no significant use to date
Municipal Transit Administration	Clinton, Iowa	29000	NA	9	67	4800	3	NA	Yes	100	have always done; 1/2 hr headways; will deviate a few blocks; will deviate on all routes
Ottumwa Transit Authority	Ottumwa, Iowa	25000	50	7	86	4200	4	1984	No	NA	40 min. headways; deviate on all 4 local routes; generally operate during off-peak; typically deviate 2-3 blocks

Table B-3. Selected Transit Providers Presently Operating Route Deviation Services (Continued)

Agency Name	City State/Province	Total Population	Service Area (mi.²)	Fixed Route Fleet Size	% FR Fleet Accessible	Paratransit Trips/Year	Route Dev. Effectiveness	Date Route Dev. Implem.	Deviate for Gen. Public?	# of Dev. Requests/Mo.	Route Dev. General Info.
Preston Co. Sr. Citizens, Inc. dba Buckwheat Express	Kingwood, West Virginia	30000	654	7	100	32000	4	1992	Yes	NA	Deviation over entire FR system; will deviate 1/4 mile; can call ahead to arrange; for general public; not used frequently (no #s)
Rapid Transit System	Rapid City, South Dakota	60000	35	5	100	60000	4	1992	Yes	50	will deviate to certain locations; prompted by problems in winter in certain areas; maximum deviation is 3 blocks
Richmond Hill Transit	Richmond Hill, Ontario	82000	NA	21	0	11000	NA	NA	NA	NA	Done in conjunction with service routes; limited use
The T	Fort Worth, Texas	500000	286	150	25	183000	NA	1989	No	300	prescheduled deviations (ongoing) for groups or certain individuals; each request evaluated; if not possible, will consider when routes changed; coordinated w/ paratransit
York County Transportation Authority	York, Pennsylvania	180000	NA	22	93	193000	4	1990	Yes	1200	rural routes only, city routes offer adequate coverage; can call until noon day before; allow standing orders; 1st come 1st serve (not guaranteed) service

"Route Dev. Effectiveness" = effectiveness rating provided in survey
"Deviate for Gen Public?" = indicates if deviation requests are accepted from the general public

"Date Route Dev. Implem." = date when the service was implemented
"# of Dev. Requests/Mo." = number of requests for deviations per month
NA = not available

Table B-4. Selected Transit Providers Presently Operating Point Deviation Services

Agency Name	City State/Province	Total Population	Service Area (mi.²)	Fixed Route Fleet Size	% FR Fleet Accessible	Paratransit Trips/Year	Point Dev. Effectiveness	Date Point Dev. Implem.	# of Points in System	General Public Served?	Point Dev. General Info.
Ashtabula County Transportation System	Ashtabula, Ohio	99821	723	3	100	56911	NA	July, 1993	23	Yes	1 hr headways; have zones within which they deviate; if beyond, will use paratransit; 25 cents charge to deviate
Guam Mass Transit Authority	Agana, Guam	133152	214	27	80	40000	3	March, 1993	NA	NA	one hour headways; doesn't serve a substantial number of persons with disabilities
Transit Management of Hamilton, Inc. (AKA The Bus Co.)	Hamilton, Ohio	NA	NA	10	NA	5,900	NA	1993	NA	NA	service area divided into 6 sectors; six "routes" serviced by vehicles which arrive at designated checkpoints in each sector; "pulse" system with central transfer; replaced traditional radial fixed route system; have seen increase in ridership

"Point Dev. Effectiveness" = effectiveness rating provided in survey
"# of Points in System" = the number of checkpoints designated in the system

"Date Point Dev. Implem." = date the program was implemented
"General Public Served" = indicates if all riders can request pick-up/drop-off at places other than checkpoints
NA = not available

Table B-5. Selected Transit Providers Presently Providing Feeder Service

Agency Name	City State/Province	Total Population	Service Area (mi.²)	Fixed Route Fleet Size	% FR Fleet Accessible	Paratransit Trips/Year	Feeder Effectiveness	Date Feeder Implem.	Transfer Required?	# of Transfers/Month	Feeder General Info.
Broward County Transit	Pompano Beach, Florida	1200000	410	200	50	NA	2	1991	NA	NA	service routes in local communities feed into regional routes
Fairmont Marion County Transit Authority	Fairmont, West Virginia	45000	NA	21	18	1500	2	NA	No	5	thinking of requiring transfers; feeder service done in conjunction with route deviation
Greater Attleboro-Taunton Regional Transit Authority	Attleboro, Massachusetts	100000	80	13	100	220000	NA	April, 1992	NA	30	use paratransit to take individuals who work at local workshop from downtown fixed routes to workshop; coordinated with travel training program
Island Transit	Coupeville, Washington	40000	NA	8	100100	72000	5	March, 1992	Yes	3000	started feeder at same time started paratransit; trips on fixed route can be 40 mi. long; commonly do double feeders; half of all paratransit trips feed into fixed route
Lane Transit District	Eugene, Oregon	180000	76	77	100	75000	4	1993	Depends on situation	100	focus on conditionally ADA paratransit eligible riders for inbound trips; find return trips to hard to coordinate; both required & volunteer based on situation
Lassen Rural Bus System	Susanville, California	12500	6	6	100	6950	5	1992	No	50	use on rural route coming into Susanville; buses also will deviate from route if more convenient than feeder; ridership has been increasing
LACMTA	Los Angeles, California	9400000	3114	3250	93	5800000	NA	1994	NA	NA	Primarily geared toward trips from San Bernardino to downtown.
MTA of Black Hawk County	Waterloo/Cedar Falls, Iowa	104000	NA	14	28	73300	NA	July, 1993	Yes	500	for trips between cities; fixed route portion of trip typically 10-15 miles; many riders with developmental disabilities going to sheltered workshops

Table B-5. Selected Transit Providers Presently Providing Feeder Service (Continued)

Agency Name	City State/Province	Total Population	Service Area (mi.²)	Fixed Route Fleet Size	% FR Fleet Accessible	Paratransit Trips/Year	Feeder Effectiveness	Date Feeder Implem.	Transfer Required?	# of Transfers/ Month	Feeder General Info.
Madison County Transit	Granite City, Illinois	227000	390	78	81	85000	5	1990	Yes	200	hub & spoke time transfer system; paratransit to fixed route as well as service route to fixed route feeders employed; feed mainly into hubs; will feed along route, but difficult
Pioneer Valley Transit Authority	Springfield, Massachusetts	551000	115	178	14	275000	NA	1992	Yes	10	large service area (2 counties); feed into fixed route for trips from outlying areas; need better data and scheduling system for schedulers in order to expand use of feeder
Regional Public Transportation Authority	Phoenix, Arizona	2100000	400	360	40	900000	NA	1985	No	1600	most feeder trips over 2 zones (> 5 miles); feeder at both ends only rarely
Rogue Valley Transportation District	Medford, Oregon	111000	158	26	74	48000	5	1993	No	675	eliminated inefficient fixed route buses in rural areas; offer direct paratransit service for $1.50 or feeder for $.35; contract w/ taxi for feeder; 60% savings in rural areas
Tidewater Transportation District Commission	Norfolk, Virginia	900000	1000	135	50	168000	4	1979	No	100	started as feeder for general public dial-a-ride service, now expanding to ADA paratransit service; several transfer points (zonal system with one transfer point in each zone); transfer centers serve fixed route as well as demand-responsive vehicles.
Transit Authority of North Kentucky	Ft. Wright, Kentucky	208000	84	97	50	32000	5	1992	Yes	100	2 people regularly every day; trips typically 5 miles on paratransit and 10-15 miles on fixed route

"Feeder Effectiveness" = effectiveness rating provided in survey
"Transfer Required?" = indicates if riders are required to use the feeder service

"Date Feeder Implem." = date the program was implemented
"# of Transfers/Mo." = the number of trips on the feeder service per month
NA = not available

Table B-6. Selected Transit Providers Presently Using Low-Floor Buses

Agency Name	City State/Province	Total Population	Service Area (mi.²)	Fixed Route Fleet Size	% FR Fleet Accessible	Paratransit Trips/Year	Low-Floor Bus Effectiveness	Date Low Floor Implem	# of LF Buses/% of Fleet	Low-Floor Bus General Information
AJAX Transit	Ajax, Ontario	60000	NA	27	0	27000	NA	Sept., 1992	2 buses	Used on community bus program; Elf by Overland; perimeter seating for 18, 3 w/c; also have 1 Elf for Paratransit (12 amb, 5 w/c)
Altoona Metro Transit	Altoona, Pennsylvania	67000	NA	31	35	10200	3	June, 1993	3/10%	Orion II's; plan to use in FR deviation service in Spring of 1994
Ann Arbor Transportation Authority	Ann Arbor, Michigan	189000	71	57	92	337000	3	1985	18/32%	10 New Flyers, 16 Orions (of which 8 are used in fixed route); customer reaction very positive; AATA sees numerous additional benefits
BC Transit	Victoria, British Columbia	302000	250	163	15	144000	5	1992	25/15%	200 trips by wheelchair users monthly; most shifted from paratransit; New Flyer buses
Calgary Transit	Calgary, Alberta	NA	NA	550	NA	NA	NA	1993	50/9%	40-foot New Flyer buses
Champaign-Urbana Mass Transit District	Champaign-Urbana, Illinois	115,000	NA	70	NA	NA	NA	1993	15/21%	40-foot New Flyers. Use on busiest routes.
Coast Transit Authority	Gulfport, Mississippi	250000	NA	30	73	NA	4	1989	4/18%	Orion II's in FR operation; used on major routes; had to make substantial changes to buses to make work on FR but public reaction has been very positive
Edmonton Transit	Edmonton, Alberta	NA	NA	NA	NA	NA	NA	NA	43/NA	
Jefferson Transit	Port Townsend, Washington	21000	3000	14	71	12000	3	1987	2/14%	Orion II's; "passengers love them, drivers hate them"
Kitchener Transit	Kitchener, Ontario	250000	NA	108	NA	NA	NA	1992	14/13%	Non-accessible 40-foot New Flyer buses

Table B-6. Selected Transit Providers Presently Using Low-Floor Buses (Continued)

Agency Name	City State/Province	Total Population	Service Area (mi.²)	Fixed Route Fleet Size	% FR Fleet Accessible	Paratransit Trips/Year	Low-Floor Bus Effectiveness	Date Low Floor Implem	# of LF Buses/% of Fleet	Low-Floor Bus General Info.
MTA of Black Hawk County	Waterloo/Cedar Falls, Iowa	104000	NA	14	28	73300	NA	Oct., 1992	4/28%	4 Orion II ramp-equipped low-floor buses
Madison County Transit	Granite City, Illinois	227000	390	78	81	85000	5	1989	20/26%	Orion IIs; great from customer perspective and for operations; high maintenance cost and initial capital cost
Municipal Transit Administration	Clinton, Iowa	29000	NA	9	67	4800	NA	1993	2/22%	Orion II's in fixed route service
Richmond Hill Transit	Richmond Hill, Ontario	82000	NA	21	0	11000	NA	1989	2/10%	On service routes and paratransit; Orion II's;
St. Albert Transit	St. Albert, Alberta	NA	NA	NA	NA	NA	NA	NA	4/NA	
Sonoma County Transit	Santa Rosa, California	NA	NA	33	NA	NA	NA	NA	6/18%	Orion II's on fixed route service
Winnipeg Transit System	Winnipeg, Manitoba	640000	NA	560	2	330000	NA	Feb., 1993	9/2%	Elf buses; 20 passenger; 6 in fixed route, 3 in paratransit; rough ride, small ramp; also buying larger Flyers

"Low-Flr Bus Effectiveness" = effectiveness rating provided in the survey
"# of LF Buses/% of Fleet" = the number of low-floor buses in the fleet and the percentage of the fleet that is low-floor

"Date Low-Flr. Implem" = date the program was implemented
NA = not available

Table B-7. Selected Transit Providers Presently Using Accessible Taxis

Agency Name	City State/Province	Total Population	Service Area (mi.?)	Fixed Route Fleet Size	% FR Fleet Accessible	Paratransit Trips/Year	Access Taxi Effectiveness	Date Access Taxi Implem.	# of Accessible Taxis	Integrated w/ Gen Public?	Access Taxi General Info
AJAX Transit	Ajax, Ontario	60000	NA	27	0	27000	NA	April. 1992	7	NA	for paratransit only; used off-peak and Saturday; purchase service from taxis
City of Benicia	Benicia, California	NA	NA	NA	NA	NA	NA	NA	3	Yes	Operated by Benicia Yellow Cab. Used for both City subsidized service and general public
BC Transit	Vancouver, British Columbia	1600000	1125	950	29	800000	NA	June, 1991	66	No	dedicated contract service; 50% user-side subsidy; immediate response; also offer advance reservation dial-a-ride w/ 92% subsidy; taxis do about 50,000 trips per year
Capital Area Transit	Raleigh, North Carolina	250000	88	36	100	18000	NA	1989	3	Yes	3 accessible taxis leased to 2 companies; transit agency uses user-side subsidy program to provide paratransit service; currently 5-10 wheelchair users use daily
Greater Attleboro-Taunton Regional Transit Authority	Attleboro, Massachusetts	100000	80	13	100	220000	3	Sept., 1992	2	Yes	no subsidy provided for operation; transit bought cabs and leases to local taxi company; used as general public cabs
Lane Transit District	Eugene, Oregon	180000	76	77	100	75000	NA	1991	2	Yes	next day scheduling, no operating subsidy; 430 trips by wheelchair users in 1993; also use for contracted service

Table B-7. Selected Transit Providers Presently Using Accessible Taxis (Continued)

Agency Name	City State/Province	Total Population	Service Area (mi.²)	Fixed Route Fleet Size	% FR Fleet Accessible	Paratransit Trips/Year	Access Taxi Effectiveness	Date Access Taxi Implem.	# of Accessible Taxis	Integrated w/ Gen Public?	Access Taxi General Info
LACMTA	Los Angeles, California	NA	NA	NA	NA	NA	NA	NA	5	NA	Leased to two cab companies. Used primarily for subsidized contract service.
Monmouth County DOT	Freehold, New Jersey	NA	NA	NA	NA	NA	4	1990	1	Yes	local taxi company purchased 1 accessible taxi; uses separate from work done for transit agency
MUNI	San Francisco, California	NA	NA	NA	NA	NA	NA	NA	4	Yes	Accessible minivans leased to one local cab company. Subsidized taxi script program through MUNI
City of Napa	Napa, California	NA	NA	NA	NA	NA	NA	NA	2	Yes	Operated by two local cab companies. City does provide some subsidy for riders
Pioneer Valley Transit Authority	Springfield, Massachusetts	551000	115	178	14	275000	NA	1991	2	Yes	have had problems w/ vehicle reliability; accessible minivans bought by transit agency and leased to 2 local taxi companies
Red Rose Transit Authority	Lancaster, Pennsylvania	250000	NA	41	NA	28000	3	1977	17	Yes	lease vehicles to taxi companies; subsidize ADA paratransit trips but vehicles used for general public service as well
Richmond Hill Transit	Richmond Hill, Ontario	82000	NA	21	0	11000	5	1989	2	NA	purchase some paratransit trips through local accessible taxi service; subsidy provided; other paratransit requires 2 day notice; 460 trips/month provided by taxis
Santa Cruz Transportation	Santa Cruz, California	NA	NA	NA	NA	NA	NA	NA	3	Yes	Operated by Yellow Cab. Used for both publicly subsidized service and general public

Table B-7. Selected Transit Providers Presently Using Accessible Taxis (Continued)

Agency Name	City State/Province	Total Population	Service Area (mi.²)	Fixed Route Fleet Size	% FR Fleet Accessible	Paratransit Trips/Year	Access Taxi Effectiveness	Date Access Taxi Implem.	# of Accessible Taxis	Integrated w/ Gen Public?	Access Taxi General Info
Saskatoon Transit System	Saskatoon, Saskatchewan	185000	NA	130	0	120000	4	1992	2	NA	local taxi company bought accessible vehicle on own; no capital or operating subsidy provided; charges standard fare for all trips
System of Barrie - B.A.C.T.S.	Barrie, Ontario	66000	271	21	0	26400	5	April, 1992	3	Yes	2 taxi companies; fixed rate negotiated for contract work; supplements paratransit on Saturdays, evenings, and during peak hours; companies use for general public; taxis do 10% of transit agency paratransit service
Winnipeg Transit System	Winnipeg, Manitoba	640000	NA	560	2	330000	5	Nov., 1992	10	Yes	2 local companies bought taxis w/ no subsidy; transit buys some paratransit trips from them; contract 100 trips/day; also open to general public

"Access Taxi Effectiveness" = effectiveness rating provided in the survey
"# of Accessible Taxis" = the number of accessible taxis in use

"Date Access Taxi Implem." = date that accessible taxis were introduced in service
"Integrated w/ Gen Public?" = indicates if accessible taxis provide general public taxi service
NA = not available

Table B-8. Selected Transit Providers Presently Using Travel Training

Agency Name	City State/Province	Total Population	Service Area (mi.²)	Fixed Route Fleet Size	% FR Fleet Accessible	Paratransit Trips/Year	Trav. Trng. Effectiveness	Date Trav. Trng. Implem.	Integrated with Elig?	# of People Trained	Travel Training General Info.
Aiken Area Council on Aging, Inc.	Aiken, South Carolina	140000	NA	3	100	NA	3	NA	NA	NA	bus demos at local agencies and schools
Augusta Public Transit	Augusta, Georgia	198000	26	30	85	12000	NA	1992	No	20 total	for vision-impaired, mobility-impaired, elderly, hearing-impaired; provide bus passes to local human service agencies to allow them to do additional training
BC Transit	Victoria, British Columbia	302000	250	163	15	144000	2.5	1992	Yes	NA	various populations; little response; advertised on application form and in newsletter
Ben Franklin Transit	Richland, Washington	125000	110	54	22	133000	4	1982	No	300	paratransit applicants determined ineligible are referred to trainers automatically; others reviewed for referral; 90% success rate in training; mainly developmentally disabled, some sensory-impaired
Capital District Transportation Authority	Albany, New York	780000	2261	229	NA	66000	5	1990	NA	1/month	training by independent living center w/ full-time instructor; utilize fees from agencies to offset cost; for vision-impaired, developmentally disabled, mobility impaired; had bus buddy program in 1983
Central Ohio Transit Authority	Columbus, Ohio	960000	543	342	31	85200	5	1991	NA	600	1st round Project ACTION; held 22 "Mobility Fairs" demonstrating accessible vehicles to 600 people; monthly lift trips have increased from 700 to 1350
Central Oklahoma Transportation & Parking Authority	Oklahoma City, Oklahoma	900000	500	89	10	24546	5	1992	No	750	program combines local demonstrations at agencies and schools with one-on-one rider training; mainly educational, though (promotional)

Table B-8. Selected Transit Providers Presently Using Travel Training (Continued)

Agency Name	City State/Province	Total Population	Service Area (mi.²)	Fixed Route Fleet Size	% FR Fleet Accessible	Paratransit Trips/Year	Trav. Trng. Effectiveness	Date Trav. Trng. Implem.	Integrated with Elig?	# of People Trained	Travel Training General Info.
City Utilities of Springfield	Springfield, Missouri	90000	NA	29	50	18000	4	1991	No	500	do group demonstrations and training as well as train the trainer for human service agency staff who can then do one-on-one training; 1 group/mo, about 500 people total trained to date
City of Jackson Transportation Authority	Jackson, Mississippi	149000	1500	19	100	NA	2	June, 1992	No	176	transit authority trains human service agency staff to train clients; have trained 23 staff who have trained 176 clients; train for both fixed route and paratransit
City of Santa Rosa	Santa Rosa, California	388000	1600	39	100	42776	NA	1993	Yes	4	primarily seniors
City of Waukesha Transit System Utility	Waukesha, Wisconsin	62000	NA	17	0	13000	5	1983	NA	100/year	part-time in-house trainer; work with local Training Center and public schools; train persons with developmental disabilities and children w/ disabilities
Coast Transit Authority	Gulfport, Mississippi	250000	NA	30	73	NA	NA	1991	No	100	for developmentally disabled and mobility impaired populations
Cobb Community Transit (CCT)	Marietta, Georgia	480000	NA	36	100	0	5	1990	No	NA	transit trains human service agency staff (train the trainer); training is in how to use system; trainers provided w/ free fare; clients include vision-impaired, developmentally disabled, and mobility-impaired; trained 200 staff to date
Danville Mass Transit	Danville, Illinois	35000	15	9	100	1500	3	1992	No	10	offered paratransit riders travel training; generally have trained persons with mobility-impairments

Table B-8. Selected Transit Providers Presently Using Travel Training (Continued)

Agency Name	City State/Province	Total Population	Service Area (mi.²)	Fixed Route Fleet Size	% FR Fleet Accessible	Paratransit Trips/Year	Trav. Trng. Effectiveness	Date Trav. Trng. Implem.	Integrated with Elig?	# of People Trained	Travel Training General Info.
Erie Metropolitan Transit Authority	Erie, Pennsylvania	170000	39	62	40	192000	3	1991	Yes	NA	MTA does presentations on using buses to local groups; local agencies do one-on-one training
Greater Attleboro-Taunton Regional Transit Authority	Attleboro, Massachusetts	100000	80	13	100	220000	5	April, 1991	Yes	85	full-time trainer on staff; trainer works with ADA eligibility coordinator; gets agency referrals as well; various groups (developmentally disabled, seniors)
Island Transit	Coupeville, Washington	40000	NA	8	100	72000	5	1992	Yes	50	ask applicants if they "Would like to learn to use fixed route" on applications; various populations trained
Janesville Transit System	Janesville, Wisconsin	53000	225	23	100	1400	4	1978	NA	50/year	started by working with local State school for vision-impaired; system is now a model for the State of Wisconsin; training done on demand as requested
Lane Transit District	Eugene, Oregon	180000	76	77	100	75000	4	1980	Yes	25/mo.	for vision-impaired, mobility-impaired, just starting to work with developmentally disabled; 12 drivers trained as trainers, take bus to person's home
Logan Transit District	Logan, Utah	50000	NA	12	83	5400	4	1992	NA	NA	use in-house staff, mainly group training (senior centers, etc.); also offer trip planning; will do for anyone (general public)
MTA of Black Hawk County	Waterloo/Cedar Falls, Iowa	104000	NA	14	28	73300	5	1991	No	10/year	have trained 50 riders to date; mainly developmentally disabled and mentally retarded; training by local agencies; transit provides bus passes

Table B-8. Selected Transit Providers Presently Using Travel Training (Continued)

Agency Name	City State/Province	Total Population	Service Area (mi.?)	Fixed Route Fleet Size	% FR Fleet Accessible	Paratransit Trips/Year	Trav. Trng. Effectiveness	Date Trav. Trng. Implem.	Integrated with Elig?	# of People Trained	Travel Training General Info.
Madison County Transit	Granite City, Illinois	227000	390	78	81	85000	5	1990	NA	180	for developmentally disabled and mobility-impaired; in-house as well as by local agencies; local mental health agency trained 100 clients; recently a school for developmentally disabled started sending classes out on FR; train about 20 riders/year
Madison Metro Transit System	Madison, Wisconsin	240000	100	170	25	150000	4	1993	NA	NA	"very positive results"
Marquette County Transit Authority	Marquette, Michigan	70000	1864	27	100	NA	NA	1988	No	35/year	travel training is part of intermediate education program for persons with disabilities
Memphis Area Transit Authority	Memphis, Tennessee	700000	347	161	2	130000	4	1987	No	100/year	work with 4 local human service agencies; provide ride coupons for trainers; mainly train developmentally disabled and vision-impaired
Merrimack Valley Regional Transit Authority	Haverhill, Massachusetts	281000	325	45	91	130000	4	1990	Yes	20/year	have questions in paratransit eligibility forms re: interest in receiving training; assist vision-impaired, developmentally disabled, some mobility-impaired riders; initially trained 45 riders, now 20/year
Metro-Dade Transit Agency	Miami, Florida	2000000	300	550	27	1010000	NA	1978	No	2000	various populations; training for bus, rail, people mover; "thousands" trained; very successful

Table B-8. Selected Transit Providers Presently Using Travel Training (Continued)

Agency Name	City State/Province	Total Population	Service Area (mi.²)	Fixed Route Fleet Size	% FR Fleet Accessible	Paratransit Trips/Year	Trav. Trng. Effectiveness	Date Trav. Trng. Implem.	Integrated with Elig?	# of People Trained	Travel Training General Info.
Miami Valley Regional Transit Authority	Dayton, Ohio	600000	458	258	100	121000	5	1991	No	180/year	hired person with disability to do one-on-one and group training; 1-2 meetings/month with 10-15 people at each; primarily for developmentally disabled, schools, mobility-impaired; 2000 wheelchair boardings/month (40% increase) on fixed route
Norwalk Transit District	Norwalk, Connecticut	78000	23	24	100	35000	5	NA	No	NA	provide free fixed route transportation to trainers and trainees; training done by local agencies
Ottumwa Transit Authority	Ottumwa, Iowa	25000	50	7	86	4200	4	1992	No	20/year	transit agency trains trainers at agencies; also provide free tickets to agencies; various populations
Pecos Trails Transit	Roswell, New Mexico	45000	29	9	100	13000	4	Nov., 1992	No	100	primarily developmentally disabled
Peninsula Transportation District Commission	Hampton/Newport News, Virginia	200000	116	118	33	56000	4	1992	No	15	a one-time training conducted; both developmentally disabled and mobility-impaired
Pioneer Valley Transit Authority	Springfield, Massachusetts	551000	115	178	14	275000	5	1992	Yes	25/year	full-time in-house trainer; primarily for developmentally disabled; training of vision-impaired done by state commission for the blind; joint effort w/ statewide transit authority program
Port Authority of Allegheny County	Pittsburgh, Pennsylvania	1400000	729	887	35	2032000	3	1992	No	10	primarily persons with mobility impairments

Table B-8. Selected Transit Providers Presently Using Travel Training (Continued)

Agency Name	City State/Province	Total Population	Service Area (mi.²)	Fixed Route Fleet Size	% FR Fleet Accessible	Paratransit Trips/Year	Trav. Trng. Effectiveness	Date Trav. Trng. Implem.	Integrated with Elig?	# of People Trained	Travel Training General Info.
Regional Transportation District	Denver, Colorado	1800000	2406	733	92	0	NA	1990	No	150	two different programs: (1) eight times per year conduct 2-day class w/ local rehabilitation center; (2) individual training as requested
SPAN, Inc.	Denton, Texas	60000	NA	4	50	24000	5	1992	Yes	NA	in-house trainer; one-on-one training for developmentally disabled, mobility-impaired, elderly; also provide free tokens to outside trainers; persons denied ADA paratransit eligibility are contacted
Sacramento Regional Transit District	Sacramento, California	1000000	500	200	60	300000	4	NA	Yes	400/year	offered free as part of eligibility process; primarily developmentally disabled and senior; 80% of participants continue to ride fixed route buses
Sarasota County Area Transit (SCAT)	Sarasota, Florida	287000	620	35	50	37500	NA	1991	No	100	work with local Easter Seal Society as part of Project ACTION grant; primarily developmentally disabled population
Saskatoon Transit System	Saskatoon, Saskatchewan	185000	NA	130	0	120000	4	NA	NA	NA	work w/ National Institute for the Blind; make vehicles available for training
Sioux Falls Transit/Paratransit	Sioux Falls, South Dakota	108000	52	27	0	105000	3	1987	NA	NA	Transit agency trains human service agency staff who then train clients; transit training focuses on use of system and system information, not detailed mobility instruction
Societe de Transport de Ville de Laval	Laval, Quebec	320000	245	215	0	184000	4	1991	No	40/year	through local school for developmentally disabled children; transit provides free passes for 1 year to students and fare for teachers; training in groups of 20-25

Table B-8. Selected Transit Providers Presently Using Travel Training (Continued)

Agency Name	City State/Province	Total Population	Service Area (mi.²)	Fixed Route Fleet Size	% FR Fleet Accessible	Paratransit Trips/Year	Trav. Trng. Effectiveness	Date Trav. Trng. Implem.	Integrated with Elig?	# of People Trained	Travel Training General Info.
The T	Fort Worth, Texas	500000	286	150	25	183000	5	1989	Yes	50/year	through local human service agency for vision-impaired and independent contractors; for vision-impaired, developmentally disabled, and mobility impaired; 25000 trips/year transferred; combined eligibility and travel training staff; target frequent riders
Tidewater Transportation District Commission	Norfolk, Virginia	900000	1000	135	50	168000	4	1992	NA	NA	various populations
Topeka Metropolitan Transit Authority	Topeka, Kansas	120000	NA	33	0	26000	5	1991	No	NA	work w/ local human service agencies; provide free passes to trainers who train clients; also make presentations on using fixed route to local agencies; "effective way to promote"
Transit Authority of North Kentucky	Ft. Wright, Kentucky	208000	84	97	50	32000	3	1981	No	NA	started in earnest in 1992, transit agency provided training 3 times in past year; other training done by local agencies
Visalia City Coach	Visalia, California	95000	33	12	100	36000	5	1991	No	NA	regional mental health center buys monthly fixed route passes and travel trains clients
Worcester Regional Transit Authority	Worcester, Massachusetts	290000	700	63	30	305000	4	1988	Yes	20/year	started primarily w/ developmentally disabled riders; now include elderly and mobility-impaired; full-time in-house trainer, will soon hire 2nd trainer; use trained riders to assist as peers

Table B-8. Selected Transit Providers Presently Using Travel Training (Continued)

Agency Name	City State/Province	Total Population	Service Area (mi.²)	Fixed Route Fleet Size	% FR Fleet Accessible	Paratransit Trips/Year	Trav. Trng. Effectiveness	Date Trav. Trng. Implem.	Integrated with Elig?	# of People Trained	Travel Training General Info.
York County Transportation Authority	York, Pennsylvania	180000	NA	22	93	193000	5	1982	No	40/year	transit trains trainers and provides bus passes; local agencies do training; mainly work with agencies serving developmentally disabled but also coordinate with program for vision-impaired, starting to work with agency serving mobility-impaired

"Trav. Trng. Effectiveness" = effectiveness rating provided in the survey   "Date Trav. Trng. Implem." = date the travel training program was implemented

"Integrated with Elig?" = indicates if the provision of travel training is coordinated with determinations of paratransit eligibility

"# of People Trained" = a measure of the number of riders trained (time period varies); if not otherwise indicated, the number is a total number since program inception   NA = not available

Table B-9. Selected Transit Providers Presently Using Fare Incentives

Agency Name	City State/Province	Total Population	Service Area (mi.²)	Fixed Route Fleet Size	% FR Fleet Accessible	Paratransit Trips/Year	Fare Incen. Effectiveness	Date Fare Incen. Implem.	Ongoing?	Fare Incen. General Info.
Austin-Capital Metropolitan Transportation Authority	Austin, Texas	605000	572	305	NA	430000	NA	1991	Yes	free fare for persons determined paratransit eligible; very successful; 5,000 wheelchair boardings on fixed route reported in July 1993
BC Transit	Vancouver, British Columbia	1600000	1125	950	29	800000	3	1990	Yes	initially offered free fare to persons with disabilities; after 1st year switched to 1/2 fare and free attendant
Chicago Transit Authority (CTA)	Chicago, Illinois	3700000	220	2175	44	1000000	NA	1993	Yes	allowing attendants to ride free as incentive for persons with disabilities to ride
City of Jackson Transportation Authority	Jackson, Mississippi	149000	1500	19	100	NA	4	NA	Yes	1/2 fare extended to all hours
Erie Metropolitan Transit Authority	Erie, Pennsylvania	170000	39	62	40	192000	4	1975	Yes	started as part of state lottery program in the 1970s; seniors ride free during off-peak; persons with disabilities pay half fare during off-peak
Grays Harbor Transportation Authority	Hoquiam, Washington	65400	2000	38	28	69000	5	NA	NA	25 cents for all riders
Greater Bridgeport Transit District	Bridgeport, Connecticut	282000	90	53	75	56000	5	May, 1993	NA	introduced free fare as promotional program in May, 1993; continued through 1993 and 1994; also aggressive marketing effort and travel training; fixed route use by persons with disabilities increased from 300 in May to 5000 in Sept., 1993

Table B-9. Selected Transit Providers Presently Using Fare Incentives (Continued)

Agency Name	City State/Province	Total Population	Service Area (mi.²)	Fixed Route Fleet Size	% FR Fleet Accessible	Paratransit Trips/Year	Fare Incen. Effectiveness	Date Fare Incen. Implem.	Ongoing?	Fare Incen. General Info.
Indiana County Transit Authority	Indiana, Pennsylvania	90000	830	9	100	NA	4	1992	Yes	ADA paratransit eligible persons ride free on fixed route at all times; seniors free during off-peak; paratransit fare is twice fixed route
Livermore Amador Valley Transit	Livermore, California	140000	NA	34	100	NA	5	1992	Yes	1/3 fare on fixed route; ticket booklets even greater discount; also free bus card for elders to travel 10am-2pm, has freed up paratransit capacity
Lowell Regional Transit Authority	Lowell, Massachusetts	200000	67	35	80	90000	5	NA	NA	have extended half fare to all hours
Lynx Orange-Seminole-Osceola Transportation Authority	Orlando, Florida	1178000	2700	130	14	76000	5	1992	Yes	33% of base fare ($.25 compared to $.75 base fare)
Madison Metro Transit System	Madison, Wisconsin	240000	100	170	25	150000	5	1992	Yes	half fare for standard fixed route; 25% of fixed route fare charged for service route; has encouraged ridership on service routes; $1 fixed routes, $1.50 paratransit, $.25 service routes
Metro-Dade Transit Agency	Miami, Florida	2000000	300	550	27	1010000	NA	May, 1993	No	free pass for paratransit eligible individuals (pilot); have seen 47 people who make 30-40 trips/month transfer; also "Medical Metro" pass for medicaid eligible riders

101

Table B-9. Selected Transit Providers Presently Using Fare Incentives (Continued)

Agency Name	City State/Province	Total Population	Service Area (mi.²)	Fixed Route Fleet Size	% FR Fleet Accessible	Paratransit Trips/Year	Fare Incen. Effectiveness	Date Fare Incen. Implem.	Ongoing?	Fare Incen. General Info.
Metropolitan Transit Authority of Harris County	Houston, Texas	3323000	1225	1100	33	NA	NA	April, 1993	Yes	Free fares on fixed route for ADA paratransit eligible persons
Metropolitan Tulsa Transit Authority	Tulsa, Oklahoma	380000	175	84	NA	174000	NA	NA	Yes	Free fare on fixed route for persons with disabilities
Miami Valley Regional Transit Authority	Dayton, Ohio	600000	458	258	100	121000	4	1975	Yes	have extended half fare program to all hours
Municipal Transit Administration	Clinton, Iowa	29000	NA	9	67	4800	4	July, 1992	NA	give free ride coupons as a service promotion; done for general public as well but target riders with disabilities
Pecos Trails Transit	Roswell, New Mexico	45000	29	9	100	13000	5	NA	Yes	in addition to half fare, seniors and persons with disabilities can buy 9 ride tickets and get 10th free; 30% of fixed route rides made by persons with disabilities (also reflects success of service routes)
People Mover - Municipality of Anchorage	Anchorage, Alaska	240000	300	60	0	52000	NA	March, 1992	Yes	base fare is $1; fare for persons with disabilities is 25 cents; customers must get an ID for $2; paratransit fare is $1
Port Authority of Allegheny County	Pittsburgh, Pennsylvania	1400000	729	887	35	2032000	3	July, 1993	NA	paratransit riders ride 1/2 fare all times not just off peak; also promotion: elderly ride free off-peak; also offer 2 free trips to everyone as intro to program.
Regional Transportation District	Denver, Colorado	1800000	2406	733	92	0	NA	NA	Yes	25 cents off-peak only; very often less than half fare given that base fares range from $.50 to $2.50

Table B-9. Selected Transit Providers Presently Using Fare Incentives (Continued)

Agency Name	City State/Province	Total Population	Service Area (mi.²)	Fixed Route Fleet Size	% FR Fleet Accessible	Paratransit Trips/Year	Fare Incen. Effectiveness	Date Fare Incen. Implem.	Ongoing?	Fare Incen. General Info.
Rogue Valley Transportation District	Medford, Oregon	111000	158	26	74	48000	3	1993	Yes	reduced fixed route fares for all riders from $.75 to $.25
Sacramento Regional Transit District	Sacramento, California	1000000	500	200	60	300000	5	NA	NA	is less than half fare, but moving to half fare for financial reasons (success w/ travel training is allowing agency to consider raising fares)
The T	Fort Worth, Texas	500000		150	25	183000	NA	NA	NA	when riders agree to switch to paratransit, will trade paratransit pass for fixed route pass (1 month of paratransit buys 5 months of fixed route service)
Utah Transit Authority	Salt Lake City, Utah	1000000	1800	520	60	250000	3	1991	No	as new accessible buses are added, fixed route passes are distributed as a promotion; good for 30 days of travel

"Fare Incen. Effectiveness" = effectiveness rating provided in the survey
"Ongoing?" = indicates if the fare incentive is provided on an ongoing basis or only as a promotion

"Date Fare Incen. Implem." = date the program was implemented
NA = not available

Table B-10. Selected Transit Providers Presently Using Audio/Visual Systems

Agency Name	City	State/ Province	Contact Person	Phone #	A/V Systems Effectiveness
Ohio Valley Regional Transportation Authority	Wheeling	WV	Mr. Chester J. Sokol	(304)232-2190	5
Richmond Hill Transit	Richmond Hill	Ontario	A. Evans	(416)771-2419	5
Sonoma County Transit (Countywide Service)	Santa Rosa	CA	Ms. Priscilla Kays	(707)585-7516	4
Danville Mass Transit	Danville	IL	Mr. Karl Gnadt	(217)431-0653	2
Metropolitan Transit System	San Diego	CA	Mr. Thomas F. Larwin	(619)231-1466	2
North San Diego County Transit District	Oceanside	CA	Ms. Leslie Blanda	(619)967-2828	2
Wichita Metropolitan Transit Authority	Wichita	KS	Mr. Michael D. Vinson	(316)265-1450	2
Municipal Transit Administration	Clinton	IA	Ms. Cheryl Williams	(319)242-3721	1
Rogue Valley Transportation District	Medford	OR	Mr. Doug Pilant	(503)779-5821	1
AJAX Transit	Ajax	Ontario	Terry Barnett	(416)427-5710	
Area Transportation Authority of NC PA	Johnsonburg	PA	Mr. Richard A. Viglione	(814)965-3211	
Athens Transit System	Athens	GA	Mr. Tom Lett	(706)613-3430	
Augusta Public Transit	Augusta	GA	Ms. Heather Jenia	(706)821-1819	
BC Transit	Vancouver	British Columbia	Mr. Bruce Chown	(604)264-5005	
Bi-State Development Agency	St. Louis	MO	Mr. Donald W. Maag	(314)982-1578	
Blue Water Area Transit	Port Huron	MI	Mr. Jim Wilson	(313)987-7373	
Brockton Area Transit Authority	Brockton	MA	R. Ledoux	(508)588-2240	
Central Oklahoma Transportation & Parking Authority	Oklahoma City	OK	Ms. Jeanette Sheets	(405)297-2056	
Chicago Transit Authority (CTA)	Chicago	IL	Ms. Nancy Isaac	(312)521-1427	

Table B-10. Selected Transit Providers Presently Using Audio/Visual Systems (Continued)

Agency Name	City	State/ Province	Contact Person	Phone #	A/V Systems Effectiveness
Chillicothe Transit System	Chillicothe	OH	NA	(614)773-1569	
City of East Grand Forks	East Grand Forks	MN	Kerry Knoff	(218)773-2371	
City of Regina, Transit Department	Regina	Saskatchewan	Ms. Beverly DeJong	(306)777-7815	
City of Saginaw Transit System	Saginaw	MI	Mr. Sylvester Payne	(517)759-1679	
DTOP/AMA/ACT - Metropolitan Bus Authority	San Juan	PR	Ms. Adaline Torres	(809)767-7979	
Dallas Area Rapid Transit	Dallas	TX	L. G. Fuller	(214)749-2770	
DuBois, Falls Creek, Sandy TWP Joint Transp. Authority	DuBois	PA	Ms. Edith E. Swisher	(814)371-3940	
Five Seasons Transportation	Cedar Rapids	IA	Mr. William Hoekstra	(319)398-5367	
Golden Empire Transit District	Bakersfield	CA	Ms. Jill Smith	(805)324-9874	
Lake Charles Transit System	Lake Charles	LA	Mr. Michael McCauley	(318)491-1210	
Lane Transit District	Eugene	OR	Micki Kaplan	(503) 741-6100	
Los Angeles County Metropolitan Transp. Authority	Los Angeles	CA	Mr. Richard DeRock	(213)244-6524	
Metro RTA	Akron	OH	Avon R. Smith	(216)762-7267	
Metro Transit Division, Metropolitan Authority	Halifax-Dartmouth	Nova Scotia	Ms. Lori Patterson	(902)421-6609	
Metro-Dade Transit Agency	Miami	FL	Mr. Mario G. Garcia	(305)637-3756	
Metropolitan Evansville Transit System	Evansville	IN	Ms. Rose M. Zigenfus	(812)426-5230	
Mid-County Transit Authority	Kittanning	PA	Mr. James McFarland	(412)548-8696	

Table B-10. Selected Transit Providers Presently Using Audio/Visual Systems (Continued)

Agency Name	City	State/ Province	Contact Person	Phone #	A/V Systems Effectiveness
Monterey - Salinas Transit	Monterey	CA	Mr. Thomas Hiltner	(408)899-2558	
OMNITRANS	San Bernardino	CA	Mr. Daniel Brogan	(909)889-0811	
S.T.C.U.M.	Montreal	Quebec	Mr. Richard D. Daneau	(514)280-6307	
Transit Authority of River City (TARC)	Louisville	KY	Tina Morris	(502)561-5117	
Venango County Transportation	Franklin	PA	Ms. Denise Pickens	(814)437-6871	
Wilson Transit System	Wilson	NC	NA	(919)399-2488	

Table B-11. Selected Transit Providers Presently Using Fare Simplification Mechanisms

Agency Name	City	State/Province	Contact Person	Phone #	Simpl. Fare Effectiveness
Albany Transit System	Albany	GA	Mr. Mike Crittenden	(912)430-5182	5
Bay Metro Transit	Bay City	MI	Mr. Michael Stoner	(517)894-2900	5
Cornwall Transit	Cornwall	Ontario	Mr. Gerry Godard	(613)930-2636	5
Logan Transit District	Logan	UT	Mr. Michael L. Noonchester	(801)750-7108	5
Memphis Area Transit Authority	Memphis	TN	Ms. Lynn Everett	(901)722-7145	5
Metropolitan Transit System	San Diego	CA	Mr. Thomas F. Larwin	(619)231-1466	5
Pecos Trails Transit	Roswell	NM	Mr. Dave McKay	(505)624-6769	5
Ashland Bus System	Ashland	KY	Mr. Michael Rogers	(606)327-2025	4
Danville Mass Transit	Danville	IL	Mr. Karl Gnadt	(217)431-0653	4
Eureka Transit Service	Eureka	CA	Ms. Marie Liscom	(707)441-4117	4
Lassen Rural Bus System	Susanville	CA	Mr. John Shoun	(916)257-8311	4
Marquette County Transit Authority	Marquette	MI	Mr. Howard Schweppe	(906)225-1283	4
Municipal Transit Administration	Clinton	IA	Ms. Cheryl Williams	(319)242-3721	4
Norwalk Transit District	Norwalk	CT	Ms. Nancy Carroll	(203)853-3338	4
TALTRAN	Tallahassee	FL	Ms. Donna Peacock	(904)891-5200	4
The Metro	Cincinnati	OH	Mr. Douglas Herkes	(513)632-7590	4
Wichita Metropolitan Transit Authority	Wichita	KS	Mr. Michael D. Vinson	(316)265-1450	4
Winnipeg Transit System	Winnipeg	Manitoba	Mr. Jarvis Kohut	(204)986-5726	4
Sonoma County Transit (Countywide Service)	Santa Rosa	CA	Ms. Priscilla Kays	(707)585-7516	3.5
Canton Regional Transit Authority	Canton	OH	Ms. Sharon A. Kasunic	(216)454-6132	3

Table B-11. Selected Transit Providers Presently Using Fare Simplification Mechanisms (Continued)

Agency Name	City	State/ Province	Contact Person	Phone #	Simpl. Fare Effectiveness
City of Jackson Transportation Authority	Jackson	MI	Mr. Garrett Erb	(517)787-8363	3
Corvallis Transit System	Corvallis	OR	Ms. Bernadette D. Barrett	(503)757-6916	3
Janesville Transit System	Janesville	WI	Mr. David J. Mumma	(608)755-3150	3
Miami Valley Regional Transit Authority	Dayton	OH	Mr. Wayne Barnett	NA	3
North San Diego County Transit District	Oceanside	CA	Ms. Leslie Blanda	(619)967-2828	3
Pinellas Suncoast Transit Authority	Clearwater	FL	Mr. Michael J. Siebel	(813)530-9921	3
VOTRAN, Volusia Transit Management, Inc.	South Daytona	FL	Mr. David Hope	(904)761-7600	3
Worcester Regional Transit Authority	Worcester	MA	Mr. Robert E. Ojala	(508)791-2389	3
BC Transit	Victoria	British Columbia	Mr. Ron Drolet	(604)385-2551	2.5
Duluth Transit Authority	Duluth	MN	Mr. Dennis Jensen	(218)722-4426	2
Sioux Falls Transit/Paratransit	Sioux Falls	SD	Mr. John Roberts	(605)339-7130	2

Table B-12. Selected Transit Providers Presently Using Marketing Programs

Agency Name	City	State/ Province	Contact Person	Phone #	Marketing Effectiveness
Central Oklahoma Transportation & Parking Authority	Oklahoma City	OK	Ms. Jeanette Sheets	(405)297-2056	5
City of East Grand Forks	East Grand Forks	MN	Kerry Knoff	(218)773-2371	5
Duluth Transit Authority	Duluth	MN	Mr. Dennis Jensen	(218)722-4426	5
Marquette County Transit Authority	Marquette	MI	Mr. Howard Schweppe	(906)225-1283	5
Muskegon Area Transit System	Muskegon	MI	P. Varona	(616)724-6420	5
Richmond Hill Transit	Richmond Hill	Ontario	A. Evans	(416)771-2419	5
Sonoma County Transit (Countywide Service)	Santa Rosa	CA	Ms. Priscilla Kays	(707)585-7516	4.5
BC Transit	Victoria	British Columbia	Mr. Ron Drolet	(604)385-2551	4
Basin Transit Service	Klamath Falls	OR	Ms. Cynthia Thompson	(503)883-2877	4
City of Astoria Transit	Astoria	OR	Ms. Cindy L. Howe	(503)325-5821	4
Cornwall Transit	Cornwall	Ontario	Mr. Gerry Godard	(613)930-2636	4
Durham Area Transit Authority	Durham	NC	Mr. John Gardner	(919)688-2611	4
GATRA	Attleboro	MA	Mr. Frank Gay	(508)226-1102	4
Madison Metro Transit System	Madison	WI	Mr. Paul J. Larrousse	(608)267-8777	4
Metropolitan Transit System	San Diego	CA	Mr. Thomas F. Larwin	(619)231-1466	4
North San Diego County Transit District	Oceanside	CA	Ms. Leslie Blanda	(619)967-2828	4
Piedmont Wagon Transit System	Hickory	NC	Mr. John C. Tippett	(704)322-9191	4
Prince George's County Dept. of Public Works & Transp.	Landover	MD	Mr. James E. Raszewski	NA	4
Riverside Transit Agency	Riverside	CA	Cis Seroy	(909)684-0850	4

109

Table B-12. Selected Transit Providers Presently Using Marketing Programs (Continued)

Agency Name	City	State/ Province	Contact Person	Phone #	Marketing Effectiveness
Stevens Point Transit	Stevens Point	WI	Ms. Joanne Cummings	(715)341-4490	4
Aiken Area Council on Aging, Inc.	Aiken	SC	Ms. Lynnda C. Bassham	NA	3
Altoona Metro Transit	Altoona	PA	Mr. Thomas W. Klevan	(814)944-4074	3
BC Transit	Vancouver	British Columbia	Mr. Bruce Chown	(604)264-5005	3
Bay Metro Transit	Bay City	MI	Mr. Michael Stoner	(517)894-2900	3
Central Ohio Transit Authority	Columbus	OH	Lynn Rathke	(614)275-5800	3
City of Jackson Transportation Authority	Jackson	MI	Mr. Garrett Erb	(517)787-8363	3
CityLink Abilene	Abilene	TX	Ms. Martha Ontiveros Castillo	(915)676-6403	3
Community Transit	Lynnwood/ Everett	WA	Ms. Gretchen Weber-Schlobohm	(206)348-7196	3
Fayetteville Area System of Transit	Fayetteville	NC	Ms. Kimberly Sledge	(919)433-1748	3
Housatonic Area Regional Transit District	Danbury	CT	Mr. Lewis May	NA	3
Indiana County Transit Authority	Indiana	PA	Mr. Gerald L. Blair	(412)465-2140	3
Los Angeles County Metropolitan Transp. Authority	Los Angeles	CA	Mr. Richard DeRock	(213)244-6524	3
Merrimack Valley Regional Transit Authority	Haverhill	MA	Ms. Patricia Monahan	(508)372-2427	3
Norwalk Transit District	Norwalk	CT	Ms. Nancy Carroll	(203)853-3338	3
OC Transpo	Ottawa	Ontario	Ms. Helen Gault	(613)741-6440	3
Ottumwa Transit Authority	Ottumwa	IA	Ms. Pam Ward	(515)683-0695	3
Pecos Trails Transit	Roswell	NM	Mr. Dave McKay	(505)624-6769	3
Peninsula Transportation District Commission	Hampton/ Newport News	VA	Ms. Karen Burnette	(804)722-2837	3

Table B-12. Selected Transit Providers Presently Using Marketing Programs (Continued)

Agency Name	City	State/ Province	Contact Person	Phone #	Marketing Effectiveness
Pima County Rural Transit	Tucson	AZ	Mr. Ben Goff	(602)740-6403	3
Pinellas Suncoast Transit Authority	Clearwater	FL	Mr. Michael J. Siebel	(813)530-9921	3
Sarasota County Area Transit (SCAT)	Sarasota	FL	Mr. Jay Goodwill	(813)951-5850	3
The Metro	Cincinnati	OH	Mr. Douglas Herkes	(513)632-7590	3
Toronto Transit Commission	Toronto	Ontario	Ms. Katherine Biggart	(416)393-4501	3
VOTRAN, Volusia Transit Management, Inc.	South Daytona	FL	Mr. David Hope	(904)761-7600	3
Worcester Regional Transit Authority	Worcester	MA	Mr. Robert E. Ojala	(508)791-2389	3
Capital District Transportation Authority	Albany	NY	Ms. Cary Roessel	(518)482-4199	2
City of Pullman Transit Service	Pullman	WA	Mr. Jim Hudak	(509)334-4555	2
Danville Mass Transit	Danville	IL	Mr. Karl Gnadt	(217)431-0653	2
Guam Mass Transit Authority	Agana	Guam	Mr. Mack N. Ezzell	(671)475-4682	2
James City County Transit	Williamsburg	VA	Mr. Richard Drumwright	(804)220-1621	2
Municipal Transit Administration	Clinton	IA	Ms. Cheryl Williams	(319)242-3721	2
Portage Area Regional Transportation Authority	Akron	OH	Mr. Charles A. Nelson	(216)836-2672	2
Rapid Transit System	Rapid City	SD	Mr. Rich Sagen	(605)394-6631	2
Rockland County Dept. of Public Transportation (T.R.I.P.S.)	Rockland	NY	Mr. William Chase	(914)364-2064	2
Rogue Valley Transportation District	Medford	OR	Mr. Doug Pilant	(503)779-5821	2
San Luis Obispo Regional Transit Authority	San Luis Obispo	CA	Mr. Alan Cantrell	(805)781-4465	2

Table B-13. Selected Transit Providers with Accessible Bus Stop Programs

Agency Name	City	State/ Province	Contact Person	Phone #	Access. Bus Stop Effect.
Albany Transit System	Albany	GA	Mr. Mike Crittenden	(912)430-5182	5
BC Transit	Vancouver	British Columbia	Mr. Bruce Chown	(604)264-5005	5
Miami Valley Regional Transit Authority	Dayton	OH	Mr. Wayne Barnett	NA	5
BC Transit	Victoria	British Columbia	Mr. Ron Drolet	(604)385-2551	4
Pecos Trails Transit	Roswell	NM	Mr. Dave McKay	(505)624-6769	4
Sarasota County Area Transit (SCAT)	Sarasota	FL	Mr. Jay Goodwill	(813)951-5850	4
Capital District Transportation Authority	Albany	NY	Ms. Cary Roessel	(518)482-4199	3
Central Ohio Transit Authority	Columbus	OH	Lynn Rathke	(614)275-5800	3
Community Transit	Lynnwood/ Everett	WA	Ms. Gretchen Weber-Schlobohm	(206)348-7196	3
Grays Harbor Transportation Authority	Hoquiam	WA	Mr. Dave Rostedt	(206)532-2770	3
Metropolitan Transit System	San Diego	CA	Mr. Thomas F. Larwin	(619)231-1466	3
Municipality of Metropolitan Seattle (Seattle Metro)	Seattle	WA	Ms. Karen Rosenzweig	(206)689-3103	3
Pinellas Suncoast Transit Authority	Clearwater	FL	Mr. Michael J. Siebel	(813)530-9921	3
Santa Barbara Metropolitan Transit District	Santa Barbara	CA	Mr. John Murdoch	(805)963-9571	3
Santa Cruz Metro	Santa Cruz	CA	Mr. Mark Dorfman	(408)426-6080	3
Simi Valley Transit	Simi Valley	CA	Hibbie Hayslett	(805)527-2141	3
James City County Transit	Williamsburg	VA	Mr. Richard Drumwright	(804)220-1621	2
Rogue Valley Transportation District	Medford	OR	Mr. Doug Pilant	(503)779-5821	2

Table B-13. Selected Transit Providers with Accessible Bus Stop Programs (Continued)

Agency Name	City	State/ Province	Contact Person	Phone #	Access. Bus Stop Effect.
Madison Metro Transit System	Madison	WI	Mr. Paul J. Larrousse	(608)267-8777	1
Athens Transit System	Athens	GA	Mr. Tom Lett	(706)613-3430	
Augusta Public Transit	Augusta	GA	Ms. Heather Jenia	(706)821-1819	
Basin Transit Service	Klamath Falls	OR	Ms. Cynthia Thompson	(503)883-2877	
C-Tran	Vancouver	WA	Mr. Barry Cavanaugh	(206)695-9893	
Calgary Transit	Calgary	Alberta	Mr. Dave Colquhoun	(403)277-9794	
Capital Area Transit	Raleigh	NC	Mr. Robert Olason	(919)890-3440	
Chapel Hill Transit	Chapel Hill	NC	Mr. Robert Godding	(919)968-2755	
City of Greeley "The Bus"	Greeley	CO	Mr. John Lee	(303)350-9280	
City of Rochester	Rochester	MN	Mr. Anthony Knauer	(507)287-1976	
City of Santa Rosa	Santa Rosa	CA	Mr. Bruce Eisert	(707)524-5121	
City of South Portland Bus Service	South Portland	ME	Mr. Leroy Beaver, Jr.	(207)767-5556	
City of St. Albert Transit	Edmonton	Alberta	R. Findlay	(403)463-7520	
CMTA	Austin	Texas	Ms. Nancy Crowther	(512)389-7583	
Cobb Community Transit (CCT)	Marietta	GA	Ms. Lynne Christian	(404)528-1610	
Columbus Transit	Columbus	IN	Ms. Sue Chapple	(812)376-2506	
Dallas Area Rapid Transit	Dallas	TX	L. G. Fuller	(214)749-2770	
Eastern Contra Costa Transit Authority	Pittsburg & Antioch	CA	Ms. Anne Muzzini	NA	
Escambia County Transit System	Pensacola	FL	Mr. Kenneth Westbrook	(904)436-9386	
Fairfield/Suisun Transit	Fairfield	CA	Mr. Kevin S. Daughton	(707)428-7590	

Table B-13. Selected Transit Providers with Accessible Bus Stop Programs (Continued)

Agency Name	City	State/ Province	Contact Person	Phone #	Access. Bus Stop Effect.
Farmville Area Bus	Farmville	VA	Mr. Michael J. Socha	(804)392-7433	
Five Seasons Transportation	Cedar Rapids	IA	Mr. William Hoekstra	(319)398-5367	
GATRA	Attleboro	MA	Mr. Frank Gay	(508)226-1102	
Greater Portland Transit District	Portland	ME	Mr. John Tibbetts	(207)774-0351	
Honolulu Public Transit Authority	Honolulu	HI	Mr. James L. O'Sullivan	(808)527-6890	
Kansas City Area Transportation Authority	Kansas City	MO	Ms. Donna Brown	(816)346-0311	
La Crosse Municipal Transit Utility (MTU)	La Crosse	WI	Mr. Tim Schick	(608)789-7375	
Lane Transit District	Eugene	OR	Micki Kaplan	(503)741-6100	
Metro-Dade Transit Agency	Miami	FL	Mr. Mario G. Garcia	(305)637-3756	
Monterey - Salinas Transit	Monterey	CA	Mr. Thomas Hiltner	(408)899-2558	
MUNI	San Francisco	CA	Mr. Paul Fishera	(415)923-6142	
OC Transpo	Ottawa	Ontario	Ms. Helen Gault	(613)741-6440	
OMNITRANS	San Bernardino	CA	Mr. Daniel Brogan	(909)889-0811	
Park City Transit - Park City Municipal Corporation	Park City	UT	Ms. Kae Draper	(801)645-5129	
People Mover - Municipality of Anchorage	Anchorage	AK	Ms. Brenda Bergsrud	(907)786-8209	
Peterborough Transit	Peterborough	Ontario	J. N. Kimble	(705)748-8895	
Port Arthur Transit (PAT)	Port Arthur	TX	Mr. Charles Airiohuodion	(409)983-8140	
Regional Transit Board	Minneapolis/ St. Paul	MN	Ms. Debra Sorenson Nelles	(612)229-2716	
Regional Transportation District	Denver	CO	Mr. Dave Shelley	(303)299-2408	

Table B-13. Selected Transit Providers with Accessible Bus Stop Programs (Continued)

Agency Name	City	State/ Province	Contact Person	Phone #	Access. Bus Stop Effect.
San Mateo County Transit District	San Carlos	CA	Mr. Mark Whitefield	(415)508-6247	
St. Albert Transit	St. Albert	Alberta	W. D. Liggett	(403)459-1589	
Star Trak	Lincoln	NE	Mr. Larry Worth	(402)441-8600	
Sun Line Transit Agency	Thousand Palms	CA	Mr. Dennis Guinaw	(619)343-3456	
The University of Iowa - Cambus	Iowa City	IA	Mr. Brian McClatchey	(319)335-8632	
Transit Authority of River City (TARC)	Louisville	KY	Tina Morris	(502)561-5117	
Transit Management of Hamilton, Inc. (AKA The Bus Co.)	Hamilton	OH	Mr. Michael Melaniphy	(513)867-1660	

Table B-14. Selected Transit Providers Presently Using Bus Identifier Kits

Agency Name	City	State/ Province	Contact Person	Phone #	Bus ID Effectiveness
Municipality of Metropolitan Seattle (Seattle Metro)	Seattle	WA	Ms. Karen Rosenzweig	(206)689-3103	5
CityLink Abilene	Abilene	TX	Ms. Martha Ontiveros Castillo	(915)676-6403	4
Los Angeles County Metropolitan Transp. Authority	Los Angeles	CA	Mr. Richard DeRock	(213)244-6524	4
OC Transpo	Ottawa	Ontario	Ms. Helen Gault	(613)741-6440	4
Sheboygan Transit System	Sheboygan	WI	Mr. Steven Billings	(414)459-3285	4
Westmoreland Transit	Greensburg	PA	Executive Director	(412)834-9282	4
Ben Franklin Transit	Richmond	WA	Ed Frost	(509)735-4131	3
C-Tran	Vancouver	WA	Mr. Barry Cavanaugh	(206)695-9893	2
Grand Rapids Area Transit Authority	Grand Rapids	MI	Mr. Steve Kantz	(616)456-7514	2
Mid Mon Valley Transit Authority	Charleroi	PA	Mr. David N. Lint	(412)489-0880	2
GO Transit	Toronto	Ontario	Ian Cale	(416)665-9211	1
Richmond Hill Transit	Richmond Hill	Ontario	A. Evans	(416)771-2419	1
Capital District Transportation Authority	Albany	NY	Ms. Cary Roessel	(518)482-4199	
City of Tucson Mass Transit System	Tucson	AZ	NA	NA	
DART	Wilmington	DE	Mr. Robert Taylor	(302)658-8960	
Five Seasons Transportation	Cedar Rapids	IA	Mr. William Hoekstra	(319)398-5367	
Fort Wayne Public Transportation Corporation	Fort Wayne	IN	Mr. Robert E. Morton	(219)432-4977	
Indianapolis Public Transportation Corp.	Indianapolis	IN	Mr. Jim Maslanka	(317)635-2100	
Lane Transit District	Eugene	OR	Micki Kaplan	(503)741-6100	
Metro Transit Division, Metropolitan Authority	Halifax-Dartmouth	Nova Scotia	Ms. Lori Patterson	(902)421-6609	

Table B-14. Selected Transit Providers Presently Using Bus Identifier Kits (Continued)

Agency Name	City	State/ Province	Contact Person	Phone #	Bus ID Effectiveness
Sonoma County Transit (Countywide Service)	Santa Rosa	CA	Ms. Priscilla Kays	(707)585-7516	
Suburban Mobility Authority for Regional Transp. (SMART)	Detroit	MI	Mr. Dan Dirks	(313)362-0924	
The Metro	Cincinnati	OH	Mr. Douglas Herkes	(513)632-7590	
The T	Fort Worth	TX	Ms. Carla Forman	(817)871-6219	
Topeka Metropolitan Transit Authority	Topeka	KS	Mr. Craig Cole	(913)233-2011	
Utah Transit Authority	Salt Lake City	UT	Ms. Kathy McCune	(801)262-5626	

Table B-15. Selected Transit Providers Presently Using Destination Cards

Agency Name	City	State/ Province	Contact Person	Phone #	Dest. Card Effectiveness
CityLink Abilene	Abilene	TX	Ms. Martha Ontiveros Castillo	(915)676-6403	4
Municipality of Metropolitan Seattle (Seattle Metro)	Seattle	WA	Ms. Karen Rosenzweig	(206)689-3103	4
Portage Area Regional Transportation Authority	Akron	OH	Mr. Charles A. Nelson	(216)836-2672	4
Grand Rapids Area Transit Authority	Grand Rapids	MI	Mr. Steve Kantz	(616)456-7514	2
VOTRAN, Volusia Transit Management, Inc.	South Daytona	FL	Mr. David Hope	(904)761-7600	2
Ames Transit Agency	Ames	IA	Mr. Bob Bourne	(515)292-1105	
Beloit Transit System	Beloit	WI	Mr. Kevin Davies	(608)364-2870	
Bettendorf Transit	Bettendorf	IA	Ms. Margaret Lake	(319)344-4085	
Central Ohio Transit Authority	Columbus	OH	Lynn Rathke	(614)275-5800	
Chapel Hill Transit	Chapel Hill	NC	Mr. Robert Godding	(919)968-2755	
City of St. Albert Transit	Edmonton	Alberta	R. Findlay	(403)463-7520	
Farmville Area Bus	Farmville	VA	Mr. Michael J. Socha	(804)392-7433	
Five Seasons Transportation	Cedar Rapids	IA	Mr. William Hoekstra	(319)398-5367	
Los Angeles County Metropolitan Transp. Authority	Los Angeles	CA	Mr. Richard DeRock	(213)244-6524	
Metro RTA	Akron	OH	Avon R. Smith	(216)762-7267	
Red Deer Transit	Red Deer	Alberta	Grant Beattie	(403)342-8225	
The Metro	Cincinnati	OH	Mr. Douglas Herkes	(513)632-7590	
The T	Fort Worth	TX	Ms. Carla Forman	(817)871-6219